Basic
K'ichee'
Grammar

Basic K'ichee' Grammar

Thirty-Eight Lessons
Revised Edition

James L. Mondloch

UNIVERSITY PRESS
OF COLORADO
Boulder

Published by University Press of Colorado
5589 Arapahoe Avenue, Suite 206C
Boulder, Colorado 80303

 The University Press of Colorado is a proud member of
the Association of American University Presses.

The University Press of Colorado is a cooperative publishing enterprise supported, in part, by Adams State University, Colorado State University, Fort Lewis College, Metropolitan State University of Denver, Regis University, University of Colorado, University of Northern Colorado, Utah State University, and Western State Colorado University.

∞ This paper meets the requirements of the ANSI/NISO Z39.48-1992 (Permanence of Paper).

ISBN 978-1-60732-389-1 (cloth)
ISBN 978-1-60732-451-5 (ebook)
ISBN 978-1-60732-530-7 (paper)
DOI: 10.5876/9781607324515

Library of Congress Cataloging-in-Publication Data

Names: Mondloch, James L., author.
Title: Basic K'ichee' grammar : 38 lessons / James L. Mondloch.
Description: Revised edition. | Boulder : University Press of Colorado, [2016] | English and K'ichee'.
Identifiers: LCCN 2015043077 | ISBN 9781607323891 (cloth) | ISBN 9781607324515 (ebook) | ISBN 9781607325307 (paper)
Subjects: LCSH: K'ichee' language—Grammar.
Classification: LCC PM4231 .M66 2016 | DDC 497/.415—dc23
LC record available at https://lccn.loc.gov/2015043077

Contents

Foreword

Among the indigenous languages of the Americas, the K'ichee'an languages occupy a prominent place both in regard to number of speakers and in their historical significance. Presently the speakers of K'ichee'an languages (K'ichee', Kaqchikel, Tz'utujil, Sakapulteko, and Sipakapense) number almost one million, compared with approximately 600,000 speakers of *all* the Amerindian languages of the United States and Canada. The *Popol Vuh*, written by a K'ichee' noble in the sixteenth century, is considered our most valuable firsthand account of the myths and oral history of pre-Hispanic Mesoamerica. *The Title of the Lords of Totonicapan*, the *Rabinal Achi* dance drama, and the *Annals of the Cakchiquels* are other K'ichee'an documents of the highest significance for scholars dealing with the history and mythology of pre-Columbian America.

Despite the importance of K'ichee'an languages, modern linguistic descriptions of these languages are relatively scanty. For example, there is no published connection of K'ichee' texts, nor is there an adequate dictionary of the modern dialects. Although some reasonably accurate pedagogical materials are available (Stanley A. Wick and Remigio Cochojil Gonzalez, *Spoken Quiche Maya*; David Fox, *Lecciones Elementales en Quiche*), they are either unsuited for nonlinguists (Wick) or offer only a superficial introduction to the grammar of the language.

Basic K'ichee' Grammar, by James L. Mondloch, fills a gap in our descriptive materials by providing an extensive and accurate survey of the principal grammatical structures of K'ichee', explained in a thorough yet nontechnical manner. The author has spent more than nine years in K'ichee'-speaking communities and so is able to provide a wealth of examples and detailed commentaries on actual usage. This is a pedagogical rather than a reference grammar; it is organized around graded grammatical lessons accompanied by drills and exercises. It should prove extremely valuable both to linguists and nonlinguists alike who wish to acquire a speaking and reading knowledge of modern K'ichee' or to those who want only to find out about the structure of the language.

WILLIAM NORMAN AND LYLE CAMPBELL

Introduction

This grammar is presented with the goal of making available a much more complete and useable presentation of the K'ichee' language than has yet been published. It is my hope that this work will be of value to its readers in their study of K'ichee'.

After studying and speaking the K'ichee' language for some eight years, in 1973 I decided it was time to write down in an orderly fashion some of my ideas about the structure of the language. Much of the analysis found in this grammar is not mine, but rather is the work of other dedicated students of K'ichee'. Some few of the ideas are my own.

When I began my study of K'ichee', I used the available works written on the language, especially the grammars of David Fox, Stanley Wick, Adrian Chávez, and Charles Étienne Brasseur de Bourbourg. As I progressed in my knowledge of the language I came upon many points of grammar, especially in the verb structure, that were not touched upon in these works. For this reason I began constructing my own grammatical analysis of the language. In this study I have attempted to make a rather complete analysis of the K'ichee' verb system based on the everyday speech of the people. Many of the unresolved grammatical problems that I encountered while studying the language have been resolved, at least to my satisfaction, in this present analysis. Another problem I had to face in attempting to describe the

Nahualá-Ixtahuacán dialect of K'ichee' was that of vowel length. The modern grammars of the language (Fox, Wick) are of dialects with a six-vowel system. However, the Nahualá-Ixtahuacán dialect has a ten-vowel system. With the help of Dr. William Norman I have attempted to accurately record vowel length in this present work.

Needless to say, no grammatical analysis of any language is ever complete. This grammar is intended to be a pedagogical rather than a reference work. A more thorough treatment of the phonology of the language is necessary (e.g., vowel shortening, contractions, the phonological properties of the phoneme /h/, etc.). Yet this grammar should serve as a useful complement to the already existing works.

I wish to express my gratitude to all who have helped me in the preparation of this work. Above all, I thank the K'ichee' speakers, especially those from Nahualá, Santa Catarina Ixtahuacán, and Santo Tomás la Unión, Suchitepéquez, who have so patiently mentored me in their language. A greater gift they could not have given me. For in sharing with me their language they opened their hearts in friendship.

My thanks to Father Eugene Hruska, who so patiently and with much effort helped me to formulate my ideas in the clearest possible fashion. It was his prodding that made me begin constructing this grammar, and it was his continual help and encouragement that enabled me to finally finish it. These lessons bear the mark of his careful revision and constructive criticism.

I also owe a debt of gratitude to Dr. William Norman for the long hours he invested in the correction and revision of this grammar. And finally, I especially thank my wife, Maria Tahay Carrillo, herself a native K'ichee' speaker, who so patiently helped me in formulating this work.

In 1998 Mark Potter and his wife, Hilaria Xu'm, a native of Santa Catarina Ixtashucan, on their own initiative, transcribed the entire grammar into a Word document and rewrote all of the K'ichee' entries into the now commonly used alphabet of the Academia de Lenguas Mayas de Guatemala (ALMG). I am deeply indebted to them for undertaking that laborious task.

Abbreviations and Symbols

ADJ	adjective
ADV	adverb
CONJ	conjunction
DEM	demonstrative
DEM ART	demonstrative article
DEM PRO	demonstrative pronoun
DIR	direction
EXCLAM	exclamatory word
FORM	formal address form
INDEF ART	indefinite article
INTER	interrogatory word
IVP	positional intransitive verb
IVS	simple intransitive verb
MANNER, DIR	manner or direction
N	noun

NUM	number
PART	particle (not translatable)
PER PRO	personal pronoun
PL	plural
PLU FAM	second person plural, familiar address form (*ix*)
PLU FORM	second person plural, formal address form (*alaq*)
PN	obligatorily possessed noun
POSS PRO	possessive pronoun
PREP	preposition
PRO	pronoun
REL PRO	relative pronoun
SING	singular
SING-FAM	second person singular, familiar address form (*at*)
SING-FORM	second person singular, formal address form (*laal*)
SPAN	Spanish loan word
TV	transitive verb
TVR	radical transitive verb
TVD	derived transitive verb

Basic
K'ichee'
Grammar

LESSON

1

The K'ichee' Alphabet

The K'ichee' alphabet consists of the following sounds:

aa Closely resembles the *a* in "father."

aaj	reed	paar	skunk
chaaj	ash	laal	you (sing-form)

(See note 1.)

a A rapidly pronounced *a* resembling the *u* in "but."

aj	fresh ear of corn	ak'	chicken
kar	fish	jal	dried ears of corn

b' There are two forms of *b'*:

b'₁ FORMATION: This sound is formed by pulling air from the mouth back into the throat while pronouncing an English *b* and at the same time momentarily closing the throat before opening the lips to say the *b* sound.

OCCURRENCE: Before vowels.

b'e	road	ab'aj	rock
b'a	gopher	ub'een	tamale with beans inside

b'₂ FORMATION: Made by holding the breath while making a *p* sound and releasing the air in the mouth between the lips with a small puff of air or without releasing the air.

OCCURRENCE: Before consonants or at the end of an utterance.

jab'	rain	sib'	smoke
sub'	corn tamale	aab'	hammock

ch Like the *ch* in "church."

cho	lake	chiim	woven bag
wach	face, front	wo'ch	my house

ch' Pronounced with the tongue in the same position as for the *ch*, but now the throat is closed; only the air remaining in the mouth is used to produce this "glottalized" (produced with the throat closed) sound.

Hold your breath and practice making *ch'* and *ch'o*:

ch'   ch'   ch'   ch'   ch'   ch'   ch'o   ch'o   ch'o   ch'o   ch'o   ch'o

ch'o	mouse	puuch'	matter from eyes
jach'	corn harvest	ch'iich'	any metallic object

ee Pronounced like the *ai* in "bait."

cheech	for him	wee	mine (belonging to me)
eera	place where wheat is thrashed		

(See note 1.)

e A rapidly pronounced (short) *e* approximately like the *e* in "bet."

k'el	a small parrot	le	the (DEM ART)

ii Like the *ee* in "deed."

piim	thick	riib'	himself
siip	woodtick	wiij	my back

(See note 1.)

i A rapidly pronounced *i*.

sib'	smoke	in	I

j Somewhat resembles the *h* sound in "hot" but pronounced deep in the throat with a scraping sound.

jat	go!	jooj	a black bird
ajiij	sugar cane	iij	measles

k Like the *c* in "cat."

| ko | hard | keem | weaving |
| kuuk | squirrel | ki | maguey plant |

(See note 2.)

k' Pronounced with the tongue in the same position as for the *k*, but now the throat is closed and only the air in the mouth is used to produce this glottalized" (produced with throat closed) sound.

Hold your breath and practice making *k'* and *k'a*:

k' k' k' k' k' k' k' k' k' k'a k'a k'a k'a k'a k'a k'a

k'a	bitter	k'ook'	fragrant
k'i	many	k'olok'ik	spherical
k'aak'	new	k'ab'ak'ik	gaping (mouth)

l There are two *l*'s:

l_1 FORMATION: Like an English *l* but with the tip of the tongue placed immediately behind the upper front teeth.

OCCURRENCE: Before vowels.

| lo | perhaps | lawalo | seriously sick |
| Luu' | Peter (name) | lik'ilik | spread out |

l_2 FORMATION: Formed with the tongue in the same position as it is for l_1 but said without voicing (whispered); the air in the mouth is blown out over the top sides of the tongue while saying this sound.

OCCURRENCE: Before consonants or at the end of utterances.

| aal | heavy | yaab'iil | sickness |
| jul | hole | te'l | torn |

m Like the *m* in English.

| am | spider | amoolo | fly |
| poom | copal | maam | grandfather |

n Closely resembles the English *n*.

| naan | ma'am | nuwaa | my tortilla |
| siin | bamboo | aninaq | quickly |

oo Like the *o* in "phone."

| ooj | avocado | pooy | scarecrow |
| lool | grasshopper | q'ooq' | type of squash |

(See note 2.)

o A rapidly pronounced (short) *o*.

oj	we	kon	foolish
koj	lion	ch'ok	blackbird

p Like the *p* in "spot."

poom	copal	puum	dove
poop	straw mat	peepe	butterfly, moth

(See note 2.)

p vs. b': It is often hard for a beginner in the language to distinguish between *p* and *b'*. The following contrasting words will help in hearing and pronouncing the difference:

sib'	smoke	b'o'j	clay cooking pot
siip	woodtick	po'j	a type of coastal tree
jab'	rain	kolob'	rope
poop	straw mat	ch'oop	pineapple

q A *k* sound produced deep in the throat. In order to produce this sound, it may help to place the tip of the tongue down near the root of the tongue and then, forcing the back of the tongue as deep as possible into the throat, pronounce a *k*.

aaq	pig	waaqib'	six
b'aaq	bone	b'aqiil	body

(See note 2.)

q' Pronounced with the tongue in the same position as for the *q*, but now the throat is closed and only the air remaining in the mouth is used to produce the "glottalized" (produced with the throat closed) sound. In Nahualá the mouth air is pulled back into the throat to produce this sound. In some dialects the mouth air is forced outward to produce the sound.

Hold your breath and practice making *q'* and *q'a*:

q'   q'   q'   q'   q'   q'   q'   q'   q'a   q'a   q'a   q'a   q'a   q'a   q'a

q'an	yellow	aq'ab'	night
q'iij	day, sun	q'eq	black
waaq'	my tongue	q'aaq'	fire

r There are two *r*'s:

r₁ FORMATION: Like the Spanish *flip r* (as in "pero") or the *tt* in the English name "Betty."

OCCURRENCE: Between two vowels.

toroom	open	eera	place for thrashing wheat
waraal	here	joron	cold

r₂   FORMATION: Like the Spanish trilled *r* (as in "perro") but without voicing (whispered).

OCCURRENCE: Whenever the *r* is not found between two vowels.

rax	green	paar	skunk
ri'	that one	karna't	passion fruit

s Like the *s* in English.

t A *t* pronounced with the tip of the tongue directly behind the upper front teeth.

tap	crab	ataam	early
jat	go!	taat	sir

(See note 2.)

t' Pronounced with the tongue in the same position as for the *t*, but now the throat is closed and only the air remaining in the mouth is used to produce this "glottalized" (produced with the throat closed) sound.

Hold your breath and practice making *t'* and *t'a*:

t'   t'   t'   t'   t'   t'   t'   t'   t'a   t'a   t'a   t'a   t'a   t'a   t'a

b'it'	a tearing sound	t'u'y	cooking pot
t'oot'	snail	jat'iim	tied

tz Like the *ts* in "sits."

tzi	soaked kernels of corn (hominy)	tzatz	thick
tzaam	liquor	patzapik	shaggy

tz' Pronounced with the tongue in the same position as for the "tz," but now the throat is closed and the air remaining in the mouth is used to produce this "glottalized" (produced with the throat closed) sound.

Hold your breath and practice making *tz'* and *tz'a*:

tz'   tz'   tz'   tz'   tz'   tz'   tz'a   tz'a   tz'a   tz'a   tz'a   tz'a   tz'a

tz'i'	dog	suutz'	cloud
atz'aam	salt	patz'an	dried plant stalk

uu Like the *oo* of "boot."

uul	landslide	puum	a kind of bird
suuq	scum	puuch'	matter from eyes

(See note 2)

u A rapidly pronounced (short) *u*.

us	gnat	jul	hole
sub′	corn tamale	k′uch	buzzard

w There are two *w*'s:

w₁ FORMATION: Like the *w* in English.

OCCURRENCE: Before vowels.

wa	tortilla	yawaab′	sick one
awaal	your child (woman)	oyowaal	anger

w₂ FORMATION: Somewhat like the *oof* in "aloof," but the *f* is pronounced with the two lips rather than with the lower lip and upper front teeth.

OCCURRENCE: Before consonants or at the end of utterances.

teew	cold	ulew	land, earth
rajaaw	its owner	utiw	coyote

x Like the *sh* in "ship."

xaan	adobe	aweex	corn planting
oxib′	three	xoot	earthen shingles or cooking plate

y There are two y's:

y₁ FORMATION: Like the *y* in "yes."

OCCURRENCE: Before vowels.

yaab′iil	sickness	iyoom	midwife
yaak	fox	saniyeb′	sand

y₂ FORMATION: Like the *ee* of "beet" immediately followed by the *h* of "hot," but with the *h* pronounced directly behind the upper front teeth.

OCCURRENCE: Before consonants or at the end of utterances.

pooy	scarecrow	xu′y	stingy
t′o′y	woven cap	t′u′y	cooking pot

′ Glottal stop, formed by quickly closing and opening the throat, as if saying the word "bottle" as *bo′l*. To pronounce "bottle" this way, first the *bo* of "bottle" is said, then the breath is held for a short moment before relaxing the throat muscles and saying the *l*: "bo" — hold breath — *l*.

b'aa'	well! oh!	tapa'l	a type of fruit
ja'	water	t'u'y	cooking pot
wachi'iil	my companion	kin'eek*	I go
ub'e'eel	correctness	kix'eek*	you go

* In this grammar glottal stops are almost never written before vowels, even though any word beginning with a vowel in K'ichee' is preceded by a glottal stop (e.g., 'ak' "chicken").

NOTES TO LESSON 1

1. Final short vowels: Any short vowel that occurs at the end of an utterance is followed by a breathy *h* almost as if the vowel were said a second time in a whispered manner.

b'ah	gopher	choh	lake
b'eh	road	puupu	balloon
tzih	soaked kernels of corn		

2. Aspiration: If the consonants *k*, *p*, *q*, and *t* occur before vowels, they are pronounced with a minimum of air escaping from the mouth (unaspirated), as in the *c* of "scare," the *p* of "spot," and the *t* of "stake."

kaa'	grinding stone	pooy	scarecrow
ko	hard	apanoq	over there
qeech	ours	tap	crab
aqan	foot	maataam	late

If the consonants *k*, *p*, *q*, and *t* occur before other consonants or at the end of an utterance, they are pronounced with a noticeable amount of air escaping from the mouth (aspirated), as in the *c* of "tic," the *p* of "up," and the *t* of "at."

pa'k	cracked hands	tap	crab
xok la'	that one entered	siip	woodtick
aaq	pig	at	you
uq	skirt	po't	woven blouse

OPTIONAL DRILLS

Listed below are some exercises to further the mastery of some of the more difficult sounds for those needing extra drill.

A. Regular vs. Short Vowels

aa, a

| aaj | reed | chaaj | ash |
| aj | fresh corn | chaj | pine |

b'aatz'	calendar day	k'aat	cargo net
b'atz'	thread	k'at	calendar day
aak'	type of grain	oq'aab'	an edible green
ak'	chicken	uq'ab'	his hand
kaawaaj	you want it	pataan	service
kawaaj	I want it	patan	head strap

ee, e

eek'	bromeliad	cheech	for him
		k'el	a green parrot

ii, i

siip	woodtick
sib'	smoke

oo, o

ooj	avocado	poom	copal
oj	we	kon	stupid
q'inoom	rich	k'ook'	fragrant
q'inom	a type of fruit	ch'ok	blackbird
k'ooj	mask	q'oor	corn dough
koj	lion	q'or	lazy

uu, u

uul	landslide	k'uul	blanket
us	gnat	jul	hole
suuq	scum	puuch'	matter from eyes
sub'	corn tamale	k'uch	buzzard

B. Distinguishing *k*, *k'*, *q*, and *q'* in Hearing and Speaking

kook	turtle		
kook'	finely ground	kuuk	squirrel
k'ook'	fragrant	kuuk'	with them
q'ooq'	large squash	quuk'	with us
q'aaq'	fire	kuq	their skirts
qaaq'	our tongues	quq	our skirts
kaaq'	their tongues	q'uuq'	quetzal bird
k'aak'	new		
kaaq	their pig	kolik	to be defended, saved
qaaq	our pig	k'olik	to be put away
kaak'	their chicken	qolik	to be scraped, scratched
qaak'	our chicken	q'olik	to be picked (apples, coffee, etc.)
kaq	red	k'aq	flea

C. Glottal Stops

chee	for him	kuulik	he arrives
chee'	tree, wood	ku'lik	they arrive
ja	house	kab'alka'tik	he rolls over and over
ja'	water	kaab'alkatiij	you roll it over and over
tzi	soaked kernels of corn	ixoqiib'	women
tz'i'	dog	i'xoqiib'	women (third person plural)

STRESS RULES

In K'ichee' words are generally stressed on the last syllable (e.g., tina<u>mit</u> "town"; kixqatzu<u>kuuj</u> "we look for you"). However, small particle-like words are generally not stressed unless are the last word in an utterance (e.g., with the adverbial particle *na* "later": kim<u>b'ee</u> na chw<u>ee</u>'q; utterance-final: kim<u>bee na</u>). If a word ends in a short vowel, then the stress is on the penultimate syllable of that word (e.g., kojee<u>wa</u>ra jee la' "We'll go sleep over there"; <u>chu</u>wa ja "in front of the house"). The stress rules for the language are more complex than what has just been stated, but since this is an introductory grammar, no more will be said about stress here.

USEFUL EXPRESSIONS

1. Xsaqirik.
   Good morning. (greeting)

2. Xe q'iij.
   Good afternoon. (greeting)

3. Xok aq'ab'.
   Good evening. (greeting)

4. La utz awach?*
   How are you?

5. Utz, maltyoox. E k'u ri at?*
   Fine, thank you. And you?

* All expressions using second person singular or plural will here be found in the familiar *at* and *ix* forms. If these same expressions are to be said in the formal *laal* and *alaq* forms, the appropriate changes must be made.

The Nonverbal Sentence

In K'ichee' there is no verb "to be" (*ser* in Spanish). Sentences that normally depend on the verb "to be" in English are formed in K'ichee' simply by using the subject and a modifier without expressing the verb "to be."

MODELS

Saq le ja.
(white the house)
or The house is white.

K'a'n le tz'i'.
(mean the dog)
or The dog is mean.

VOCABULARY

ja	(N)	house, building
tz'i'	(N)	dog
chee'	(N)	tree, wood

achi	(N)	man
ixoq	(N)	woman
awach	(N)	external appearance, face, front, state of being
elaq'oom	(N)	thief
utz	(ADJ)	good
itzeel	(ADJ)	bad, evil
k'a'n	(ADJ)	mean, ill-tempered
niim	(ADJ)	big
ch'uti'n	(ADJ)	small
niich'	(ADJ)	small
saq	(ADJ)	white, clear
kaq	(ADJ)	red
q'eq	(ADJ)	black
le	(DEM ART)	the (visible to the speaker or spoken of as if present)

K'ICHEE' TO ENGLISH

1. Q'eq le tz'i'.
2. Elaq'oom le achi.
3. Niich' le ixoq.
4. K'a'n le elaq'oom.
5. Niim le ja.
6. Utz le achi.
7. Saq le chee'.
8. Niich' le tz'i'.

NOTE: Frequently words ending in a vowel followed by words beginning in a vowel will fuse these two vowels in the following manner:

$V_1 V_2 c$ > V_2'c: e.g., le ach > la'chi "the man"
le elaq'oom > le'laq'oom "the thief"
ri utaat > ru'taat "his/her father"

Such vowel fusion, however, does not occur with monosyllabic nouns that begin with a vowel; e.g., *le ak'* "the chicken" or *le uul* "the landslide" would never be contracted to *la'k'* or *lu'l*.

ENGLISH TO K'ICHEE'

1. The house is big.
2. The woman is white.
3. The dog is mean.

4. The man is big.
5. The man is mean.
6. The dog is white.
7. The man is good.
8. The tree is big.
9. The woman is good.
10. The tree is small.
11. The dog is good.
12. The tree is white.
13. The thief is bad.
14. The dog is a thief.
15. The man is a thief.
16. The woman is a thief.
17. The house is white.

USEFUL EXPRESSIONS

1. Jas kuub'iij?
   What do you say? (What's new?)

   Maaj or na k'oo taj.
   Nothing.

2. Chaaya'aa rutzil uwach ri awachajiil.
   Give greetings to your husband.

3. La maaj k'ax chaawee?
   Are you feeling well?

   Xaq jee wa' nub'anoom, maltyoox chee ri Dyoos.
   I'm doing alright, thanks be to God.

4. K'ate' oj wa'.
   Here we are (we just arrived).

LESSON

3

Pluralization of Nonverbal Sentences

In general, there are three different elements that may be used to pluralize nonverbal sentences. Sometimes all of these elements are present, and sometimes only one or two are present.

MODELS

Some nouns and some adjectives have their own proper plural forms:

achi	man	achijaab'	men
ak'aal	child	ak'alaab'	children
ch'uti'n	little	ch'uti'q	little ones
niim	big	nima'q	big ones

As a general rule, only human nouns have plural forms. And since these plurals are formed quite irregularly, in each instance they must be memorized. E.g.:

ali	girl	altomaab′	girls
ala	boy	alab′oom	boys

The pluralizer for "living (moving) things" in the third person is *ee*. Sometimes this precedes the word to be pluralized. The pluralizer *ee* can often be glossed in English as "they."

Ee nima′q (taq) le tz′i′.
(they big the dog)
The dogs are big.

The particle *taq*, which is a pluralizer, can be inserted into the sentence. If nothing else in the plural sentence/clause indicates plural, then *taq* must be used:

Saq taq le ja.
The houses are white.

NOTE: Should a noun begin with a vowel, when pluralizing, the *ee* is not expressed. But the first vowel of the noun has a glottal stop following it (see note on page 13).

Ee elaq′omaab′ (taq) le achijaab′ > E′laq′omaab′(taq) le achijaab′.
The men are thieves.

VOCABULARY

ak′aal	(N)	child
ak′alaab′	(N)	children
ajchaak	(N)	worker
ajchakiib′	(N)	workers
kotz′i′j	(N)	flower, candle
sak′aaj	(ADJ, N)	ambitious, ambitious one
sak′ajiib′	(ADJ, N)	ambitious, ambitious ones
q′or	(ADJ, N)	lazy, lazy one
q′oriib′	(N)	lazy ones
kaq	(ADJ)	red
rax	(ADJ)	green, blue
niim	(ADJ)	big
nima′q	(ADJ)	big (PL)
ch′uti′n	(ADJ)	small (SING)
ch′uti′q	(ADJ)	small (PL)
ixoq	(N)	woman
ixoqiib′	(N)	women
achijaab′	(N)	men
elaq′oom	(N)	thief
elaq′omaab′	(N)	thieves

FIGURE 3.1. *Ak'alaab'* (children). Photograph by John Edvalson.

| ee | (PRO) | they |
| taq | (PART) | pluralizer |

K'ICHEE' TO ENGLISH
1. Rax taq le kotz'i'j.
2. Ee nima'q (taq) le ak'alaab'.
3. Saq taq le ja.
4. Ee q'oriib' (taq) le ak'alaab'.
5. A'jchakiib' (taq) le achijaab'.
6. Rax taq le chee'.
7. Ee k'a'n (taq) le tz'i'.
8. Ee sak'ajiib' (taq) le ixoqiib'.
9. Ee sak'ajiib' taq le ajchakiib'.
10. Ee nima'q (taq) le tz'i'.

ENGLISH TO K'ICHEE'
1. The children are good.
2. The workers are lazy.
3. The women are ambitious.
4. The men are workers.
5. The workers are thieves.
6. The children are lazy ones.

FIGURE 3.2. *Ixoqiib'* (women). Photographs by James Mondloch.

7. The women are ambitious ones.
8. The dogs are mean.
9. The trees are big.
10. The flowers are red.
11. The trees are small.
12. The houses are red.
13. The candles are white.
14. The flowers are blue.
15. The dogs are white.

USEFUL EXPRESSIONS

1. La xatpeetik?
   Did you come? (small talk, asked when someone arrives)
   Xinpeetik.
   I came.

2. La ix k'olik?
   Are you there? (asked when approaching a house to enter)
   Oj k'olik.
   We're here.

3. Ee na.
   So long. (a short greeting when meeting someone on the road or passing by someone's house)

Personal Pronouns and the Nonverbal Sentence

There are eight independent personal pronouns. These, used in conjunction with a predicate noun or a predicate adjective, form another type of nonverbal sentence. It should be noted that the model and schema below are not the only correct way of forming these types of nonverbal sentences.

MODEL

In in achi. I am a man.

SCHEMA OF PERSONAL PRONOUNS

In (in) achi.	I am a man.	Oj (oj) achijaab'.	We are men.
At (at) achi.	You are a man.	Ix (ix) achijaab'.	You are men.
Ri are' achi.	He is a man.	Ri a're' a'chijaab'.	They are men.
Laal (laal) achi.	You (FORM) are a man.	Alaq (alaq) achijaab'.	You (FORM) are men.

The personal pronoun can be doubled to emphasize the subject:

In in achi. I myself am a man.
In achi. I am a man.

VOCABULARY

in	(PER PRO)	I
at	(PER PRO)	you
ri are'	(PER PRO)	he/she/it
laal	(PER PRO, FORM)	you (FORM)
oj/uj	(PER PRO)	we
ix	(PER PRO)	you (PL)
ri a're' (ri ee are')	(PER PRO)	they
alaq	(PER PRO, FORM)	you (FORM)

K'ICHEE' TO ENGLISH

1. Oj oj nima'q.
2. Ri are' elaq'oom.
3. In in utz.
4. Alaq alaq ixoqiib'.
5. At at ch'uti'n.
6. At at elaq'oom.
7. Ri a're' ee tz'i'.
8. Laal laal niim.
9. Ix ix utz.
10. Ri are' k'a'n.

ENGLISH TO K'ICHEE'

1. I am a woman.
2. They are women.
3. She is a woman.
4. You (FORM) are a woman.
5. We are women.
6. You (PL) are women.
7. You (SING) are a woman.
8. You (FORM) are women.
9. I am a thief.
10. You (FORM) are a thief.
11. We are thieves.
12. You are thieves.
13. They are thieves.
14. You (FORM) are thieves.
15. You are a thief.
16. It is a dog.

17. They are dogs.
18. I am good.
19. You are good.
20. She is good.
21. He is good.
22. They are small.
23. She is mean.
24. I am bad.
25. You (SING-FORM) are good.
26. They are good.
27. He is a thief.
28. You (PL) are mean.
29. We are big.
30. They are bad.

USEFUL EXPRESSIONS

1. Jas ab'i'?
   What is your name?

   In alWe'l.
   I'm Manuela.

2. Janipa' ajunaab'?
   How old are you?

   B'elejeb' nujunaab'.
   I'm nine years old.

3. Jawii k'o wi le awo'ch?
   Where is you house?

   Pa Niwala' k'o wi.
   It's in Nahualá.

4. Jawii katpee wi?
   Where do you come from?

   Pa Niwala' (kimpee wi).
   (I come) from Nahualá.

5. Jachin ri ataat?
   Who is your father?

5

Adjectives Modifying Nouns

We saw previously the sentence *Niim le ja* "The house is big." Now we will modify *ja* with the adjective *saq* "white." We put the adjective first, followed by the noun, generally with an *a* between the two to aid in pronunciation. Therefore *saq* + *ja* becomes *saqa ja* "the white house." If the noun begins with a vowel, the *a* between the adjective and noun becomes a glottal stop after the first vowel of the noun, e.g., *niima achi* > *niim a'chi* "big man." (See asterisked note, p. 12.)

If we pluralize the noun and its modifier, then we use the particle *taq* between the adjective and the noun:

le saqa ja	the white house
le saqa taq ja	the white houses
le utz a'chi	the good man
le utza taq achijaab'	the good men

It should be noted that to say "the white houses" *saqa taq ja* is not the same as saying "the houses are white" *saq taq le ja*, as we saw in lesson 3.

If the adjective has a plural form, it must be used with a plural noun, e.g.:

nimaq taq ja	the big houses
ch'utiq taq chee'	the small trees

Note that in the above examples, before *taq* the plural forms like *nima'q* become *nimaq* and *ch'uti'q* becomes *ch'utiq*.

VOCABULARY

ala	(N)	boy
ali	(N)	girl
alab'oom	(N)	boys
altomaab'	(N)	girls
ab'aj	(N)	rock
tz'ikin	(N)	bird
yawaab'	(ADJ, N)	sick, sick one
yawab'iib'	(N)	sick ones
ko	(ADJ)	strong, hard
q'an	(ADJ)	yellow

K'ICHEE' TO ENGLISH

1. Kaqa taq ja.
2. Saqa taq kotz'i'j.
3. Ala le yawaab' a'k'aal.
4. Ko le q'eq a'b'aj.
5. Laal laal sak'aaj a'jchaak.
6. Ch'uti'n le saqa kotz'i'j.
7. Ee utz le q'ana taq tz'ikin.
8. Ix ix sak'aja taq ixoqiib'.
9. Yawaab' le niim a'chi.
10. Nima'q taq le chee'.

ENGLISH TO K'ICHEE'

1. Red house
2. Big man
3. Mean dog
4. Lazy woman
5. Yellow bird
6. Sick child
7. Ambitious worker
8. Black rock
9. White flower
10. Red houses
11. Big men

FIGURE 5.1. *Ali* (girl). Photograph by John Edvalson.

12. Mean dogs
13. Lazy women
14. Yellow birds
15. Sick children
16. Ambitious workers
17. Black rocks
18. White flowers
19. The red house is big.
20. The big man is mean.
21. The mean dog is white.
22. The ambitious women are good.
23. The yellow birds are bad.
24. The black rock is hard.
25. The sick child is a boy.
26. The lazy worker is a man.
27. The big men are mean.
28. The white flower is small.
29. The red houses are big.
30. The mean dogs are white.
31. The lazy women are small.
32. The yellow birds are bad.

33. The sick children are boys.
34. The black rocks are hard.
35. The white flowers are small.
36. The lazy workers are men.

USEFUL EXPRESSIONS

1. La ee k'as ataat, anaan?
   Are your father and mother living?

2. La ee k'o awachalaal?
   Do you have brothers and sisters?

   Je', ee k'olik.
   Yes, I do. (literally, "Yes, there are.")

3. Ix janipa' ix k'o pa ja?
   How many of you are in the family?

   Oj waqiib'.
   We are six.

4. La ix alaxik ruuk'?
   Are you related to him/her?

   Je', oj alaxik.
   Yes, we are related.

5. Jas kixk'aman ruuk'?
   How are you related to him/her?

   Aree inchaaq'.
   He's my younger sibling.

6

Converting Affirmative Sentences into Questions

Note that in the preceding lessons we learned to say *saq le nima ja* "the big house is white." This is a simple statement. To make this a question, one merely places the question word *la* in front of the utterance.

La questions require a "yes" or "no" answer, as in the basic sentence below:

La saq chi le nima ja?
(is white now the big house)
Is the big house white now?

VOCABULARY

juyub'	(N)	mountain
tinamit	(N)	town, nation
chaak	(N)	work
b'e	(N)	road
ab'i'	(N)	your name
ri'j	(ADJ, N)	grown, grownup, old; old one
ri'jaab'	(N)	the grown-up ones, old ones
chi, chik	(ADV)	now, again

FIGURE 6.1. *B'e* (road). Photograph by John Edvalson.

k'ax (ADV, N) difficult, painful, suffering
jas, jasa (INTER) what

K'ICHEE' TO ENGLISH
1. La k'a'n chi le ixoq?
2. La niim le achi?
3. La ee nima'q le elaq'omaab'?
4. La kaq a'b'aj le juyub'?
5. La ch'uti'n le ixoq?
6. La saq le chee'?

FIGURE 6.2. *Tinamit* (town). Photograph by John Edvalson.

7. La yawaab' le ri'j?
8. La nima'q taq le tinamit?
9. La ee q'orib' taq le alab'oom?
10. La saq taq le kotz'i'j?
11. La yawaab' chi le achi?
12. Jasa le ab'i'?
13. La at at ajchaak?

ENGLISH TO K'ICHEE'

1. The work is difficult.
2. Is the work difficult?
3. The town is big.
4. Is the town big?
5. The child is grown up now.
6. Is the child grown up now?
7. The man is sick now.
8. Is the man sick now?
9. The mountain is red rock.
10. Is the mountain red rock?
11. The white dog is mean now.
12. Is the white dog mean now?

13. The boys are lazy now.
14. Are the boys lazy now?
15. The little girls are good.
16. Are the little girls good?
17. The roads are difficult.
18. Are the roads difficult?
19. The men are good workers.
20. Are the men good workers?

USEFUL EXPRESSIONS

1. La at k'ulanik?
   Are you married?

   Jee', in k'ulanik.
   Yes, I'm married.

2. La ee k'o awalk'u'aal?
   Do you have children? (asked of a man)
   Ee k'olik.
   I do have (literally, "there are").

3. La ee k'o awaal?
   Do you have children? (asked of a woman)
   Ee k'olik.
   I do have. (literally, "There are.")

4. Ee janipa'?
   How many (children do you have)?
   Ee jo'ob'.
   Five.

5. La konojel ee k'ask'oj?
   Are they all alive?

LESSON

7

Possessive Pronouns

We recognize the sentence *k'a'n le tz'i'* "the dog is mean." In the model below we see a new element appearing with *tz'i'*. The *nu-* indicates "my."
    *Sib'alaj k'a'n le <u>nu</u>tz'ii'.

> *Sib'alaj k'a'n le nutz'ii'.   My dog is very mean.

The possessive pronouns are:

nu-	my	qa-	our
a-	your	i-	your
u-	his/hers/its	ki-	their
la	your (FORM)	alaq	your (FORM)

SCHEMA OF POSSESSIVE PRONOUNS

nutz'ii'	my dog	qatz'ii'	our dog
atz'ii'	your dog	itz'ii'	your dog
utz'ii'	his/her dog	kitz'ii'	their dog
tz'i' la	your (FORM) dog	tz'i' alaq	your (FORM) dog

The *nu-* occasionally becomes *in-*, e.g.:

intaat "my father"
inchaaq' "my younger sibling"

*Notice that when the word *tz'i'* "dog" is possessed, the vowel is lengthened: *nutz'ii'*. A large number of nouns in K'ichee' undergo vowel lengthening when possessed: *wa* "tortilla," *nuwaa* "my tortilla," *laq* "clay dish," *alaaq* "your clay dish." Other nouns do not undergo this vowel-lengthening process: *tz'ikin* "bird," *kitz'ikin* "their bird." There is no rule to predict which nouns undergo vowel lengthening when possessed.

Phrases with nouns as the possessors of the possessed nouns, such as "the boy's dog" or "the girls' birds," are formed as follows:

u-tz'ii' le ala   ki-tz'ikin   le altomaab'
his-dog   the boy   their-bird(s) the girls

VOCABULARY

taat	(N)	father, sir (term of direct address)
naan	(N)	mother, ma'am (term of direct address)
pwaq	(N)	money, precious metal
keej	(N)	horse
me's	(N)	cat
b'aaq	(ADJ, N)	thin; bone, needle
joron	(ADJ, N)	cold, cool; water
rax	(ADJ)	green, blue
choom	(ADJ)	fat
sib'alaj	(ADV)	very, a lot

K'ICHEE' TO ENGLISH

1. Sib'alaj niim le akeej.
2. La k'a'n le me's la?
3. Ee q'eq taq le nukeej.
4. La utz chi le ichaak?
5. La ee b'aaq chi le tz'i' alaq, taat?
6. Sib'alaj niim chi nupwaaq.
7. Niim a'chi le intaat.

ENGLISH TO K'ICHEE'

1. Your dog is very mean.
2. His horse is white.
3. Our father is very good.
4. Her cat is small.

5. Their work is very difficult.
6. My cat is yellow.
7. Your (SING-FORM) horse is thin.
8. Their mother is sick.
9. Our cat is very fat.
10. The man's horses are big.
11. Your (PLU FORM) money is much (big).
12. Their fathers are mean.
13. Your mothers are good.
14. My dogs are sick.
15. Your (PLU FORM) works are difficult.
16. The workers' trees are very green now.
17. The rocks are very cold.
18. The men's town is big.
19. My horse is white.
20. The boys' father's trees are green.

USEFUL EXPRESSIONS

1. Janipaa chi rik'iil le nee'?
   How many months old is the baby?

2. La k'o awulew?
   Do you have land?

   Jee', k'olik.
   Yes, I do.

3. Janipaa k'a'aam awulew?
   How many cuerdas of land do you have?

   Xaa kajib' k'a'aam.
   Just four cuerdas.

4. Jas aatikom chuwach?
   What have you planted on it?

8

Possessive Pronouns (Continued)

In the preceding lesson we studied possessive pronouns. The possessive pronouns used in that lesson are the forms that are used when the object possessed started with a consonant, (e.g., *tz'i'*, *taat*, etc.). If the object possessed begins with a vowel, then a different set of possessives is used.

The possessive pronouns are:

w-	my	q-	our
aw-	your	iw-	your
r-	his/her	k-	their
la	your (FORM)	alaq	your (FORM)

SCHEMA OF POSSESSIVE PRONOUNS

wixoqiil	my wife	qixoqiil	our wives
awixoqiil	your wife	iwixoqiil	your wives
rixoqiil	his wife	kixoqiil	their wives
ixoqil la	your (FORM) wife	ixoqil alaq	your (FORM) wives

MODEL

Utz le wixoqiil.
My wife is good.

If the owner or possessor is a noun, then the ownership or possession is expressed in the following way:

Utz'ii' le ala.   Le rixoqil le watz.
(his dog the boy) (his wife my older brother)
The boy's dog.   My older brother's wife.

VOCABULARY

wa	(N)	tortilla, corn substance, food in general
riki'l	(N)	dish of food that accompanies tortillas
atz'iyaq	(N)	clothing, cloth
winaq	(N)	person, people
Ixoqiil	(PN)	wife
achajiil	(PN)	husband
atz	(PN)	older sibling (of the same sex)
chaaq'	(PN)	younger sibling (of the same sex)
o'ch	(PN)	house, home
k'aak'	(ADJ)	new
k'i	(ADJ)	much, many
lawalo	(ADJ)	bad from sickness or nature
pa	(PREP)	in, into, toward, to, from
kamik	(ADV)	today
iwir	(ADV)	yesterday
chwe'q	(ADV)	tomorrow

K'ICHEE' TO ENGLISH

1. Yawaab' le rachajiil le watz.
2. Saq le ro'ch le achi.
3. La ee utz le kixoqiil le achijaab'?
4. Sib'alaj nima'q taq le o'ch alaq.
5. Saq taq le qatz'iyaaq.
6. La k'aak' le saqa o'ch la?
7. Ee k'a'n taq le kachajiil le ixoqiib'.
8. Sib'alaj lawalo le taat la kamik.
9. Sib'alaj q'or a'chi le rachajiil le watz.
10. La yawaab' chi le uchaaq' le ixqiil la?

ENGLISH TO K'ICHEE'

1. The worker's wife is mean.

2. The woman's husband is sick.
3. The woman's clothes are new.
4. The boy's food is much. (The boy has much food.)
5. Yesterday the girl's mother was sick.
6. Our father's white house is new.
7. Their mother's older sister is a fat woman.
8. The children's dog is small.
9. The cat's house is wood.
10. The woman's mother is very sick.
11. The boy's dogs are many.
12. Are you the man's older brother?
13. Are the people's houses big in the town?
14. Are your (FORM) father's clothes new?
15. Does their father have much money? (Is their father's money much?)
16. Is the girl's dish of food cold now?
17. Are you the child's father?
18. Was the boy's father sick yesterday?
19. Is his horse sick?
20. The worker's food is cold.
21. Yesterday the flowers were white.

USEFUL EXPRESSIONS

1. Kojee b'a na.
   We have to go now. (when departing)

2. Ee b'a'.
   Well, I'm going. (when departing)

3. Ja'ee.
   Alright.

4. Jat b'a'.
   Well, go then.

9

Simple Intransitive Verbs in Incomplete Aspect

In K'ichee' there are two main types of verbs, transitive and intransitive.

Simple Intransitive Verbs are verbs that express an aspect and the subject of the aspect (e.g., I run). In verbs there is both an incomplete aspect and a completed aspect. In this lesson we will be dealing with Simple Intransitive Verbs in incomplete aspect.

Transitive Verbs express a subject, the action, and the receiver of the action, or subject, verb, and object. We will study these verbs in later lessons beginning in lesson 15.

SIMPLE INTRANSITIVE VERBS IN INCOMPLETE ASPECT

The Simple Intransitive Verb of this type is made up of the following elements:

+ *aspect*   + *person*   + *root*   ± *termination*

(The + sign before an element means that it must be present. The ± sign before an element means that it may be present.)

ASPECT

We will be using the word "aspect" rather than the word "time" or "tense." It seems better to speak of an incomplete aspect rather than a present time.

The idea here is that the action has not yet been done or, if begun, is not yet finished. This aspect is always marked by the prefix *k-*.

PERSON

Person is the second element of the Simple Intransitive Verb. The person in these verbs is expressed by the personal pronouns that we learned in lessons 7 and 8:

in	I	oj	we
at	you	ix	you
ri are'	he/she/it	ri a're'	they
laal	you (FORM)	alaq	you (FORM)

These same person markers are used in the Simple Intransitive Verb with the exception of the third persons and the *laal*, which becomes *la*:

in	I	oj	we
at	you	ix	you
Ø*	he	ee	they
la	you (FORM)	alaq	you (FORM)

* The symbol Ø indicates that there is no marker (i.e., "zero").

ROOT

The root is the heart of the verb, which gives it meaning and is unchanging if the verb is regular (most K'ichee' verbs are regular).

TERMINATION

If the Simple Intransitive Verb is the final word of the sentence or clause, it will be terminated with *-ik*, or *-k* if the last sound of the root happens to be a vowel (e.g., *keeb'eek* "they go"). This termination marker *-k* or *-k* does not appear to mean anything—it simply indicates that the verb is at the end of the sentence or independent clause.

MODEL

Chwe'q keeb'ee le achijaab' pa tinamit.
Tomorrow the men go to town.

In the model the verb is *keeb'ee* "they go."

+ *aspect*	+ *person*	+ *root*	± *termination*
+ k	+ "ee"	+ b'ee	– no termination here

SCHEMA OF THE SIMPLE INTRANSITIVE VERB

+ ASPECT	+ PERSON	+ ROOT	± TERMINATION	
k	in	b'ee	k	I go
k	at	b'ee	k	you go
ka	Ø	b'ee	k	he/she goes
ka	—	b'ee la	—	you go (FORM)
k	oj	b'ee	k	we go
k	ix	b'ee	k	you go
k	ee	b'ee	k	they go
ka	—	b'ee alaq	—	you go (FORM)

As we have said above, there is no third person singular marker. So in the third person singular we would get $k + Ø + b'ee + k$, which means we would have *kb'eek*. Since the *kb'* is too difficult to pronounce, an *a* inserted. This is also true with the *laal* and *alaq* forms.

The person in the verb is ordinarily sandwiched between the aspect and the root. However, with the formal forms the *la* and *alaq* person markers always come after the verb root. Hence the *-ik* disappears (e.g., *kab'ee la* or *kab'ee alaq*).

In sentences or clauses in which the main verb is intransitive and the subject is a noun, the preferred word order appears to be: verb-subject, as in the model sentence above: *keeb'ee le achijaab'* "the men go."

Study the conjugations of the verbs "to go" and "to walk."

kimb'eek*	I go	kojb'eek	we go
katb'eek	you go	kixb'eek	you go
kab'eek	he/she/it goes	keeb'eek	they go
kab'ee la	you go (FORM)	kab'ee alaq	you go (FORM)
kimb'iinik*	I walk	kojb'iinik	we walk
katb'iinik	you walk	kixb'iinik	you walk
kab'iinik	he/she/it walks	keeb'iinik	they walk
kab'iin la	you walk (FORM)	kab'iin alaq	you walk (FORM)

* When the verb root begins with the sound *b'* or the sound *p*, the first person singular element *in* becomes *im*: i.e., *kimb'eek* "I go"; *kimpeetik* "I come."

VOCABULARY

b'ee	(IVS)	to go
b'iin	(IVS)	to walk, to travel
peet	(IVS)	to come
koos	(IVS)	to become tired
qaaj	(IVS)	to go down

FIGURE 9.1. *Keech'aaw le achijaab'* (the men talk). Photograph by John Edvalson.

wa'	(IVS)	to eat
ch'aw	(IVS)	to talk
ka'y	(IVS)	to see, to look
nuum	(IVS)	to be hungry
chakun	(IVS)*	to work
kam	(IVS)	to die
war	(IVS)	to sleep
jab'	(N)	rain
aninaq	(ADV)	fast

* *chakun* is actually a transitive verb, but in this form it is conjugated like an intransitive verb.

K'ICHEE' TO ENGLISH

1. Kojb'ee pa tinamit chwe'q.
2. Keewar le ak'alab' pa le nima ja.
3. Keekam le itzel taq tz'i' pa juyub'.
4. Sib'alaj aninaq kixch'awik.
5. La kawa' alaq pa qo'ch kamik?
6. Keekoos le ixoqiib' pa b'e.

FIGURE 9.2 *Keewa' le achijjab'* (the men eat). Photograph by John Edvalson.

7. Kapee nima jab' kamik.
8. La kanuum chi la?
9. Keepee chi le kixoqiil le achijaab' kamik.
10. Sib'alaj kinka'y pa b'e.
11. Keeb'ee le a'jchakiib' pa chaak chwe'q.
12. La kachakun la pa tinamit?

ENGLISH TO K'ICHEE'

1. The man goes to work today.
2. I'll come again tomorrow.
3. We go down to the house.
4. You (SING-FORM) become tired on the road.
5. The big horse walks fast.
6. The boy will come from town tomorrow.
7. The rain will come today.
8. We will go again to the white house.
9. The thin man will go to work tomorrow.
10. I am a worker.
11. I'll come to work tomorrow.
12. Will your father travel in the hills today?
13. We are sick. We will become tired on the road.

14. The little boy is hungry.
15. The man talks fast.
16. The children eat fast.
17. The little girl sleeps in her older sibling's house.
18. The old man (*niim a'chi*) goes down to the town.

USEFUL EXPRESSIONS

1. Chaawila' awiib'.
   Watch yourself. (when departing)

2. Mattzaaqik.
   Don't fall. (said to one departing or met on the road)

3. Chaab'anaa kwenta.
   Be careful. (said to one departing)

4. K'oo b'a ri Dyoos, Taat.
   There is a God (to protect you), Sir. (said when departing)

   Ja'ee Taat, k'oo ri Dyoos.
   Yes, sir, there is a God. (to protect you)

5. Ch'aab'ej chik.
   We'll talk again. (when departing)

6. Chwe'q chik.
   Until tomorrow. (when departing)

10

Simple Intransitive Verbs in Completed Aspect;
Declension of the Prepositions *-umaal* and *-uuk'*

SIMPLE INTRANSITIVE VERBS IN COMPLETED ASPECT

We saw that for the Simple Intransitive Verbs in incomplete aspect, the *k-*
(ka-) was the marker. To form the Simple Intransitive Verb in completed
aspect, just substitute *x-* for the marker *k- (ka-)*. The remainder of the verb
remains unchanged.

Review the formula given in the last chapter:

+ *aspect*   + *person*   + *root*   ± *termination*

CONJUGATION IN COMPLETED ASPECT

kamik "to die"

xinkamik	I died	xojkamik	we died
xatkamik	you died	xixkamik	you died
xkamik	he/she/it died	xeekamik	they died
xkam la	you died (FORM)	xkam alaq	you died (FORM)

Remember it is better not to think of the aspect or aspect markers as time
markers. They are not, strictly speaking, showing time but rather whether
an action is completed or incomplete. Note that the *ka-* in the third person
singular in incomplete aspect becomes *x-* only in completed aspect and not
xa-. The *a* is no longer needed to facilitate pronunciation.

THE PREPOSITIONS -*UMAAL* AND -*UUK'*

Prepositions such as these — *umaal* "by," "because of," "by agency of," and -*uuk'* "with" — are declined in K'ichee'. To decline these prepositions, use the same person markers as used for the possessive pronouns. Since the roots of these prepositions begin with a vowel (*umaal, uuk'*), use the same person markers that were used for possessives that precede vowels.

Declension of -*umaal*:

w-umaal	by me	q-umaal	by us
aw-umaal	by you	iw-umaal	by you
r-umaal	by him, her, it	k-umaal	by them
umal la	by you (FORM)	umal alaq	by you (FORM)

Declension of -*uuk'*:

w-uuk'	with me	q-uuk'	with us
aw-uuk'	with you	iw-uuk'	with you
r-uuk'	with him, her, it	k-uuk'	with them
uk' la	with you (FORM)	uk' alaq	with you (FORM)

NOTE: Many words in K'ichee' end in vowel-vowel-consonant when they occur at the end of an utterance. When these words are not final in an utterance, the final vowel is frequently shortened: vowel-consonant. The prepositions *umaal* and *uuk'* follow this pattern:

rumaal	"by him"	rumal le achi	"by the man"
ruuk'	"with him"	ruk' le achi	"with the man"

MODEL

Xb'ee le wuuj wumaal.   The document went by me (i.e., I sent it).

VOCABULARY

q'ab'ar	(IVS)	to become drunk
tzaaq	(IVS)	to fall
k'ulel	(N)	enemy
wuuj	(N)	paper, book
ja'	(N)	water, river, aguardiente
aal	(PN)	a woman's child
noojiim	(ADV)	slowly (alternate form of *noojimaal*)
umaal	(PREP)	by, by the agency of, because of
uuk'	(PREP)	with (declined like *umaal*)
we	(CONJ)	if
y	(CONJ, SPAN)	and

K'ICHEE' TO ENGLISH

1. Xq'ab'ar le achi y xtzaaq pa ja.
2. We katb'ee wuuk', aninaq kojb'eek.
3. Sib'alaj k'ax le nima b'e we kaqaaj jab'.
4. La katb'ee pa chaak chwe'q?
5. We ee yawab'iib'chi le ak'alaab', utz keepeetik.
6. Iwir xojwa' ruk' le achi pa ro'ch.
7. Noojimaal xpee le ajchaak pa b'e.
8. Xeeb'ee le nimaq taq winaq pa tinamit kuk' le ak'alaab'.
9. Xtzaaq le q'ana me's pa le ja' rumal le k'a'na tz'i'.
10. Noojiim kab'iin le achi pa taq b'e.
11. We kab'ee la wuk' pa chaak, kakoos la.

ENGLISH TO K'ICHEE'

1. I slept yesterday in the mountains (*pa juyub'*).
2. I went to town with my mother.
3. The man became drunk because of me.
4. Did you eat with the people yesterday?
5. If you (PL) come quickly, I'll eat with you.
6. Because of the rain, the children fell on the road.
7. We will go with you (*laal*) to town.
8. Your father will die if you go.
9. The workers got drunk because of their enemies.
10. The woman slept in the house with her child.

SUBSTITUTION DRILL

1. I came with him from town yesterday.
   Ximpee ruk' pa tinamit iwir.

2. You (*at*) came with him from town yesterday.

3. The girls came with him from town yesterday.

4. You (*alaq*) came with him from town yesterday.

5. We walked with him from town yesterday.

6. The workers traveled with him from town yesterday.

7. The letter was sent (went) by him.
   Xb'ee le wuuj rumaal.

8. The letter was sent (went) by the boys.

9. The letter was sent (went) by you (*ix*).

10. The letter was sent (went) by us.

11. The letter was sent (went) by you (*alaq*).

12. Will you go with me tomorrow?
    La katb'ee wuk' chwe'q?

13. La _____ _____ chwe'q?
         the boys go   with the man

14. La _____ _____ chwe'q?
         the dog goes with the boy

15. Xqaaj le achi quk' pa tinamit iwir.
    The man went down with us to town yesterday.

16. _____ _____ pa tinamit iwir.
        You went down (*ix*)   with your mother.

17. _____ _____ pa tinamit iwir.
        The children went down   with us.

18. _____ _____ pa tinamit iwir.
        You went down (*laal*) with your horses.

19. _____ _____ pa tinamit iwir.
        I went down with the big people.

20. _____ _____.
        I ate   with the sick child yesterday.

USEFUL EXPRESSIONS

1. Dyoos katuk'a'nik.
   God is the one who sustains you. (to one departing)

2. Jo'.
   Let's go.

3. Joo wuuk'.
   Go with me.

4. Jat.
   Go.

5. Katojo'.
   Come here.

Simple Intransitive Verbs Whose Roots Begin with Vowels

If you look back at the last two lessons, you will notice that all of the verb roots that we used began with consonants (e.g., *wa'*, *koos*, *b'iin*). There are also many Simple Intransitive Verbs whose roots begin with vowels.

The vowel-initial verbs are conjugated the same in the incomplete and completed aspect as the verbs starting with a consonant, except in the third persons. In the third person singular of verbs beginning with consonants, the *a* is added to facilitate pronunciation. It comes between the aspect and the root (e.g., *ka̲b'iinik* "he walks"). In Simple Intransitive Verbs whose roots begin with a vowel, the *a* is no longer necessary to aid pronunciation because the root already begins with a vowel (e.g., *kuxlanik* "he rests"; *koopanik* "he arrives there"). This is also true in the *laal* and *alaq* forms (*kuxlan la* "you rest"; *koopan alaq* "you all arrive there").

In the third person plural we have seen that the person marker is *ee*. However, in Nahuala and Santa Catarina Ixtahuacan, when the verb root begins with a vowel, the *ee* disappears and is replaced by a glottal stop immediately after the initial vowel of the root (e.g., *kee'uxlanik > ku'xlanik* "they rest").

CONJUGATION OF SIMPLE INTRANSITIVE VERB

uxlan "to rest"

Incomplete Aspect

kinuxlanik	I rest	kojuxlanik	we rest
katuxlanik	you rest	kixuxlanik	you rest
kuxlanik	he rests	ku'xlanik	they rest
kuxlan la	you rest (FORM)	kuxlan alaq	you rest (FORM)

Completed Aspect

xinuxlanik	I rested	xojuxlanik	we rested
xatuxlanik	you rested	xixuxlanik	you rested
xuxlanik	he rested	xu'xlanik	they rested
xuxlan la	you rested (FORM)	xuxlan alaq	you rested (FORM)

MODEL

Rajawaxik kinuxlan pa q'iij.
It is necessary that I rest at noon.

VOCABULARY

uxlan	(IVS)	to rest
ul	(IVS)	to arrive (here)
oopan	(IVS)	to arrive (over there)
aatin	(IVS)	to bathe
k'ayib'al	(N)	market place
b'enaq'iij	(ADJ)	afternoon, in the afternoon
pa q'iij	(ADV)	at noon, daytime, during the daytime
chaaq'ab'	(ADV)	at night
rajawaxik	(ADV, N)	necessary; necessity
ya	(ADV-SPAN)	now
waraal	(ADV)	here
jee la'	(ADV)	over there

K'ICHEE' TO ENGLISH

1. Ku'xlan le winaq pa taq ko'ch chaaq'ab'.
2. La kojaatin pa ja' kamik?
3. La koopan la pa tinamit kamik?
4. Ku'l le kitaat le ak'alaab' kamik b'enaq'iij.
5. Xuxlan alaq pa b'e iwir.
6. Kinoopan pa k'ayib'al pa q'iij.
7. Rajawaxik kojoopan jee la' chaaq'ab'.
8. La kul la waraal chwe'q?
9. We kuxlan le ala pa b'e, koopan pa ro'ch chaaq'ab'.

FIGURE 11.1. *Keetz'an le ali* (the girl plays). Photograph by
John Edvalson.

10. Ka'tin le ak'alaab' pa ja'.
11. Rajawaxik aninaq koopan alaq pa k'ayib'al.

ENGLISH TO K'ICHEE'
1. The man rested yesterday in the afternoon.
2. The man rests today in the afternoon.
3. The woman arrived here at home (*pa ja*).
4. The woman arrives here at home.
5. The children arrived over there at noon yesterday.
6. The children arrive over there at noon today.
7. You (*laal*) bathed in the river at night.
8. You (*ix*) bathe in the river at night.
9. It is necessary that I arrive here at the market place at noon.
10. They arrived here in town yesterday.
11. They will arrive here in town tomorrow.

USEFUL EXPRESSIONS
1. La katb'ee wuuk'?
   Are you going with me?

2. Kimb'ee awuuk'.
   I'm going with you. (I want to go with you.)

3. Kimb'eek, ri'.
   I'm going right away.

4. Jawii katb'ee wi?
   Where are you going?

5. Kimb'ee chuwa ja.
   I'm going home.

LESSON

12

Imperative Mood for the Simple Intransitive Verbs

We have seen that the Simple Intransitive Verbs in completed aspect have the aspect marker x- and those in incomplete aspect have the aspect marker k-.

The marker for the imperative is ch- or k-. In the imperative of the third person there is no aspect marker in the singular form (see special note below).

Likewise, we have seen that there is an -ik termination marker in both the incomplete and completed aspects. Remember that this disappears when the verb is not in the utterance-final position.

In the imperative of these verbs, the termination marker is -oq when the verb is in the utterance-final position; it is -a when the imperative is not utterance-final.

SCHEMA OF THE IMPERATIVE (UTTERANCE-FINAL)

chinwaroq (kinwaroq)*	let me sleep	kojwaroq	let us sleep
katwaroq	sleep	kixwaroq	sleep
waroq	let him sleep	cheewaroq/keewaroq	let them sleep
wara la	sleep	war a'laq†	sleep

* The first person singular imperative form is rarely found.

† In the second person formal plural, the normal form would be *wara alaq*, but a fusion of the vowels takes place, giving us the form *war a'laq*.

Using the same verb below, we will use the exclamatory *b'a'* following the imperative. Note now how the *-oq* termination changes to *-a* when another word follows the imperative.

SCHEMA OF THE IMPERATIVE (NOT UTTERANCE-FINAL)

chinwara b'a'	well, let me sleep	kojwara b'a'	well, let us sleep
katwara b'a'	well, sleep	kixwara b'a'	well, sleep
wara b'a'	well, let him sleep	cheewara b'a'/ keewara b'a'	well, let them sleep
wara b'a la*	well, sleep	wara b'a' laq†	well, sleep

* Note that *b'a'* loses the glottal stop if another word or particle follows it in the clause or sentence (e.g., *katwara b'a chaaniim* "Go to sleep right now!").

† Note that the same vowel fusion takes place in this second person formal plural form, as noted above. Note that the non-utterance final imperative forms of these verbs are stressed on the penultimate syllable in the word (e.g., *kat<u>wa</u>ra b'a'* "well, sleep!").

SPECIAL NOTE: In the third person singular form of the imperative, there is no aspect marker for those verbs that start with a consonant. However, for those verb roots that begin with a vowel, either *ch-* or *k-* is prefixed to the verb word. This rule is also applicable to the *laal* and *alaq* forms.

Below is the conjugation of a verb in the imperative whose root begins with a vowel: *uxlan* "to rest."

SCHEMA OF THE IMPERATIVE *UXLAN* (UTTERANCE-FINAL)

chinuxlanoq	let me rest	kojuxlanoq	let us rest
katuxlanoq	rest	kixuxlanoq	rest
chuxlanoq/ kuxlanoq	let him rest	chu'xlanoq/ ku'xlanoq	let them rest
chuxlana la/ kuxlana la	rest	chuxlan a'laq/ kuxlan a'laq	rest

SCHEMA OF THE IMPERATIVE *UXLAN* (NOT UTTERANCE-FINAL)

chinuxlana b'a'	well, let me rest	kojuuxlana b'a'	well, let us rest
katuxlana b'a'	well, rest	kixuuxlana b'a'	well, rest
chuxlana b'a'/	well, let him rest	chu'xlana b'a'/	well, let them rest

kuxlana b'a'   ku'xlana b'a'
chuuxlana b'a la/ well, rest   chuuxlana b'a'laq   well, rest
kuxlana b'a la   kuxlana b'a'laq

VOCABULARY

etz'an	(IVS)	to play
el	(IVS)	to leave
aq'an	(IVS)	to climb
q'i'taj	(IVS)*	to become bored
pax	(IVS)	to break
laq	(N)	clay bowl
warab'al	(N)	sleeping place
wo'qib'al	(N)	eating place
nimaq'ab'	(ADV)	in the morning
b'a'	(ADV)	well, oh!
puwi'	(PREP)	on top of it, on his head
panuwi'		above me, on my head, on top of me
paawi'		above you, on your head, on top of you
puwi'		above him (her, it), on top of him (her, it)
pawi' la		above you, on your head, on top of you
paqawi'		above us, on our heads, on top of us
piiwi'		above you, on your heads, on top of you
pakiwi'		above them, on their heads, on top of them
pawi' alaq		above you, on your heads, on top of you

* q'i'taj is actually a transitive verb, but in this form it is conjugated exactly like
an intransitive verb.

K'ICHEE' TO ENGLISH

1. Achijaab', kixela pa le warab'al.
2. Kojb'iina pa k'ayib'al nimaq'ab'.
3. Paxa le laq we kapaxik.
4. Kataatina pa q'iij.
5. Ch'awa le achi wuuk'.
6. Chu'xlana le winaq pa le wo'qib'al chaaq'ab'.
7. Kojwara b'a jee la' kamik.
8. Ak'alaab', kixaq'ana puuwi' le chee'.
9. Chuxlana la waraal, taat.
10. Ka'y a'laq waraal, naan.

ENGLISH TO K'ICHEE'

1. Let's rest here in the marketplace.
2. Let the children play in the eating place.
3. Rest (*laal*) in the sleeping place, sir.
4. Climb up (*at*) in the tree.
5. Go out of the town, sirs (*alaq*).
6. Let the cat climb up on top of the house.
7. Play in the market, children (*ix*).
8. Well, look (*at*) over there!
9. If you get bored, get bored. (This sentence in K'ichee' is structured like no. 3 in the K'ichee' to English sentences of this lesson.)

SPECIAL EXERCISES

Change the verbs in the following sentences into imperatives, rewriting the entire sentence.

1. Ke'tz'an le ak'alaab' pa k'ayib'al.
2. Kojaq'an puwi' le chee'.
3. Kaqaaj alaq pa le tinamit.
4. Kul le achi waraal pa q'iij.
5. Xpax le laq pa ja.
6. Kuxlan la jee la', taat.
7. Xixel pa ja.
8. Katwar waraal pa le wo'qib'al chwe'q.
9. Xeq'i'taj le ak'alaab' pa juyub'.

USEFUL EXPRESSIONS

1. Jampaa chi katpeetik?
   When are you coming again?

2. Kimpee chi chwe'q.
   I'll come again tomorrow.

3. Chaakowij b'iik.
   Hurry along. (said to someone departing)

4. Kataan u'loq.
   Come here quickly.

5. Chaakowij loq.
   Come here quickly. (or Hurry back.)

Negatives

The negativizing form in K'ichee' is *na . . . ta(j)*, with the word or words to be negativized sandwiched between them. Not only verbs, but nouns, pronouns, adjectives, adverbs, and prepositions can be negativized.

The negative form *na . . . taj* is used if *taj* is the last word in the utterance.

The negative form *na . . . ta* is used when the *ta* is followed by some other word in the utterance.

MODELS

WITH VERBS

Na kojwar taj.	We don't sleep.
Na kojwar ta waraal.	We don't sleep here.
Na kawar ta la.*	You don't sleep.

* With the *laal* and *alaq* forms, the second element of the negative goes between the verb and the pronoun.

WITH NOUNS

Na ee winaq taj.	(They are) not people.
Na ee winaq ta la'.	(They are) not people, those ones.
Na niim i'xoq taj.	(She is) not a big woman.
Na niim i'xoq ta le ali.	The girl (is) not a big woman.

WITH PRONOUNS

Na in taj.	It is not I.
Na in elaq'oom taj.	I am not a thief.

WITH ADJECTIVES

Le achi, na k'a'n taj.	The man, he is not mean.
Na k'a'n ta le achi.	The man is not mean.
Na niim ta le ixoq.	The woman is not big.
Na ee nima'q ta le ixoqiib'.	The women aren't big.

WITH ADVERBS

Na chwe'q taj.	(It is) not tomorrow.
Na chwe'q ta kimpeetik.	(It is) not tomorrow that I come.

WITH PREPOSITIONS

Na wuk' taj.	Not with me.
Na ruk' ta le achi.	Not with the man.

NOTE: These are just some of the possible word orders in the models. Word order and which words are negativized can be changed for emphasis.

VOCABULARY

ok	(IVS)	to enter
oq'	(IVS)	to cry
ux	(IVS)	to become
kar	(N)	fish
chikop	(N)	animal
ajk'aay	(N)	seller
ajk'ayiib'	(N)	sellers
chaaniim	(ADV)	right now, quickly
wa'	(DEM PRO)	this one, these (very close to the speaker)
la'	(DEM PRO)	that one, those (visible to the speaker or spoken of as if it were present

K'ICHEE' TO ENGLISH

1. Na yawaab' ta le saqa keej.
2. Na kakam ta le ak'uleel.
3. Na kojb'ee ta pa k'ayib'al chaaniim.
4. Na ke'tz'an ta le alab'oom pa juyub'.
5. Na kixoq' taj, ak'alaab'.
6. La', na kab'ee ta pa chaak nimaq'ab'.
7. Na me's ta la'.
8. Na kitaat ta wa'.
9. Na nuwuuj taj.

10. Na tz'i' taj.
11. Na k'ax taj.
12. Na oj elaq'omaab' taj.
13. Na a're' taj.
14. Na ix taj.
15. Na b'eenaq'iij taj.
16. Na aninaq ta keeb'iin le ixoqiib'.
17. Na niim ta le chee'.
18. Na ee saq ta le tz'i'.

ENGLISH TO K'ICHEE'
1. I am not going.
2. That one will not die.
3. The sick one does not go out from (*pa*) the house.
4. We do not become tired because of the work.
5. Boys, don't play here.
6. You (*laal*) will not go over there today.
7. You (*at*) will not eat in the market tomorrow.
8. Those are not animals.
9. This is not my book.
10. The worker is not a lazy one.
11. The woman is not an ambitious one.
12. The men are not thieves.
13. The mountain is not rock.
14. That is not a dog.
15. You (*at*) are not good.
16. We are not lazy.
17. He is not sick.
18. You (*alaq*) are not big.
19. You (*ix*) are not workers.
20. I am not a child.
21. They are not women.
22. We are not thieves.
23. She is not fat.
24. The horses are not white.
25. The children are not sick.
26. Not quickly do the boys come.
27. Not in the morning are we going to the market.
28. Not slowly do I go.
29. Not today will you (*laal*) die.
30. Not yesterday did you (*ix*) come.

DRILL

Change the following underlined parts of the sentences into negatives, rewrite the entire sentence, and translate to English.

1. <u>Keekam</u> le kar aninaq.
2. <u>Kojb'ee</u> awuk' pa k'ayib'al.
3. <u>Kab'iin la</u> pa b'e.
4. <u>Keeb'ee</u> le achijaab' pa juyub'.
5. <u>Ka'tin</u> le i'xoqiib' pa ja'.
6. <u>Kixetz'an</u> nimaq'ab' pa iwo'ch.
7. <u>Kab'ee</u> <u>alaq</u> pa chaak b'eenaq'iij.
8. <u>Tz'i'</u> la'.
9. <u>Elaq'oom</u> le ak'aal.
10. <u>Niim</u> <u>i'xoq</u> le rixoqiil.
11. <u>Q'or</u> a'chi.
12. <u>Chooma</u> <u>tz'i'</u> le chikop.
13. <u>Nuwaa</u> la'.
14. <u>At</u> elaq'oom.
15. <u>Alaq</u> ajk'ayiib'.
16. <u>In</u> yawaab'.
17. <u>Are'</u> elaq'oom.
18. <u>Oj</u> q'oriib'.
19. <u>Laal</u> choom.
20. <u>In</u> k'a'n.
21. <u>Aninaq</u> xeeb'ee le ak'alaab'.
22. <u>Chaaniim</u> xo'k le ajk'ayiib' pa ja.
23. <u>Iwir</u> ximpee pa k'ayib'al.

USEFUL EXPRESSIONS

1. Chinaawiye'j na jub'iq'.
   Wait for me a second.

2. Kinteri' b'i chaawiij.
   I'm going to tag along after you.

3. Xpee nuwaraam.
   I've become sleepy.

4. Xinkoosik. Kojuxlana na jub'iq'.
   I've become tired. Let's rest a minute.

5. Jasa ora chaaniim?
   What time is it now?

14

The Particle *wi* (*u, wu*) with Direction and Location Words

In K'ichee' there are a number of direction words or phrases, such as "where," "to," "from," "into," etc., that indicate movement toward or away from a person, object, or place. Also there are words or phrases that indicate locations: "here," "there," "where," "in," "on," "under," "besides," etc.

In a clause, if these direction or location words are placed before the verb of the clause, then the direction or location particle *wi* generally follows immediately after the verb, as in the first model below.

If the direction or location word or phrase follows the verb, the *wi* particle is not used.

At times, if this particle is followed by other words and spoken at an ordinary or fast pace, it becomes *u* or *wu*. For the sake of simplicity, we shall for now only use *wi*.

The particle *wi* performs a number of other functions in the language that are beyond the scope of this basic grammar.

MODELS

Jawi' katb'ee wi?	Pa k'ayib'al kimb'ee wi.
Where you go (to)?	To marketplace I go (to).
Where are you going?	I am going to market.

VOCABULARY

ok'ow	(IVS)	to pass by, to go by
wa'kat	(IVS)	to take a pleasure walk (pasear in Spanish)
k'iis	(IVS)	to end, terminate, finish
k'aslemaal	(N)	life
swaan	(N)	gully, canyon
nee'	(N)	baby
jawi'	(ADV)	where
waraal	(ADV)	here
ch-ee (ch)	(PREP)	to, from, for, at

Declension of ch-e (ch)*

chwee (ch)	at, to, from, for me	ch-q-ee (ch)	at, to, from, for us
ch-aaw-ee (ch)	at, to, from, for you	ch-iiw-ee (ch)	at, to, from, for you
ch-ee (ch)	at, to, from, for him	ch-k-ee (ch)	at, to, from, for them
ch-ee (ch) la	at, to, from, for you	ch-ee (ch) alaq	at, to, from, for you

* The last *ch* is optional.

K'ICHEE' TO ENGLISH

1. Pa tinamit ximpee wi.
2. Jawi' xeepee wi le ak'alaab'?
3. Pa juyub' kojb'iin wi.
4. Ruk' le achi xatb'ee wi.
5. Waraal kawa' wi la.
6. Pa b'e xk'iis wi uk'aslemaal le achi.
7. Cheech le ajchaak xpee wi le pwaq.
8. Jawi' kab'ee wi alaq?
9. Jee la' xtzaaq wi le nee'.
10. Chikee le winaq xojka'y wi.

ENGLISH TO K'ICHEE'

Write the following sentences in K'ichee', putting the direction or location word or phrase first.

1. Where do you (ix) come from?
2. The boy went to work.

3. We play with the children.
4. The river (*ja'*) passes through the gully.
5. I look at the man.
6. You (*alaq*) take a pleasure walk in the hills (*pa juyub'*).
7. The hardship (*k'ax*) comes from the people.
8. Where do the women walk to?
9. The women walk in the market.
10. Is it to the market that you are going today?

K'ICHEE' TO ENGLISH

Change the following sentences so that the direction or location word or phrase comes first for emphasis and place *wi* in its proper place and translate them to English.

1. Kab'ee la pa k'ayib'al.
2. Xkoos le wachajiil pa chaak.
3. Kojwa'kat pa b'e.
4. Kixka'y chqeech.
5. La kapee alaq pa tinamit?
6. La katb'ee ruk' le ataat?
7. Xinwa' kuk' le winaq.
8. Xeewar waraal iwir.
9. Ke'tz'an le tz'i' pa le ja.
10. Kok'ow le ch'iich' (*automobile*) pa le nima b'e.

USEFUL EXPRESSIONS

1. La aree b'e wa' ka'ee pa tinamit?
   Is this the road that goes to town?

2. Jasa ora xatpee chila'?
   What time did you leave from there (to come here)?

   Ximpee a las tres b'enaq'iij.
   I came (left) from there at three in the afternoon.

3. Jasa ora xatul waraal?
   What time did you arrive here?

   Xinul pa taq umooy.
   I arrived at dusk.

LESSON

15

Derived Transitive Verbs in Incomplete Aspect and Active Voice with Roots Beginning with Consonants

In this chapter. we shall begin by explaining each part of the chapter title. Then we shall show the structural makeup of these verbs. And finally we give some conjugations as models.

TRANSITIVE VERBS

We have seen that Simple Intransitive Verbs are those that express an aspect and the subject of the aspect; as a result, the verb phrase has only two main elements: subject and verb (e.g., the man fell). Transitive Verbs are those verbs that express a subject, the action, and the receiver of the action, producing a verb phrase that may have three elements: subject, verb, and object (e.g., the man sells bread).

CLASSES OF K'ICHEE' TRANSITIVE VERBS

Radical: Verbs of this class are those transitive verbs whose roots end in consonants and are of one syllable (monosyllabic). Examples are *b'an* "to do, make"; *ch'ay* "to hit, strike"; *ya'* "to give."

   Derived: Verbs of this class are those transitive verbs whose roots end in vowels and are of more than one syllable (polysyllabic). Some examples are *k'ayi* "to sell"; *sipa* "to give as a gift."

In this grammar we are first going to treat of Derived Transitive Verbs because their structure is less complex.

TRANSITIVE VERB ROOTS THAT BEGIN WITH CONSONANTS

Transitive verbs may have roots that begin with consonants. This is true both for Radical Transitive Verbs (e.g., *b'an* "to do"; *ch'ay* "to hit") as well as for Derived Transitive Verbs (e.g., *k'ayi* "to sell"; *tzuku* "to look for"). In this chapter we are treating Derived Transitive Verbs whose roots start in a consonant and end in a vowel. In a later lesson we shall treat those Derived Transitive Verbs whose roots start with a vowel.

INCOMPLETE ASPECT

We have seen the distinction between completed aspect and incomplete aspect in lesson 9. Incomplete aspect generally means that the action has not yet been done or, if begun, has not yet been finished.

ACTIVE VOICE

In this K'ichee' grammar we will describe five voices for transitive verbs. There is a sixth voice, the Instrumental Voice, which will not be covered in this book. Each of these five voices is a way of placing emphasis or focus on one or more of the main elements of the sentence or clause containing the transitive verb (i.e., subject, verb, or object).

Active Voice, with which we are dealing in this lesson, places equal emphasis on all three of the elements: subject, verb, and object. Later in this lesson we shall see the marker in the verb for Active Voice.

STRUCTURE OF DERIVED TRANSITIVE VERBS IN ACTIVE VOICE

Verbs of this type have the following structure:

+ *aspect* + *object* + *subject* + *root* + *active voice marker*

ASPECT

When we studied Simple Intransitive Verbs in lesson 9, we saw the distinction between completed and incomplete aspects. The same two aspects exist in Transitive Verbs with the same meaning and the same markers: *k-* *(ka-)* for incomplete aspect and *x-* for completed. In this lesson we are dealing with incomplete aspect.

OBJECT

When we talk of object, we should note that even though the object may be expressed as a separate word (e.g., I killed <u>the men</u>), in K'ichee' the object is also always expressed in the verb in the object position as a pronoun (it, him, her, them, etc.): for example, "I killed (them) the men," with "them" placed in the object slot of the verb.

The object markers for transitive verbs are the same as the subject markers for the Simple Intransitive Verbs.

-in-	me	-oj-	us
-at-	you	-ix-	you
-Ø-	him, her, it	-ee-	them
La	you	alaq	you

SUBJECT

The third element in the formula is the subject of the transitive verb in active voice. The following are the subject markers when the verb root begins with a consonant. In a later lesson we shall see that when the root begins with a vowel, a slightly different set of subject markers is used.

-in-	I	-qa-	we
-aa-	you	-ii-	you
-uu-	him, her, it	-ki-	they
la	you	alaq	you

It should be noted that these subject markers are the same markers that we have already learned as possessives for nouns whose roots begin with consonants (with the exception of the first person singular, for which *nu-* usually becomes *in-*).

ROOT

The root is the fourth element of the verb according to our formula, and it is the heart of the verb word, giving its meaning.

In this lesson we are dealing only with Derived Roots (i.e., polysyllabic roots terminating in vowels), which begin with consonants.

VOICE MARKER

The last element in our formula for Derived Transitive Verbs in Active Voice is that which indicates we are using Active Voice. This marker is *-j*. This *-j* never disappears from the verb.

MODEL CONJUGATION OF A DERIVED
TRANSITIVE VERB IN ACTIVE VOICE

+ ASPECT	+ OBJECT	+ SUBJECT	+ ROOT	+ VOICE MARKER		= FULL FORM
k-	-at-	-in-	-tzukuu-	-j		katintzukuuj
	you	I	look for			I look for you.
k-	-Ø-	-in-	-tzukuu-	-j		kintzukuuj
	him	I	look for			I look for him.
k-		-in-	-tzuku-	-j	la	kintzukuj la*
		I	look for		you	I look for you.
k-	-ix-	-in-	-tzukuu-	-j		kixintzukuuj
	you	I	look for			I look for you.
k-	-ee-	-in-	-tzukuu-	-j		kentzukuuj
	them	I	look for			I look for them.
		-in-	-tzuku-	-j	alaq	kintzukuuj alaq
		I	look for		you	I look for you.
k-	-in-	-aa-	-tzukuu-	-j		kinaatzukuuj
	me	you	look for			You look for me.
k-	-Ø-	-aa-	-tzukuu-	-j		kaatzukuuj
	him	you	look for			You look for him.
k-	-oj-	-aa-	-tzukuu-	-j		kojaatzukuuj
	us	you	look for			You look for us.
k-	-ee-	-aa-	-tzukuu-	-j		ka'tzukuuj*
	them	you	look for			You look for them.
k-	-in-	-uu-	-tzukuu-	-j		kinuutzukuuj
	me	he	looks for			He looks for me.
k-	-at-	-uu-	-tzukuu-	-j		katuutzukuuj
	you	he	looks for			He looks for you.[†]
k-	-Ø-	-uu-	-tzukuu-	-j		kuutzukuuj
	him	he	looks for			He looks for him.
k-	-oj-	-uu-	-tzukuu-	-j		kojuutzukuuj
	us	he	looks for			He looks for us.
k-	-ix-	-uu-	-tzukuu-	-j		kixuutzukuuj
	you	he	looks for			He looks for you.[†]
k-	-ee-	-uu-	-tzukuu-	-j		ku'tzukuuj[†]
	them	he	looks for			He looks for them.
k-	-in-		-tzukuu-	-j	la	kintzukuuj la

+ ASPECT	+ OBJECT	+ SUBJECT	+ ROOT	+ VOICE MARKER	= FULL FORM
	me		look for	you	You look for me.
ka-	-Ø-		-tzukuu-	-j la	katzukuuj la
	him		look for	you	You look for him.
k-	-oj-		-tzukuu-	-j la	kojtzukuuj la
	us		look for	you	You look for us.
k-	-ee-		-tzukuu-	-j la	keetzukuuj la
	them		look for	you	You look for them.
k-	-at-	-qa-	-tzukuu-	-j	katqatzukuuj
	you	we	look for		We look for you.
ka-	-Ø-	-qa-	-tzukuu-	-j	kaqatzukuuj
	him	we	look for		We look for him.
ka-		-qa-	-tzukuu-	-j la	kaqatzukuuj la
		we	look for	you	We look for you.
k-	-ix-	-qa-	-tzukuu-	-j	kixqatzukuuj
	you	we	look for		We look for you.
k-	-ee-	-qa-	-tzukuu-	-j	keeqatzukuuj
	them	we	look for		We look for them.
		-qa-	-tzukuu-	-j alaq	kaqatzukuuj alaq
		we	look for	you	We look for you.
k-	-in-	-ii-	-tzukuu-	-j	kiniitzukuuj
	me	you	look for		You look for me.
k-	-Ø-	-ii-	-tzukuu-	-j	kiitzukuuj
	him	you	look for		You look for him.
k-	-oj-	-ii-	-tzukuu-	-j	kojiitzukuuj
	us	you	look for		You look for us.
k-	ee-	ii-	-tzukuu-	-j	ki'tzukuuj†
	them	you	look for		You look for them.
k-	-in-	-ki-	-tzukuu-	-j	kinkitzukuuj
	me	they	look for		They look for me.
k-	-at-	-ki-	-tzukuu-	-j	katkitzukuuj
	you	they	look for		They look for you.†
ka-	-Ø-	-ki-	-tzukuu-	j	kakitzukuuj
	him	they	look for		They look for him.
k-	-oj-	-ki-	-tzukuu-	-j	kojkitzukuuj
	us	they	look for		They look for us.

+ ASPECT	+ OBJECT	+ SUBJECT	+ ROOT	+ VOICE MARKER		= FULL FORM
k-	-ix-	-ki-	-tzukuu-	-j		kixkitzukuuj
	you	they	look for			They look for you.†
k-	-ee-	-ki-	-tzukuu-	-j		keekitzukuuj
	them	they	look for			They look for them.
k-	-in-		-tzukuu-	-j	alaq	kintzukuj alaq
	me		look for		you	You look for me.
ka-	-Ø-		-tzukuu-	-j	alaq	katzukuj alaq
	him		look for		you	You look for him.
k-	-oj-		-tzukuu-	-j	alaq	kojtzukuj alaq
	us		look for		you	You look for us.
k-	-ee-		-tzukuu-	-j	alaq	keetzukuj alaq
	them		look for		you	You look for them.

* In order to avoid *ee* + *aa* for "you-them," this form becomes *a'*. This is the same logic as we saw in *ee achijaab'* = *a'chijaab'*. Likewise *ee* + *uu* becomes *u'*, and *ee* + *ii* becomes *i'*.

† "He looks for you," "They look for you," with the *laal* and *alaq* forms, are not used in this voice. Later we will see how these sentences are said in K'ichee'.

SPECIAL NOTES

1. Inanimate (nonliving) objects are not pluralized in the verb as either subject or object (e.g., *kakitzukuuj taq le ab'aj* "they look for rocks"). In K'ichee', since the object is inanimate, its corresponding object marker in the verb is singular. The plural number of the object is then expressed outside of the verb with *taq*.

2. If the subject and direct object in a transitive sentence or clause in the active voice are both nouns, then the usual word order is verb-object-subject (e.g., *xeekikamisaj le tz'ikin le achijaab'* "the men killed the birds").

VOCABULARY

k'ayi	(TVD)	to sell
chaji	(TVD)	to take care of, guard
kamisa	(TVD)	to kill
loq'o	(TVD)	to love
tzuku	(TVD)	to look for, search
jastaq	(N)	thing, things

k'isik'	(N)	goat
maltyoox	(N)	thanks
wa	(N)	tortilla, food in general
alk'u'aal	(PN)	child or children of a couple or of a man
aal	(PN)	child or children of a woman
xa	(ADV)	just (contrary to what is expected or hoped for); e.g., you just sold it (unexpected)

K'ICHEE' TO ENGLISH

1. Kink'ayij le tz'i'.
2. Kojkichajij le qataat qanaan.
3. Maltyoox kinloq'oj la, taat.
4. La xaa ki'kamisaj le tz'ikin?
5. Na kojtzukuj ta alaq, naan.
6. Le achi sib'alaj ku'loq'oj le ralk'u'aal.
7. Le kixoqiil le a'chijaab' kakik'ayij wa pa k'ayib'al.
8. Kixqatzukuj chwe'q pa tinamit.
9. Keeqachajij le qak'isiik' pa juyub'.
10. Le alab'oom kakik'ayij kijastaaq pa tinamit.

ENGLISH TO K'ICHEE'

1. Your (ix) father and mother love you.
2. The boys kill the birds.
3. We sell tortillas in the marketplace.
4. You (alaq) women really take care of your children.
5. I'll just look for you (laal) tomorrow.
6. Thanks, you (at) take care of my houses.
7. Will (do) you (alaq) take care of us, sirs?
8. The thieves look for things in the house.

SPECIAL DRILL

Change the subject and object markers in the following model sentence as indicated.

1. katkichajiij	they take care of you
you (at)	me
I	them
We	you (laal)

2. keeqatzukuuj   we look for them
    I   them
    He   you (at)
    You (alaq)   us

3. ku'k'ayiij   he sells them
                We sell houses.
                You (ix) sell your dogs.
                I sell my big horse.

EXTRA DRILL

1. Write ten sentences in K'ichee' using in each one a Derived Transitive Verb in Active Voice in Incomplete Aspect.

2. Conjugate the following Derived Transitive Verbs in Active Voice in Incomplete Aspect using all the possible subject-object combinations. Do not look at the model in this lesson while doing this exercise:

kamisa
chaji
loq'o

USEFUL EXPRESSIONS

1. La naj k'o wi le awo'ch?
   Is your house a long way away?

   Jee', naj k'o wi.
   Yes, its a long way.

2. Jasa ora kojoopanik?
   What time will we arrive?

   Ya mero kojoopanik.
   We are almost there.

3. Ya xojulik.
   We've arrived (at our destination).

16

Derived Transitive Verbs in Completed Aspect and Active Voice with Roots Beginning with Consonants

When we dealt with the idea of Completed Aspect in the Simple Intransitive Verbs, we saw that the aspect marker for the Incomplete Aspect was k- (ka-). This changed to x- for Completed Aspect. The same aspect marker x- is used for Completed Aspect in Derived Transitive Verbs whose roots begin with a consonant in Active Voice. The other components remain unchanged:

a. Kinq'aluj le ak'aal.   Xinq'aluj le ak'aal.
   I hold in arms the child.   I held in arms the child.

b. Katkiloq'ooj.   Xatkiloq'ooj.
   They love you.   They loved you.

MODEL SENTENCE

Le ajyuq'aab' xeekiyuq'uj le kikarne'l pa juyub' iwir.
(the shepherds   they herded them   their sheep in the hills yesterday)
The shepherds herded their sheep in the hills yesterday.

VOCABULARY

yuq'u   (TVD)   to shepherd

q'alu	(TVD)		to hold in arms
paxi	(TVD)		to break
sipa	(TVD)		to give as a gift
ajyuuq'	(N)		shepherd
ajyuq'aab'	(N)		shepherds
karne'l	(N)		sheep
laq	(N)		clay dish
leme't	(N)		Bottle
aretaq	(CONJ)		When
onojeel	(N)		all of, every (cf. below)
ronojeel		qonojeel	all of us
1. all of them		iwonojeel	all of you
e.g., ronojel taq chee'		konojeel	all of them
all of the trees		onojel alaq	all of you
2. every, each			

Ronojel winaq kakamik.   Every person dies.
Ronojel q'iij kapeetik.   Each day he comes.

K'ICHEE' TO ENGLISH

1. Le ixoqiib' xeekiq'aluj le kaal pa ja iwir.
2. Xaa xiipaxij ronojeel taq le leme't aretaq xixetz'anik.
3. La pa swaan xeeyuq'uj wi la le karne'l la?
4. Sib'alaj utz le kotz'i'j xqasipaaj chkee le ak'alaab'.
5. Xu'kamisaj le k'a'na taq tz'i' le ala. (Note word order: verb, object, subject.)
6. Xaa xensipaj le ch'utiq taq chikop chiiweech.
7. La xiik'ayij taq le ijastaaq pa k'ayib'al iwir?
8. Xeechajij le alk'u'al alaq pa qo'ch iwir.
9. Iwonojeel xi'yuq'uj le ichikoop.
10. Le tz'i' xeekikamisaaj konojel taq le me's pa qatinamiit.

ENGLISH TO K'ICHEE'

1. The boys gave the clay dishes as a gift to their mother.
2. All of you (alaq) herded your sheep in the gullies yesterday.
3. Did you (ix) break the bottles yesterday?
4. The bad dogs killed our sheep (PL).
5. You held my child (woman's) in your arms when you arrived here yesterday.

6. The children broke all the clay dishes when they played in the house.
7. I took care of the children in my house.
8. We gave the little dogs as gifts to the girls.
9. Every day the woman sold tortillas in the market.
10. The rocks killed the sheep.

USEFUL EXPRESSIONS

1. La k'a k'o na karaaj kojopanik?
   Is there still some to go before we get there?

   K'a k'olik.
   There's still some to go.

2. Sib'alaj k'ax le b'e waraal.
   The road is very difficult here.

3. Puqlaj le b'e.
   The road is dusty.

4. Xaq'o'l le b'e.
   The road is muddy.

17

Derived Transitive Verbs in Active Voice
Whose Roots Begin with a Vowel

When we studied possessive pronouns in lessons 7 and 8, we saw that nouns beginning with consonants took one set of possessive pronouns, and those beginning with vowels took another set, both sets having identical meaning.

When we studied Derived Transitive Verbs whose roots began with a consonant in the Active Voice, we saw that the subject pronouns corresponded almost exactly with the possessive pronouns used with nouns that began with consonants.

In K'ichee' there are a number of Derived Transitive Verbs whose roots begin with vowels. Correspondingly, we now use as subject markers those possessive pronouns that are used for nouns that begin with vowels.

-w- (-inw-)	I	-q-	we
-aaw-*	you	-iiw-*	you
-r-	He/she/it	-k-	they
la	you	alaq	you

* The vowels in the personal pronoun prefixes *aw-* and *iw-* appear to become long (*aaw* and *iiw*) when used as subject markers in transitive verbs.

The models we saw in lesson 15 remain the same except for the change of these person markers. This change occurs, then, when the root begins with a vowel.

MODEL CONJUGATION

ka-w-esaaj/ k-inw-esaaj	I take it out	ka-q-esaaj	we take it out
k-aaw-esaaj	you take it out	k-iiw-esaaj	you take it out
ka-r-esaaj	he/she/it takes it out	ka-k-esaaj	they take it out
k-esaj la	you take it out	k-esaj alaq	you take it out

MODEL SENTENCES

Le ixoq xresaj le atz'iaq puk'olib'al. (pa + uk'olib'al)
(the woman   she took it out   the clothes from [in] their place)
The woman took the clothes out from their place.

Kinwerej le sii' pa wulew.
(I haul it   the firewood   on my land)
I haul the firewood on my land.

VOCABULARY

esa	(TVD)	to remove, take out, take away
elesa	(TVD)	alternate form of esa
cabu	(TVD)	to steal, rob
oq'e	(TVD)	to cry about
eqa	(TVD)	to carry a load
ere	(TVD)	to haul
b'o'j	(N)	clay cooking pots
kamyon	(N-SPAN)	truck
kars	(N-SPAN)	jail
k'olib'al	(N)	place, dwelling place
puk'olib'al		in its place
sii'	(N)	firewood
nee'	(N)	baby
eqa'n	(N)	load, cargo
ulew	(N)	land, earth, ground, soil
q'ab'areel	(N)	drunk person
we	(CONJ)	if

FIGURE 17.1. *Reqam le si' le achi* (the man carries firewood). Photograph by Winston Scott.

K'ICHEE' TO ENGLISH

1. Le alab'oom xkelaq'aj le usii' le achi.
2. Le achi xroq'ej uwach le rixoqiil aretaq xkamik.
3. Ronojel q'iij kaqeqaj nimaq taq eqa'n.
4. La xesaj la le wa pa k'ayib'al?
5. Xaa xiiwoq'ej uwach le yawaab'.
6. Na kelaq'aj ta alaq le ulew.
7. Ix ix ajchakiib', kiiwerej le ulew pa le kamyon.
8. Pa juyub' kakelaq'aj wi le sii' le elaq'omaab'.
9. Wee kelaq'aj la le ulew, kab'ee la pa kars.
10. Xqelesaj le q'ab'areel pa ja.

ENGLISH TO K'ICHEE'

1. You (ix) carry firewood in the hills.
2. We haul rocks to the gully.
3. They cried over their mother.
4. I robbed a clay pot in the house.
5. The woman removed the dog from the house.
6. You (alaq) robbed the land from the man.
7. You (at) carry the baby in the market.
8. The workers robbed us.
9. We removed the drunk person from our house.
10. You (laal) cried over your wife.

SPECIAL DRILL

1. Conjugate the verb *oq'e* "to cry" in all eight persons, using the third person singular object pronoun in Active Voice in both Completed and Incomplete Aspects.

2. Conjugate the verb *eqa* "to carry a load" in all eight persons, combining each of the eight with all of the possible object pronouns (as in lesson 15). Do this in Active Voice in both Completed and Incomplete Aspects.

USEFUL EXPRESSIONS

1. Sib'alaj paqalik le b'e.
   The road is steep uphill.

2. Sib'alaj xulanik le b'e.
   The road is steep downhill.

3. Utz le b'e.
   The road is good.

4. Ix janipaa kixb'eek
   How many of you are going?
   Oj jo'ob'.
   We are five.

LESSON

18

Imperatives of Derived Transitive Verbs in Active Voice and the Reflexives

IMPERATIVES OF DERIVED TRANSITIVE VERBS — ACTIVE VOICE

In our study of the imperatives of Simple Intransitive Verbs in lesson 12, we saw two main points:

1. The regular imperative marker, *k-*, was replaced by *ch-* in the third person singular for verbs whose roots begin with vowels:

   c̲huxlanoq
   let him rest!

2. The termination marker that indicated the imperative was *-oq* (*-a*):

   katwar<u>oq</u>
   go to sleep!

For imperatives of transitive verbs in Active Voice, *ch-* is also the marker. However, the *-oq* is not the termination marker. Derived Transitive Verbs in Active Voice retain the *-j* termination marker.

MODEL CONJUGATION OF DERIVED
TRANSITIVE VERBS IN ACTIVE VOICE

tijo	to teach	qatijooj*	let us teach him
chaatijooj	teach him/her	chiitijooj	teach him
chuutijooj	let him teach him	chikitijooj	let them teach him
tijoj la*	teach him	tijoj alaq*	teach him

* Notice that in the first person plural and in the *la* and *alaq* forms the *ch-* marker does not occur when the object is in the third person (him/her/it). However, if the verb root begins with a vowel, the *ch-* does occur: e.g., *chesaj la* "take it out."

If the object is other than third person singular, then the *ch-* is always used:

chintijooj la	teach me
cheetijoj la	teach them

THE REFLEXIVES

The reflexive word in K'ichee' is -*iib'*, meaning "self."

DECLENSION OF REFLEXIVE -IIB'

wiib'	myself	qiib'	ourselves
awiib'	yourself	iwiib'	yourselves
riib'	himself/herself/ itself	kiib'	themselves
iib' la	yourself	iib' alaq	yourselves

In our model sentences below, we see *qatijoj qiib' chee le chaak*, which means "let's teach ourselves about the work." We see that *qatijooj qiib'* means "let's teach ourselves." In the verb the object pronoun is -Ø-, or third person singular. The reflexive word *qiib'* is a noun and is the direct object of the verb. It is therefore marked as the direct object within the verb with -Ø-.

The use of the reflexive can be seen in the conjugation below. It is used with all eight persons here with a verb in incomplete aspect:

Kintijoj wiib'.	I teach myself.	Kaqatijoj qiib'.	We teach ourselves.
Kaatijoj awiib'.	You teach yourself.	Kiitijoj iwiib'.	You teach yourselves.
Kuutijoj riib'.	He teaches himself.	Kakitijoj kiib'.	They teach themselves.
Katijoj iib' la.	You teach yourself.	Katijoj iib' alaq.	You teach yourselves.

NOTE: In the *la* and the *alaq* forms, the pronouns *la* and *alaq* are not repeated twice as logic might dictate (e.g., *katijoj la ib' la* and *katijoj alaq ib' alaq*), but as in the above conjugation (*katijoj ib' la* and *katijoj ib' alaq*). This is also true for *la* and *alaq* verb forms if the direct object is also possessed by the same pronoun: e.g., *kachajiij la le tz'i' la* "you take care of your dog" would ordinarily become *kachajiij le tz'i' la*, with the first *la* dropping out. However, it is permissible in this construction to use both *la*'s and *alaq*'s if one so wishes.

VOCABULARY

tijo	(TVD)	to teach someone
ch'aab'e	(TVD)	to talk to someone
tzijo	(TVD)	to tell about something, to talk about something
kajma	(TVD)	maintain, sustain, serve
chaku	(TVD)	to work something
chaaq'	(N)	younger sibling of the same sex
chikop	(N)	animal
jun	(INDEF ART)	an, one
-iib'	(N)	self

wiib'	myself	qiib'	ourselves
awiib'	yourself	iwiib'	yourselves
riib'	himself (herself, itself)	kiib'	themselves
iib' la	yourself	iib' alaq	yourselves

MODEL SENTENCES

1. Chaachajij le achaaq', ali.
   (take care of him   your younger sibling   girl)
   Take care of your younger sibling, girl.

2. Qatijoj qiib' chee le chaak.
   Let's teach ourselves about the work.

DRILLS

A. Change the following sentences into imperatives by changing the verb to the imperative form and then translate the entire sentence.

1. Kachajij iib' alaq.
2. Kaatijoj awiib'.
3. Keeqakajmaj le qalk'u'aal.
4. Ki'ch'aab'ej le winaq.
5. Kaloq'oj le taat la.

6. Xaakamisaj le chikop.
7. Xqach'aab'ej le achi.
8. Kiichajij le ichaaq'.
9. Xeech'aab'ej alaq konojeel le winaq.
10. Katzijoj la le utza chaak.

B. Combine each verb with the reflexive pronoun given in each exercise, putting the verbs in the imperative mood and giving translations.

Example: esa-awiib'
        chaawesaj-awiib'   Remove yourself.

1. chaji-iib' alaq
2. oq'e-iwiib'
3. kajma-iib' alaq
4. esa-qiib'
5. oq'e-riib'
6. ch'aab'e-qiib'
7. loq'o-iib' la
8. tijo-awiib'
9. kamisa-kiib'

ENGLISH TO K'ICHEE'

1. Take care of (*chaji*) yourself (*laal*), sir.
2. Teach your (*at*) children every day.
3. Work (*alaq*) the land in the hills (*pa juyub'*).
4. Let's tell about the thief.
5. Speak with (*ix*) the woman.
6. Let him carry the firewood.
7. Remove yourself (*laal*) from the house.
8. Hold (*at*) the baby in your arms.
9. Love (*ix*) one another (yourselves).
10. Let's kill the goat.
11. Take care of (*at*) me.
12. Love them (*laal*)!
13. Talk to us (*ix*)!
14. Kill (*alaq*) the animals!
15. Take care of (*laal*) your daughter, madam!
16. Talk to (*at*) me!
17. Let us talk to them!
18. Take us away (*at*)!

19. Kill it (*ix*)!
20. Work (*laal*) the land!

USEFUL EXPRESSIONS

1. Jawii katkanaj wi kanoq?
   Where are you going to get off?

2. Teren kan le qachi'iil.
   Our companion is following along behind.

3. Kattzukuxik.
   Someone is looking for you.

4. Katch'aab'exik.
   Someone is talking to you. (If the person doesn't hear.)

19

Derived Transitive Verbs in Simple Passive Voice

What is the meaning of Simple Passive Voice? We saw before that "voice" in K'ichee' transitive verbs is a way of spotlighting one or more of the three elements of the verb phrase: subject, verb, or object. For example, in Active Voice we saw that the spotlight was equally on all three of these elements.

Simple Passive Voice now switches and puts the emphasis on the object, and the verb and the object are combined in the verb phrase. For example, in the word *kinkunaxik*, *-in-* is the object, *-kuna-* is the verb root, and *-xik* is the termination. *Kinkunaxik* approximately means "I am cured." The Simple Passive Voice is somewhat similar to the passive voice in English and is usually translated that way into English.

It should be noted that with Derived Transitive Verbs, the Simple Passive Voice has its own specific termination marker, which is *-xik*. This replaces the termination marker *-j* of the Active Voice. The *-ik* of *-xik* disappears if the verb is not the final word in the utterance.

It should also be noted that the verbs in this voice are conjugated in the same way as Simple Intransitive Verbs, both in the incomplete and completed aspect as well as in the imperative mood.

CONJUGATION OF THE DERIVED TRANSITIVE VERB – SIMPLE PASSIVE VOICE

kuna "to cure"

Completed Aspect

Kinkunaxik.	I am cured.	Kojkunaxik.	We are cured.
Katkunaxik.	You are cured.	Kixkunaxik.	You are cured.
Kakunaxik.	He/she is cured.	Keekunaxik.	They are cured.
Kakunax la.	You are cured.	Kakunax alaq.	You are cured.

Completed Aspect

Xinkunaxik.	I was cured.	Xojkunaxik.	We were cured.
Xatkunaxik.	You were cured.	Xixkunaxik.	You were cured.
Xkunaxik.	He was cured.	Xeekunaxik.	They were cured.
Xkunax la.	You were cured.	Xkunax alaq.	You were cured.

Imperative Mood

		Kojkunaxoq.	Let us be cured.
katkunaxoq	be cured	kixkunaxoq	be cured
Kunaxoq.	Let him be cured.	Cheekunaxoq.	Let them be cured.
kunaxa la	be cured	kunax a'laq	be cured

In the English passive voice, we can have an agent. For example, "he was cured by the man." "By the man" is the agent. In Simple Passive Voice to express agent or by whom the action was done, we use the preposition -*umaal* (see lesson 10 for the declension). Therefore, in K'ichee' we can say:

Xkunax le yawaab' rumal le ajq'iij.
(he was cured   the sick one   by the diviner)
The sick one was cured by the diviner.

In English we can also say that someone was cured "by you," "by me," or "by us." In K'ichee' in this voice the agent can be expressed only in the third person:

Xkunax le yawaab' rumal le ajq'iij.
(he was cured   the sick one   by him   the diviner)
He (the sick one) was cured by the diviner.

Xkunax le yawaab' kumal le ajq'ijaab'.
(he was cured   the sick one   by them   the diviners)
The sick one was cured by the diviners.

In order to express the idea that "I," "we," or "you" cured someone, we must return to Active Voice:

Xinkunaj le achi. I cured the man.
Xatinkunaj. I cured you.

It is *not* correct in K'ichee' to say the following:

Xkunax le yawaab'.	wumaal	by me
He the sick one was cured.	awumaal	by you
	umaal la	by you
	qumaal	by us
	iwumaal	by you
	umaal alaq	by you

NOTE: We noted in lesson 15 that one cannot correctly have the third person subject and second person formal object combination in Active Voice. If one is speaking in the formal form and wishes to say "he cures you" or "they cure you" (formal singular or plural), then one common way to do this is to use Simple Passive Voice:

Kakunax la rumaal. You are cured by him.
Kakunax la kumaal. You are cured by them.
Kakunax alaq rumaal. You (PL) are cured by him.
Kakunax alaq kumaal. You (PL) are cured by them.

VOCABULARY

From now on, all Derived Transitive Verbs will be listed under simple passive voice with the -*xik* termination marker.

kunaxik	(TVD)	to be cured
chomaxik	(TVD)	to be thought, to be planned, to be arranged
eeta'maxik	(TVD)	to be learned
tz'aapixik	(TVD)	to be closed, locked up
josq'ixik	(TVD)	to be cleaned
majixik	(TVD)	to be begun
mulixik	(TVD)	to be gathered together
ajq'iij	(N)	diviner, Mayan priest, day keeper
ajq'ijaab'	(N)	diviners, Mayan priests, day keepers
ch'ab'al	(N)	language, Christian doctrine
ch'a'ooj	(N)	fight, dispute
uchi'	(N)	his mouth, opening
uchii ja	(N)	door (of the house)
chee'	(N)	wood, tree, jail
chee'	(ADJ)	rigid, inflexible
eskwela	(N-SPAN)	school

K'ICHEE' TO ENGLISH

1. Xmajix jun nima chaak iwir kumal le achijaab'.
2. Katz'aapix le uchii ja rumal le ixoq.
3. Xjosq'ix le ulew kumal le ajchakiib'.
4. Chwe'q kachomax le ch'a'ooj.
5. Rajawaxik keeta'max le ch'ab'al kumal konojel le winaq.
6. Chwe'q kamulix taq ab'aj pa le chaak.
7. Xelaq'ax le pwak pa ja rumal jun elaq'oom.
8. Pa eskwela keetijox wi le ak'alaab'.
9. Keech'aab'ex le yawab'iib' rumal le ajq'iij.
10. Xtzijox le ch'a'ooj kumal le alab'oom.
11. Xkamisax le nima chikop rumal le qataat.
12. Xeetz'aapix le elaq'omaab' pa chee' kumal le winaq.
13. Xojelaq'ax rumal le itzel a'chi.
14. Xelesax alaq pa chaak kumal le kitaat le ak'alaab'.
15. Xixch'aab'ex pa b'e rumal le ajyuq'.
16. Ak'aal, xa xattz'aapix pa ja rumal le anaan.
17. Xoq'ex awach rumal le awachajiil.

ENGLISH TO K'ICHEE'

1. The children are carried in arms by their fathers.
2. It is necessary that the bottles be sold.
3. The clay pots were broken by the sellers on the road.
4. We will be locked in jail by the bad men.
5. Every day the girls are taught at school.
6. You (*alaq*) were talked about by our mother yesterday.
7. You (*laal*) are served by your wife.
8. I was carried (packed on back) by the big man.
9. The firewood is hauled by the boys in the morning.
10. The land was worked by my father.
11. You (*ix*) were cried over by your mother.
12. The thief will be looked for in the hills by the men.

DRILLS

A. Fill in the appropriate words in the blanks.

Kinchajix	rumal	intaat
I am taken care of	by	my father

1. _____ rumal _____
   you are taken care of   your father

FIGURE 19.1. *Keetijox le ak'alaab'* (the children are taught). Photograph by John Edvalson.

2. _____   rumal   _____
    we are taken care of   our father

3. _____   kumal   _____
    they are taken care of   their father

4. _____   kumal   _____
    you (ix) are taken care of   your father

5. _____   rumal   _____
    he is taken care of   his father

B. Change all of the verbs from Active Voice into Simple Passive Voice, leaving the person-objects the same and substituting *rumaal* or *kumaal* for the subject.

1. Xinuutijoj le achi.
2. Katkiloq'oj le ataat anaan.
3. Le ala xreeta'maj le ch'ab'al.
4. Kojkich'aab'ej le ak'alaab'.
5. Xkimajij le ch'a'ooj le winaq.

6. Le ixoqiib' xeekimulij le ak'alaab'.
7. Le ajq'iij xixuutz'apiij pa chee'.

USEFUL EXPRESSIONS

1. La k'o ri ataat pa ja?
   Is you father at home?

   K'olik.
   He is.

   Na k'o taj.
   He isn't.

2. Jawii b'eenaq wi ri ataat?
   Where has your father gone?

   B'eenaq pa chaak.
   He has gone to work.

3. Jasa ora kulik?
   What time will he arrive here?

   Wee ne kul pa taq a las kwatro.
   Maybe he'll arrive at four o'clock.

4. Kimpee chi na pa jun rat.
   I'll come back in a while.

Derived Transitive Verbs in Completed Passive Voice

MEANING OF COMPLETED PASSIVE VOICE

Both Simple Passive and Completed Passive Voices have many of the qualities of the passive voice in English. In both of these voices the object or the recipient of the action of the verb is given emphasis. The difference between Simple Passive Voice and Completed Passive Voice is that the action done to the object receives a different emphasis.

In Simple Passive Voice the focus is placed on the object with the emphasis on the action done to the object.

In Completed Passive Voice we still have the spotlight focused on the object of the verb phrase, but now we are not concentrating so much on the action done to it as we are on emphasizing the *condition* or *state* of the object resulting from the action done to it. Therefore, in Simple Passive Voice *kak'ayixik* means "it is sold" or "someone sells it." In Completed Passive Voice *kak'ayitajik* means "it will get sold" or "it will finish being sold."

Completed Passive Voice emphasizes the "becoming" (coming to be in a state).

FORMATION OF COMPLETED PASSIVE VOICE

We saw that the marker for Active Voice is *-j*; for Simple Passive Voice the marker is *-x(ik)*. The marker for Completed Passive Voice is *-taj(ik)*.

Verbs in this voice are conjugated exactly like Simple Intransitive Verbs.

CONJUGATION OF DERIVED TRANSITIVE VERB

kunaxik "to be cured"

Incomplete Aspect

Kinkunatajik.	I shall get cured.	Kojkunatajik.	We shall get cured.
Katkunatajik.	You will get cured.	Kixkunatajik.	You will get cured.
Kakunatajik.	He will get cured.	Keekunatajik.	They will get cured.
Kakunataj la.	You will get cured.	Kakunataj alaq.	You will get cured.

Completed Aspect

Xinkunatajik.	I got cured.	Xojkunatajik.	We got cured.
Xatkunatajik.	You got cured.	Xixkunatajik.	You got cured.
Xkunatajik.	He got cured.	Xeekunatajik.	They got cured.
Xkunataj la.	You got cured.	xkunataj alaq.	You got cured.

Imperative Mood

Kojkunatajoq.	Let us get cured.		
katkunatajoq	get cured	kixkunatajoq	get cured
Kunatajoq.	Let him get cured.	Cheekunatajoq.	Let them get cured.
kunataja la	get cured	kunataj a'laq	get cured

NOTE: In English we can say such things as "it can be learned" or "it can be arranged." In K'ichee' one of the ways of expressing approximately the same idea is by using Completed Passive Voice in completed aspect—for example, *keeta'matajik* "it can be learned"; *kachomatajik* "it can be arranged."

THE POSITIONAL ASPECT

We have until now seen two aspects of Simple Intransitive and Transitive verbs, namely, incomplete completed, as well as the imperative mood.

In Completed Passive Voice there is a new aspect that is peculiar to this voice: Positional Aspect. What does this Positional Aspect mean? We saw in the first part of this lesson that in Completed Passive Voice in both incomplete and completed aspects we have emphasis on the state of the object resulting from an action to be done or that was done to it. In Positional Aspect the emphasis is still on the state of the object, but now with no mention of the action that put the object in that state.

The Positional Aspect has its own particular marker. The markers for the various aspects are shown below:

1. Completed Aspect   aspect marker   k-, ka-
2. Completed Aspect   aspect marker   x-
3. Imperative Mood   aspect marker   k/ch-ok
4. Positional Aspect   aspect marker   -tal (ik)

CONJUGATION OF POSITIONAL ASPECT

In kunatalik.	I am cured.	Oj kunatalik.	We are cured.
At kunatalik.	You are cured.	Ix kunatalik.	You are cured.
Kunatalik.	He is cured.	Ee kunatalik.	They are cured.
Kunatal la.	You are cured.	Kunatal alaq.	You are cured.

EXPRESSION OF AGENT WITH UMAAL

In Completed Passive Voice the agent of the action can be expressed in all eight persons by the preposition *umaal* "by me," "by you," "by him."

Xk'ayitaj le wa awumaal.
(finished being sold   the tortillas   by you)
The tortillas were finished being sold by you.

K'ayital le wa qumaal.)
(are sold   the tortillas   by us
The tortillas are sold (in the state of being sold) by us.

MODEL SENTENCES

1. Aretaq xk'ayitaj le kaxlan wa kumal le ajNawala'iib', xeetzalij pa kitinamiit.
(when it was finished being sold   bread   by them
the Nahualeños   they returned to their town)
When the bread was finished being sold by the Nahualenians, they returned to their town.

2. A'jlatal konojel le winaq waraal rumal q'atb'al tziij.
(they are counted   all of the people   here   by it   the government)
All the people here are counted by the government.

VOCABULARY

tzalij	(IVS)	to return
tzalixik	(TVD)	to be returned
ajlaxik	(TVD)	to be counted
b'ixik	(TVD)	to be said
poroxik	(TVD)	to be burned
rajiil	(N)	money
rajaaw	(N)	(its) owner
kaxlan wa	(N)	bread
q'atb'al tziij	(N)	courthouse, government
mayestr	(N-SPAN)	teacher
we ne'	(ADV)	perhaps, maybe
chi	(CONJ)	that
are chi	(CONJ)	in order that

K'ICHEE' TO ENGLISH

1. Aretaq xporotaj le ja rumal le rajaw, xtz'aapix pa chee'.
2. Xeechomataj le winaq pa q'atb'al tziij.
3. Aretaq xb'itaj la' rumal le achi xuumajij ch'a'ooj.
4. Xtzalitaj le rajiil chee le rajaaw rumal le elaq'oom.
5. A'jlatal le winaq waral pa tinamit rumal le mayestr.
6. Keeta'mataj le jun chaak, we sak'aaj jun.
7. Eqatal le nee' rumal unaan.
8. Aretaq xb'itaj chwee chi na kak'ayix ta le ulew, xintzalij pa wo'ch.
9. We karelaq'aj le pwaq le ak'aal, we ne katz'apitaj pa chee'.
10. Le k'isik' kakimuliij kiib' pa b'e are chi na keekamisataj ta rumal le tz'i'.

ENGLISH TO K'ICHEE'

1. When the work was finished being planned by us, we returned home.
2. The child is (in the state of) being cared for by his father.
3. We go to work in the morning in order that the land will get cleaned quickly.
4. If the fight gets resolved (*chomaxik*) quickly in the courthouse, it (the fight) will end (*k'is*) over there.
5. If you (*ix*) take care of yourselves on the road, you won't get killed.
6. The pot was returned to its place by the woman.
7. Yesterday the man's clothes got burned.

8. The man says that the children have become taught about (*chee*) the doctrine.
9. Maybe I'll go if the money gets returned to me.

ADDITIONAL DRILL

Change the following verbs from Active Voice into Completed Passive Voice, keeping the same objects and expressing the subjects by -*umaal* in its appropriate form. Translate the new sentences into English.

1. Xqaporoj le chaak iwir.
2. Le achijaab' kakitzalij le pwaq cheech le rajaaw.
3. Keechomaj la le winaq pa k'atb'al tziij.
4. Le ala xinuuch'aab'ej pa b'e.
5. Xi'mulij le chikop pa koraal (*corral*) are chi na ke'laq'ax taj.
6. Ka'jlaj alaq le winaq pa tinamit.
7. Aretaq ximb'ij wa' chkeech le ajchakiib', xeeb'ee pa chaak.
8. Xuutz'aapii uchii le ja le ala.
9. Aretaq kaqatz'aapij uchii ja, na ko'k ta le winaq.
10. Xaamajij chaak iwir.

USEFUL EXPRESSIONS

1. K'o jun nutajkiil awuuk'.
   I have an errand with you.

2. Jasa le atajkiil?
   What is your errand?

3. La k'o atajkiil?
   Do you have an errand? (Do you want something?)

4. Jasa kaawaaj?
   What do you want?

5. Jachin xataqow loq?
   Who sent you here?

21

Derived Transitive Verbs in Absolutive Antipassive Voice

We have seen that the different voices in K'ichee' verbs are ways of putting emphasis on one or more of the three elements of the transitive verb clause. We are now going to describe the Absolutive Antipassive Voice. This voice is used when one wishes to place the emphasis on the *action* of the verb clause, with secondary emphasis on the actor, and when no object is mentioned (except indirectly, as we shall see).

Since we have in this voice only subject and verb expressed, verbs in this voice resemble Simple Intransitive Verbs. It may help to think of this voice as a way of "intransitivizing" transitive verbs.

We saw that in each of the various voices, there are different markers:

Active Voice	-j	chakuu-j
Simple Passive Voice	-x	chaku-x(ik)
Completed Passive Voice	-taj	chaku-taj(ik)
Absolutve Antipassive Voice	-n	chaku-n(ik)

The marker for Absolutive Antipassive Voice is -*n(ik)*. To see how this voice works, observe the following sentences.

If we use verb *chakuxik* "to work" in active voice, we might say:

Le achijaab' kakichakuj le ulew pa juyub'.
(the men   they-work the land   in hills)
The men work the land in the hills.

Note that in Active Voice the verb expresses the object, "the land," obligatorily both in K'ichee' and in the English translation. If we use this verb
in Absolute Antipassive Voice in the same sentence, only excluding the
object, we get:

Keechakun le achijaab' pa juyub'
(they-work   the men   in hills)
The men work in the hills.

In English, as in K'ichee', we have the verb expressed along with the
subject of the verb. The object is excluded. In K'ichee', as in English, many
transitive verbs can be used without objects. To do this in K'ichee', one uses
Absolute Antipassive Voice. In the Absolute Antipassive Voice transitive verbs are conjugated exactly as Simple Intransitive Verbs.

MODEL CONJUGATION OF DERIVED TRANSITIVE
VERBS IN ABSOLUTE ANTIPASSIVE VOICE

Incomplete Aspect

+ ASPECT	+ SUBJECT	+ ROOT	+ MARKER	+ TERMINATION	
k	in	q'ojoma	n	ik	I play (music)
k	at	q'ojoma	n	ik	you play (music)
ka	Ø	q'ojoma	n	ik	he plays (music)
ka	—	q'ojoma	n la		you play (music)
k	oj	q'ojoma	n	ik	we play (music)
k	ix	q'ojoma	n	ik	you play (music)
k	ee	q'ojoma	n	ik	they play music
ka	—	q'ojoma	n alaq		you play (music)

Completed Aspect

+ ASPECT	+ SUBJECT	+ ROOT	+ MARKER	+ TERMINATION	
x	in	q'ojoma	n	ik	I played (music)
x	at	q'ojoma	n	ik	you played (music)
x	Ø	q'ojoma	n	ik	he played (music)
x	—	q'ojoma	n la		you played (music)
x	oj	q'ojoma	n	ik	we played (music)
x	ix	q'ojoma	n	ik	you played (music)
x	ee	q'ojoma	n	ik	they played music
x	—	q'ojoma	n alaq		you played (music)

Imperative Mood

+ IMP. PREFIX	+ SUBJECT	+ ROOT	+ MARKER	+ TERMINATION	
k-	at-	q'ojoma-	n-	oq (a)	play (music)
	Ø-	q'ojoma-	n-	oq (a)	let him play (music)
		q'ojoma-	n-	a la	play (music)
k-	oj-	q'ojoma-	n-	oq (a)	let us play (music)
k-	ix-	q'ojoma-	n-	oq (a)	play (music)
ch/k	ee-	q'ojoma-	n-	oq (a)	let them play (music)
		q'ojoma-	n-	a'laq	play (music)

Several peculiarities of verbs in the Absolutive Antipassive Voice should be noted.

1. Not all transitive verbs are used in this voice. They can all be theoretically formed in the Antipassive Voice, but many are not used. Apparently, to the native speaker they make no sense. Several Derived Transitive Verbs that we have seen theoretically can be formed but are not used:

Kinwesaaj.	I take it out.	CORRECT
Kinesanik.	I take out.	INCORRECT
Kinwoq'eej.	I cry over him.	CORRECT
Kinoq'enik.	I cry over.	INCORRECT

   Note that in the examples just given, their translation into English is incorrect unless the object is expressed. Many of the transitive verbs that cannot be used in this voice have corresponding Simple Intransitive Verbs that are used in their place; e.g., instead of *kinoq'enik* "I cry over," which is not used, we use the Simple Intransitive Verb *kinoq'ik*, "I cry." In the verb *ch'aab'exik* "to be spoken to," we find we cannot say *kinch'aab'enik* "I speak to." In this case the corresponding Simple Intransitive Verb is used to express the idea: *kinch'awik*, "I speak."

2. When using a verb in this voice, one must note whether the subject of the sentence is now the doer of the action or becomes the receiver of the action. For example, in the verb *kamisaxik* "to be killed," if we use this verb in Absolutive Antipassive Voice we get *kinkamisanik* "I kill." We see that the subject "I" in this case is still the active agent of the act of killing. However, if we use the verb *raqixik* "to be broken open," in Absolutive Antipassive Voice we get *kinraqinik* "I break open." Here we see that the subject is now the recipient of the action rather than the doer. Putting this verb in Active Voice, we get an active agent: *kinraqij*

le ab'aj "I break open the rock." If we reflect upon this idea, we can see that we do approximately the same in English. We don't have to look farther than the last two examples. In "I kill him" and "I kill," we have the subjects as doers of the action in both cases. In "I break open the rock" and "I break open," we have the doer of the action in the first sentence becoming the recipient of the action in the second example. And so it is in K'ichee'. Some verbs whose subjects become recipients of the actions in the Absolutive Antipassive Voice have corresponding Simple Intransitive Verbs that express the same identical meaning. For example, we saw that *karaqinik* means "it breaks open." There is a corresponding Simple Intransitive Verb, *karaqarob'ik*, which might be approximately translated as "it gets broken open." For all practical purposes these two forms are interchangeable.

3. We mentioned above that no object is expressed directly in Absolutive Antipassive Voice. However, one may use an object indirectly at times in this voice. This is done by using the preposition *ch-ee(ch)*, "to me," "to you," "to him" or "for me," "for you," "for him." We have seen that we can say: *kinuuloq'oj le intaat* "my father loves me." In Absolutive Antipassive Voice we can express the same idea by saying *kaloq'on le intaat chwee* "my father loves (to) me." The difference seems to be that in Antipassive Voice we are placing most of the emphasis on the subject's act of loving, and the one who is the object of this act is only of secondary importance. This mechanism of expressing the object indirectly with Absolutive Antipassive Voice is used very commonly in two cases:

   a. To avoid confusion that arises in Active Voice in trying to say "I + verb + you (*laal*)" (e.g., "I look for you"), as distinct from "you (*laal*) + verb + me" (e.g., "you look for me"). In K'ichee' both of these sentences come out identically in Active Voice: *Kintzukuj la*. To avoid this ambiguity, the K'ichee' speaker will often switch to Absolutive Antipassive Voice when using the first person singular *in* with the second person formal *laal* or *alaq*. Then it is immediately clear who is the subject and who is the object: *Kintzukun chee la* "I am looking for you"; *Katzukun la chwee* "You are looking for me"; *Kintzukun chee alaq* "I look for y'all"; and *Katzukun alaq chwee* "Y'all look for me."

   b. We saw when talking about Active Voice that third person subjects cannot be used with *laal* or *alaq* as objects. One cannot correctly say *kuutzukuj la* "he is looking for you." We saw that one way to express this idea is to use Simple Passive Voice: e.g., *katzukux la rumal* "you are being looked for by him." Another way to express this idea is to use Absolutive Antipassive Voice: *Katzukun chee la* "He is looking for you."

MODEL SENTENCE

Keeq'ojoman le ajq'ojomaab' pa tak nimaq'iij.
(they play   the marimba players   at fiestas)
The marimba players play at fiestas.

VOCABULARY

sik'ixik	(TVD)	to be called, to be invited
q'ojomaxik	(TVD)	to be played (as a musical instrument, especially a marimba)
raqixik	(TVD)	to be broken or burst open
taatab'exik	(TVD)	to be listened to
elaq'ik	(TVD)	Antipassive Voice of elaq'axic (TVD), to be stolen or robbed (IRREGULAR)
b'isoxik	(TVD)	to be sad about
b'ixaxik	(TVD)	to be sung
ch'o'jixik	(TVD)	to be fought over
chakuxik	(TVD)	to be worked
ajq'ojoom	(N)	marimba player
ajq'ojomaab'	(N)	marimba players
nimaq'iij	(N)	fiesta, big day
b'irin	(N)	gunny sack
paam	(PN)	stomach, inside
majaa'	(ADV)	not yet
xaq	(ADV)	no more than, only, just
jas chee	(INTER)	why?
jas chemna	(INTER)	why not?
rumal ri	(CONJ)	because

K'ICHEE' TO ENGLISH

1. Na keechakun ta le winaq pa taq nimaq'iij.
2. Keeb'ison le ak'alaab' rumal ri xkam le kinaan.
3. Majaa kasik'in le achi chee la, taat.
4. Xaq kojtaatab'enik aretaq kojch'aab'ex kumal le qamayestr.
5. Xtz'apin le uchii ja.
6. Ronojel q'iij kixk'ayin pa k'ayib'al.

7. Jasche keeb'ixan le ak'alaab' pa ja?
8. Xraqin upaam le k'isik' rumal ri xa yawaab'.
9. Keetzukun le tz'i' pa taq juyub'.
10. La keetzukun le winaq chee la, taat?
11. Jas chemna keqan alaq?

ENGLISH TO K'ICHEE'

Use only verbs in Absolutive Antipassive Voice to translate these sentences.

1. I work with my father every day in the hills.
2. The children listen to the teacher.
3. Why didn't the door to the house close?
4. The men do not think (*chomaxik*), they only rob.
5. The gunny sack burst open when it fell.
6. You (*at*) are sad because you fought with your wife.
7. The boys are looking for you (*alaq*), sirs.
8. The marimba players still do not play at the fiestas.
9. Why don't your children work with you (*laal*) in the hills, sir?
10. Where do your dogs hunt, boys?

DRILL

Change the verbs in the following sentences into Absolutive Antipassive Voice, omitting the objects. Rewrite and translate each sentence into English.

1. Le a'k'alaab' kakib'isoj uwach le kinaan.
2. Kaqachakuj le qulew ronojel q'iij.
3. Kiiq'ojomaj le q'ojoom pa le nimaq'iij.
4. Jas chee xaq ka'welaq'aj le winaq?
5. Le a'chijaab' kakik'ayij leme't pa k'ayib'al.
6. Keeqatzukuj le itzel taq chikop pa taq juyub'.
7. Ku'kamisaj le tz'ikin le me's.
8. Le achi xuuraqij le b'irin. (Make sure in this sentence that the bag is the thing that bursts.)
9. Keeqaj alaq le b'o'j pa taq b'e.
10. Cha'wajlaj le achikoop.

Change the following sentences from Active and Simple Passive Voices to Absolutive Antipassive Voice, expressing the object indirectly with *ch-ee*. Translate the new sentence into English.

1. Kaqasik'ij la, naan.
2. Xkamisax le tz'i' rumal le achi.

FIGURE 21.1. *Keeq'ojoman le achijaab'* (the men play the marimba).
Photograph by John Edvalson.

3. Katzukux alaq kumal le ak'alaab'.
4. Kintzukuj la. (*la* is the object)
5. Kinloq'oj alaq. (*in* is the object)
6. Kachajix le pwaq kumal le alab'oom.
7. Majaa kaqataatab'ej le achi.
8. Tzukuxa la rumal le ali.
9. Chiichomaj le ik'aslemaal.
10. Kojuukunaj le ajq'iij.

USEFUL EXPRESSIONS

1. Katok u'loq.
   Come on in here.

2. Kat'uyuloq.
   Sit down.

3. Katk'ola na jub'iq'.
   Stay around a while longer.

4. Jasa kulaab'anaa chi'?
   What do you come here to do?

5. Janipaa q'iij ka'b'anaa chila'?
   How long are you going to be there?

Derived Transitive Verbs in Agent-Focus Antipassive Voice

REVIEW OF THE MEANING OF VOICE

The voices in K'ichee' transitive verbs are ways of putting emphasis on one or more of the three main elements of the verb phrase: subject, verb, or object.

> *Active Voice*: emphasis is put equally on all three elements, *subject, verb,* and *object.*
>
> *Simple Passive Voice*: emphasis is put on the *object* (similar to the passive voice in English).
>
> *Completed Passive Voice*: emphasis is on the *condition* or *state* of the *object.*
>
> *Antipassive Voice*: emphasis is on the *verb* (like Simple Intransitive Verbs).

MEANING OF AGENT-FOCUS ANTIPASSIVE VOICE

This fifth voice of the K'ichee' transitive verb again places emphasis on one of the elements of the verb phrase. In Agent Focus Antipassive Voice the emphasis is placed on the *subject* or *agent* of the *action.* In English to place the emphasis on the subject of the verb phrase, we would say: "I am the one who took the boy to school." "I am the one who" is the phrase we use to emphasize the subject or agent of the action. Likewise, we can do this with the other persons in English: "you are the one who," "he is the one who," "we are the ones who," etc. To get this kind of emphasis in K'ichee', we use Agent-Focus Antipassive Voice.

FORMATION OF AGENT-FOCUS ANTIPASSIVE VOICE

In Agent-Focus Antipassive Voice all three main elements are obligatorily present: subject, verb, object. However, in every instance at least subject or object must be a third person (singular or plural) or *laal* or *alaq*. In the event that both subject and object are other than third person or other than *laal* or *alaq*, then this voice cannot be used for emphasizing the subject. We shall see in the next lesson other ways of emphasizing the persons in the verbs.

SCHEMA FOR DERIVED TRANSITIVE VERBS IN THE AGENT FOCUS ANTIPASSIVE VOICE

Incomplete Aspect

SEPARATED SUBJECT PRONOUNS		+ ASPECT	+ OBJECT		+ SUBJECT		+ ROOT	+ VOICE MARKER	± TERMINA-TION
in	I	k- (ka-)	in-	me	in-	I	—	-n	(-ik)
at	you	k- (ka-)	at-	you	at-	you	—	-n	(-ik)
are' (are)	he	k- (ka-)	Ø-	him	Ø-	he	—	-n	(-ik)
laal	you	k- (ka-)	la	you	la-	you	—	-n	(-ik)
oj	we	k- (ka-)	oj-	us	oj-	we	—	-n	(-ik)
ix	you	k- (ka-)	ix-	you	ix-	you	—	-n	(-ik)
ee-	them	k- (ka-)	ee-	them	ee-	they	—	-n	(-ik)
alaq	you	k- (ka-)	alaq	you	alaq	you	—	-n	(-ik)

Completed Aspect

SEPARATED SUBJECT PRONOUNS		+ ASPECT	+ OBJECT		+ SUBJECT		+ ROOT	+ VOICE MARKER	± TERMINA-TION
in	I	x-	in-	me	in-	I	—	-n	(-ik)
at	you	x-	at-	you	at-	you	—	-n	(-ik)
are' (are)	he	x-	Ø-	him	Ø-	he	—	-n	(-ik)
laal	you	x-	la	you	la-	you	—	-n	(-ik)
oj	we	x-	oj-	us	oj-	we	—	-n	(-ik)
ix	you	x-	ix-	you	ix-	you	—	-n	(-ik)
ee-	them	x-	ee-	them	ee-	they	—	-n	(-ik)
alaq	you	x-	alaq	you	alaq	you	—	-n	(-ik)

Imperative Mood
    Imperatives are not used in this voice.

Note in the schema above that the separated subject pronoun is to emphasize the subject of the verb and must agree with the subject within the verb in person and number. Rarely, this separated subject may appear immediately following the verb rather than before it. In the third person singular or plural, if a noun is present as the subject, then the separated subject, *are'/a're'*, may or may not be used (e.g., *aree le achi* or *le achi*).

SAMPLE CONJUGATION OF A DERIVED TRANSITIVE VERB IN AGENT-FOCUS ANTIPASSIVE VOICE IN INCOMPLETE ASPECT USING ALL POSSIBLE FORMS
Kuna: "to cure, to heal"

With *in* as subject

With object third person singular: Ø
In kinkunanik.   I am the one who cures him.

With object second person formal: *laal*
In kinkunan la.   I am the one who cures you.

With object third person plural: *ee**
In kinkunan le a'chijaab'.   I am the one who cures the men.

With the object second person plural formal: *alaq*
In kinkunan alaq.   I am the one who cures you all.

With *at* as subject

With object third person singular: Ø
At katkunan le achi.   You are the one who cures the man.

With object third person plural: *ee**
At katkunan le a'chijaab'.   You are the one who cures the men.

With Ø (third person singular) as subject

With object first person: *in*

| Aree kinkunanik. | He is the one who cures me. | Aree le achi kinkunanik. | The man is the one who cures me. |

With object second person singular — *at*

| Aree katkunanik. | He is the one who cures you. | Aree le achi katkunanik. | The man is the one who cures you. |

With object third person singular — Ø

Aree kakunanik.	He/she is the one who cures him/her/it.	Aree le achi kakunanik.	The man is the one who cures him/her/it.

With object second person singular formal — *laal*

Aree ka-kunan la.	He/she is the one who cures you.	Aree le achi kakunan la.	The man is the one who cures you.

With object first person plural — *oj*

Aree kojkunanik.	He/she is the one who cures us.	Aree le achi kojkunanik.	The man is the one who cures us.

With object second person plural — *ix*

Aree kixkunanik.	He/she is the one who cures you.	Aree le achi kixkunanik.	The man is the one who cures you.

With object third person plural — *ee*

Aree keekunanik.	He/she is the one who cures them.	Aree le achi keekunanik.	The man is the one who cures them.

With object second person plural formal — *alaq*

Aree ka-kunan alaq.	He/she is the one who cures you.	Aree le achi kakunan alaq.	The man is the one who cures you.

With *laal* as the subject

With object first person singular — *in*

Laal kinkunan la.   You are the one who cures me.

With object third person singular — Ø

Laal ka-kunan la.	You are the one who cures him/her.	Laal kakunan la le achi.	You are the one who cures the man.

With object first person plural — *oj*

Laal kojkunan la.   You are the one who cures us.

With object third person plural — *ee*

Laal keekunan la.	You are the one who cures them.	Laal keekunan la le achijaab'.	You are the one who cures the men.

With *oj* as subject

With object third person singular — Ø

| Oj kojkunanik. | We are the ones who cure him. | Oj kojkunan le achi. | We are the ones who cure the man. |

With object second person singular formal — *laal*

Oj kojkunan la.   We are the ones who cure you.

With object third person plural *ee**

| Oj kojkunanik. | We are the ones who cure them/him. | Oj kojkunan le a'chijaab'. | We are the ones who cure the men. |

With object second person plural formal — *alaq*

Oj kojkunan alaq.   We are the ones who cure you.

With *ix* as subject

With object third person singular — Ø

| Ix kixkunanik. | You are the ones who cure him. | Ix kixkunan le achi. | You are the ones who cure the man. |

With object third person plural — *ee**

| Ix kixkunanik. | You are the ones who cure them/him. | Ix kix-kunan le achijaab'. | You are the ones who cure the men. |

With *ee* (third person plural) as subject

In this person, the separated subject pronoun, *a're'* (*a'ree*), or a plural noun is often the only clue that the subject is plural.

With object first person singular — *in*

| A'ree kinkunanik. | They are the ones who cure me. |
| A're' le ixoqiib' kinkunanik. | The women are the ones who cure me. |

With object second person singular — *at*

| A'ree katkunanik. | They are the ones who cure you. |
| A're' le ixoqiib' katkunanik. | The women are the ones who cure you. |

With object third person singular — Ø

| A'ree keekunanik. | They are the ones who cure him/her/it/them. |

| A're' le ixoqiib' keekunanik. | The women are the ones who cure him/her/it/them. |

With object second person singular formal—*laal*

| A'ree keekunan la. | They are the ones who cure you. |
| A're' ixoqiib' keekunan la | The women are the ones who cure you. |

With object first person plural—*oj*

| A'ree kojkunanik. | They are the ones who cure us. |
| A're' le ixoqiib' kojkunanik. | The women are the ones who cure us. |

With object second person plural—*ix*

| A'ree kixkunanik. | They are the ones who cure you. |
| A're' le ixoqiib' kixkunanik. | The women are the ones who cure you. |

With object third person plural—*ee**

| A'ree keekunan le a'chijaab'. | They are the ones who cure the men. |
| A'ree le ixoqiib' keekunan le achijaab'. | The women are the ones who cure the men. |

With the second person plural formal—*alaq*

| A'ree keekunan alaq. | They are the ones who cure you. |
| Le ixoqiib' keekunan alaq. | The women are the ones who cure you. |

* Here, where the object is third person plural, the marker is now Ø, as in the third person singular (instead of *ee*, which is the ordinary third person plural marker). The fact that the object is plural can only be discovered from the separated object word that is plural (e.g., "men").

ADDITIONAL NOTES

It can easily be seen that the structure of Agent-Focus Antipassive Voice with Derived Transitive Verbs very closely resembles that of Absolutive Antipassive Voice, especially due to the fact that they have the same marker, *-n(ik)*. In spite of the confusingly similar structure between the two voices, their meanings are quite different and can easily be distinguished from each other in the context in which the verb is used.

To conjugate a Derived Transitive Verb in Agent Focus Antipassive Voice in completed aspect, as in all other cases we have seen, the *k- (ka-)* is changed to *x-*.

Incomplete

In kinkunanik.	I am the one who cures him.
At katkunanik.	You are the one who cures him.
Aree kakunanik.	He is the one who cures him.

Completed

In xinkunanik.	I am the one who cured him.
At xatkunanik.	You are the one who cured him.
Aree xkunanik.	He is the one who cured him.

Derived Transitive Verbs whose roots begin with vowels are conjugated in Agent-Focus Antipassive Voice exactly as those whose roots begin with consonants, e.g.:

eqaxik (TVD), to carry on the back, to pack:

In kineqan le yawaab'. I am the one who carries the sick one on my back.

SOME COMMON USES OF AGENT-FOCUS ANTIPASSIVE VOICE

1. With the interrogatory word *jachin* "who?":

| Jachin xkunan le yawaab'? | Who was the one who cured the sick one? |
| Jachin xatkunanik? | Who was the one who cured you? |

It is very common to use this voice when asking a question about the subject of the sentence/clause when the introductory word is *jachin*.

2. Commonly used to emphasize the subject:

| Aree le ajq'iij xkunanik. | The diviner was the one who cured him. |
| Le intaat xinkunanik. | My father was the one who cured me. |

3. When asking if a person did the action (and that action has an object):

La aree le achi kakunan la?	Is the man the one who cures you?
Are'.	He (is) the one.
La at katkunan le yawaab'?	Are you the one who cures the sick person?
Na in taj.	It (is) not I.

4. With *k'o*, a verb that means 'there is someone or something" and *maaj*, a verb that means "there is none," "there is nothing," "there is no one":

La k'o katkunanik.	Is there someone who cures you?
K'olik.	There is.
La maaj keekunan le winaq?	Is there no one who cures the people?
Maaj (keekunanik).	There is no one (who cures them).

VOCABULARY

k'asuxik	(TVD)	to be awakened
xib'ixik	(TVD)	to be frightened
wartisaxik	(TVD)	to be put to sleep
ramixik	(TVD)	to be cut
jat'ixik	(TVD)	to be tied
tuukur	(N)	owl
xib'ineel	(N)	ghost
xib'inelaab'	(N)	ghosts
ch'iich'	(N)	any metallic object, machete, car
kolob'	(N)	rope
alaj	(ADJ)	small (alternate form is laj; when laj is word-final in an utterance, it becomes la'j)
chee	(PREP)	with (instrumentality)
jachin(aq)	(INTER)	who?
Jachin chqee (ch)?		Who of us?
Jachin chiwee (ch)?		Who of you?
Jachin chkee (ch)?		Who of them?
Jachin cheech alaq?		Who of you?

K'ICHEE' TO ENGLISH

1. Aree le qataat xojk'asun nimaq'ab'.
2. La k'o xramin le laj chee'?
3. A'ree le xib'inelaab' keexib'in le winaq pa taq b'e.
4. La aree le alk'u'al la xsipan le pwaq chee la?
5. Jachin xjat'in le laj tz'i' pa ja?
6. Ee jachin taq le ixoqiib' keek'ayin wa pa k'ayib'al?
7. La alaq xwartisan alaq le laj ak'aal pa ja?
8. Aree Dyoos kojloq'onik.
9. Ix xixjat'in le keej chee kolob'.
10. Jachin chqeech kak'asun le qanaan?

ENGLISH TO K'ICHEE'

1. Are you (*ix*) the ones who tied the cats in the house?
2. Are you (*laal*) the one who frightens us?
3. Which one of you (*alaq*) cuts the little trees on the hill?
4. Which one of us will put the child to sleep tonight?
5. There are ghosts that frightened the children yesterday.
6. The boy's father himself killed the owl because it was an evil animal.
7. It was the thief who took the machete from its place.
8. Are you (*ix*) the ones who are going to take care of our house tomorrow?
9. No one takes care of the sick people in their house.
10. Is there no one of them to go with us to market tomorrow?

ADDITIONAL DRILL

Answer the following questions in K'ichee'.

1. La k'o xramin le kolob'?
2. La ix xixchajin le ak'alaab' iwir?
3. La aree le kitaat le ak'alaab' xk'ayin le tz'i' chiweech?
4. La alaq xporon le chaak pa juyub'?
5. Jachin chiiweech xmulin le ab'aj pa tinamit iwir?
6. La a'ree le nimaq taq a'chijaab' xeemulin le winaq pa q'atb'al tziij?
7. La aree le ataat xattijon chee le ch'ab'al?
8. La aree le ajq'iij kakunan le yawaab' chwe'q?
9. Jachin chqeech katzukun le qasii' pa swaan?
10. La laal xtz'aapin la uchii le ja aretaq xojb'ee pa k'ayib'al?

USEFUL EXPRESSIONS

1. Kojwo'oq.
   Let's eat.

2. Katwo'oq.
   Eat!

3. Chaatijaa na le awaa.
   Continue to eat your food.

4. Maltyoox chee qawaa.
   Thanks for our food.

5. Dyoos xyo'wik.
   God is the one who gave it. (response to no. 4)

23

Special Subclasses of Derived Transitive Verbs and the Use of Independent Personal Pronouns for Emphasis

■ SPECIAL SUBCLASSES OF DERIVED TRANSITIVE VERBS

We have seen that the roots of Derived Transitive Verbs end in vowels (*a, e, i, o,* and *u*). There are two subclasses of Derived Transitive Verbs whose endings vary slightly from those we have already seen whose roots simply end in vowels. One subclass consists of roots that with a vowel and a glottal stop ('); the other consists of roots ending with -*b'a*. Other than this one variation, they are conjugated exactly as the Derived Transitive Verbs we have already seen.

1. Examples of the subclass of verbs whose roots end in a vowel and glottal stop:

-a'	uk'a', "to carry"
-e'	iye', "to wait for"
-i'	tewechi', "to bless"
-o'	yo', "to shoo away"
-u'	q'u', "to cover up with"

   Now we shall see how these Derived Transitive roots that end in the vowel + glottal stop are terminated in each of the five voices.

ACTIVE VOICE ENDINGS
Utterance-Final

-a'aaj	Kinwuk'a'aaj.	I carry it.
-e'eej	Kinwiye'eej.	I wait for him.
-i'iij	Kintewechi'iij.	I bless him.
-o'ooj	Kinyo'ooj.	I shoo him out.
-u'uuj	Kinq'u'uuj.	I cover up with it.

Not Utterance-Final

- a'j	Kinwuk'a'j la'.	I carry that.
- e'j	Kinwiye'j na.	I'll wait for him a while.
- i'j	Kintewechi'j la'.	I'll bless that one.
- o'j	Kinyo'j la'.	I'll shoo that one away.
- u'j	Kinq'u'j la'.	I'll cover up with that.

Simple Passive Voice Endings

-a'x(ik)	Kuk'a'xik.	It will be carried.
-e'x(ik)	Kiye'xik.	He will be waited for.
-i'x(ik)	Katewechi'xik.	He will be blessed.
-o'x(ik)	Kayo'xik.	He will be shooed away.
-u'x(ik)	Kaq'u'xik.	It will be used to cover up with.

Completed Passive Voice Endings

-a'taj(ik)	Kuk'a'tajik.	It will become carried.
-e'taj(ik)	Kiye'tajik.	He'll become waited for.
-i'taj(ik)	Katewechi'tajik.	He will become blessed.
-o'taj(ik)	Kayo'tajik.	He will become shooed away.
-u'taj(ik)	Kaq'u'tajik.	It will become used to cover up with.

Absolutive Antipassive Voice Endings

-a'n(ik)	(lacking in this verb)	
-e'n(ik)	Kiye'nik.	He waits.
-i'n(ik)	Katewechi'nik.	He blesses.
-o'n(ik)	(lacking in this verb)	
-u'n(ik)	(lacking in this verb)	

Agent Focus Antipassive Voice Endings

-a'n(ik)	In kinuk'a'nik.	I am the one who carries it.
-e'n(ik)	In kiniye'nik.	I am the one who waits for him.
-i'n(ik)	In kintewechi'nik.	I am the one who blesses him.
-o'n(ik)	In kinyo'nik.	I am the one who shooes him away.
-u'n(ik)	In kinq'u'nik.	I am the one who covers up with it.

2. Examples of the subclass of verbs whose roots end in -b'a':

k'ulub'a' "to marry off"
t'uyub'a' "to seat"

Below are the appropriate endings for each of the five voices for this subclass. A model form of the verb k'ulub'a' "to marry off" will be given for each voice.

Active Voice Ending

-b'a'	Kuuk'ulub'a'.	He marries him off.
-b'aa	Kuuk'ulub'aa le ralk'u'aal.	He marries his child off.

Simple Passive Voice Ending

-b'ax(ik)	Xeek'ulub'axik.	They were married off.

Completed Passive Voice Ending

-b'ataj(ik)	Xixk'ulub'atajik.	You got married off.

Absolute Antipassive Voice Ending

-b'an(ik)	Kojk'ulub'anik.	We are matchmakers.

Agent-Focus Antipassive Voice Ending

-b'an(ik)	Laal xk'ulub'an la.	You are the one who married him off.

THE USE OF THE INDEPENDENT PERSONAL PRONOUNS FOR EMPHASIS

The independent personal pronouns that we saw in lesson 22—in, at, (ri) are', laal, oj, ix, (ri) a're', and alaq—can be used in any situation in which we wish to emphasize the person in some utterance.

1. In nonverbal sentences:

We have seen how to say *in in achi* "I myself am a man," which can also be said *in achi in*. The duplication of the *in* seems to give more emphasis to the person. It can also be correctly said *in achi* "I am a man," without the duplication of the pronoun to give it emphasis. This same duplication of the pronoun for emphasis can be done in all eight pronouns.

2. With Simple Intransitive Verbs and Absolutive Antipassive Voice of Transitive Verbs to emphasize the subject:

Here the pronoun is placed immediately before or immediately following the verb. *Oj kojch'awik* or *kojch'aw oj* both mean "We are the ones
who speak." The separated pronoun is also used for asking and an-
swering questions with Simple Intransitive Verbs and in Absolutive
Antipassive Voice:

La ix xixtzaaqik?	Were you the ones who fell?
Jee' oj (xojtzaaqik).	Yes, we were (the ones who fell).
Jachin kachakun wuuk'?	Who will work with me?
Aree le ala kachakun awuuk'.	The boy is the one who will work with you.

3. With Transitive Verbs in Active Voice to emphasize the subject:

In katinchajiij. or Katinchajj in.	I am the one who takes care of you.
Jachin kinloq'onik?	Who loves me?
In katinloq'ooj.	I'm the one who loves you.

4. With Transitive Verbs in Active Voice to emphasize the object:

Ix xixqach'aab'eej. or Xixqach'aab'ej ix.	You are the ones we spoke to.
Jachin xuuch'aab'eej?	Whom did he speak to?
Oj xojuuch'aab'eej.	We are the ones he spoke to.

5. In the Simple Passive and Completed Passive Voices to emphasize the
object:

Alaq xkunax alaq rumaal.	You are the ones who were cured by him.
Jachin xchomatajik?	Who was tried?
Aree le qanaan xchomatajik.	It was our mother who was tried.

6. With nouns to emphasize possession:

Nuwuuj in la'.	It is mine, that book there.

7. With prepositions to emphasize the object:

Xsipax chwee in. (Xsipax in chwee.)	To me it was given.

NOTE: Another way of emphasizing some element of a phrase is by putting it first in the utterance:

Wuk' xpee wi.	With me he came.
Pa ja kimb'ee wi.	To the house I am going.

Aninaq xpeetik.   Quickly he came.

Aree le intaat xuukunaj   It was my father the man cured.
le achi.

MODEL SENTENCES

1. Chinaawiye'j na juch'iin, k'atee k'u ri' kojb'ee pa k'ayib'al.
   (wait for me—still a bit—and after that we'll go to the market)
   Wait for me a bit yet, and then we'll go to the market.

2. Panuwi' in xtewechi'n wi Dyoos.
   (upon me myself he blessed God)
   It was upon me that God gave his blessing.

VOCABULARY

tewechi'xik	(TVD)	to be blessed
iye'xik	(TVD)	to be waited for (Antipassive Voice has two forms: iye'nik and iye'b'ik)
k'ulub'axik	(TVD)	to be married off
uk'a'xik	(TVD)	to be carried, to be in one's possession
terne'xik	(TVD)	to be followed, to be continued
ch'aqab'axik	(TVD)	to be made wet
t'uyub'axik	(TVD)	to be seated
q'u'xik	(TVD)	to be covered up with
yo'xik	(TVD)	to be shooed away
teem	(N)	chair, bench
k'uul	(N)	blanket
ak'	(N)	chicken
juch'iin	(ADV)	a bit, moment
k'atee k'u ri'	(ADV)	and after that, and then
na	(ADV)	first, still, yet, later, for a while, have to
jee'	(ADV)	yes
ja'ii'	(ADV)	no

DRILLS

A. Write out the conjugation of the following verbs for the eight persons in all aspects in all five voices. Do this exercise twice: the first time with only the verb (e.g., *kintewechi'iij*) and the second time with the verb followed by the particle *na* (e.g., *kintewechi'j na*). Give the English translation for each form.

1. iye'xik   (TVD)   to be waited for
2. terne'xik   (TVD)   to be followed
3. ch'aqab'axik (TVD)   to be made wet

B. Translate the following questions to English, then answer them in K'ichee' and translate them again into English. For example:

La at xatb'ee pa chaak iwir?	Was it you who went to work yesterday?
Jee', in.	Yes, it was I.
La ix kixkunan le yawaab' kamik?	Are you the ones who are going to cure the sick one today?
Ja'ii', na oj ta kojkunanik.	No, we aren't the ones who are going to cure him.

1. Jachin xpee iwuk' pa chaak iwir?

2. La ix xixch'aqab'ax rumal le jab'?

3. Jawii kojkiye'j wi le alab'oom chwe'q?

4. La katerne'j na la le chaak?

5. La aninaq kak'ulub'ax le ala rumal utaat?

6. Jachin kuk'a'n le wa pa k'ayib'al?

7. La xixwa'ik aretaq xixt'uyub'ataj rumal le itaat?

8. La chwe'q kaqakunaj na le qanaan?

9. La aree le k'uul kiiq'u'j chaaq'ab'?

USEFUL EXPRESSIONS

1. La xatutzirik?
   Are you finished (eating)?
   Jee', Xinutzirik.
   Yes, I'm finished.

2. Kinnuum chik.
   I'm hungry.

3. Kachaqij nuchii'.
   I'm thirsty.

4. La kak'ayix wa waraal?
   Is food sold here?

LESSON

24

The Demonstrative Articles and Relative Pronouns: *we, le, ri*

DEMONSTRATIVE ARTICLES

The articles that we translate into English as "the" also have a demonstrative quality in K'ichee' (like "this" and "that" in English). We have already frequently used in this grammar one of the demonstrative articles, namely *le,* and have translated it loosely as "the." There are three of these demonstrative articles. The proximity (physical or psychological) of the object spoken about is shown by the demonstative article used with it.

we	the (this one very near to the speaker)
le	the (that one visible to the speaker or spoken of as if visible)
ri	the (that one not present to the speaker)

In the following examples we can see how these articles are used:

1. Utz we nutz'ii'.	The (this one very near me) my dog is good.
2. Utz le nutz'ii'.	The (this one visible to me) my dog is good.
3. Utz ri nutz'ii'.	The/my dog (this one very near me) is good.

WE, LE, AND RI AS RELATIVE PRONOUNS

The three demonstrative articles are also used as relative pronouns with the following meanings:

we "who" (this one here who), "which" (this one here which); very close to speaker or an action just now done

le "who" (that one there who), "which" (that one there which); visible to the speaker or an action just recently done

ri "who" (that one who), "which" (that one which); not present to the speaker, an action not yet done, or one done in the distant past

In the following examples, we can see how the relative pronouns are used:

we "which" (used with things very close to the speaker)

Utz we nutz'ii' we xiisipaj chwee.
(good the/my dog this one you gave me)
This is a good <u>dog which</u> you gave me.
"who" (used with persons very close to the speaker)

Utz we achi we xinkunanik.
(good the man this one the one who cured me)
This <u>man who</u> cured me is good.

le "which" (used with things in the presence of or recently seen by the speaker)

Utz le nutz'ii' le xiisipaj chwee.
(good the/my dog that one you gave me)
<u>That dog there which</u> you gave me is a good one.
"who" (used with persons in the presence of or recently seen by the speaker)

Utz le achi le xinkunanik.
(good the man that one the one who cured me)
<u>That man there who</u> cured me is good.

ri "which" (used with things not present)

Utz ri nutz'i' ri xiisipaj chwee.
(good the/my dog that one you gave me)
<u>The dog which</u> you gave me is good.
"who" (used with persons not present)

Utz ri achi ri xinkunanik.
(good the man   that one   the one who cured me)
That man who cured me is good.

NOTE: In the above examples the articles used with the nouns match the relative pronouns used with them.

we achi we   this man who
le achi le   that man there who
ri achi ri   that man who

It should be noted that various combinations are possible:

le achi ri
we achi ri   the man who
we achi le

Be aware that these variations exist. In a simple grammar such as this, we will not attempt to explain this complex aspect of the grammar.

The relative pronouns can also be used with verbs:

we   Chiitaatab'eej (jasa) we kimb'iij.
(listen to [what]   this which   I say)
Listen to this which I say.

le   Chiitaatab'eej (jasa) le kimb'iij.
(listen to [what]   that which   I say)
Listen to that which I say.

ri   Chiitaatab'eej (jasa) ri kimb'iij.
(listen to [what]   that which   I say)
Listen to that which I say.

MODEL SENTENCES

1. Xpee le achi le xinkunaj kab'ijir.
   (he came the [that] man   that one who   I cured the day before yesterday)
   The man whom I cured the day before yesterday came.

2. Chiinimaaj (jasa) we kimb'ij chiiwe.
   (obey   [what]   this which   I say to you)
   Obey this which I am saying to you.

VOCABULARY

nimaxik	(TVD)	to be obeyed, respected
keej	(N)	horse
ojer	(ADV)	a long time ago
kab'ijir	(ADV)	the day before yesterday
we	(REL PRO)	this one who, this one which
we	(DEM ART)	the (this one)
le	(REL PRO)	(that one there) who, (that one there) which
le	(DEM ART)	the (that one there)
ri	(REL PRO)	that one who, that one which
ri	(DEM PRO)	the (that one)

K'ICHEE' TO ENGLISH

1. Xkam ri kitaat le ak'alaab' ojeer.
2. Utz we ak'aal; kinuunimaaj.
3. K'ax le xb'ij la chee le achi.
4. La majaa kapee ri itaat pa juyub'?
5. Ojer kaatin ri ixoq pa ja' ronojel q'iij.
6. Kamik keechakun pa tinamit le winaq le xeek'ayin le keej chwee.
7. Ri ixoq ri xixkunanik, sib'alaj kixuuloq'ooj.
8. Kaqajat'ij le tz'i' ri xkamisan ri jun me's.
9. Xul le achi ri xch'aab'en la kab'ijir.
10. Kuunimaj le ak'aal jasa ri kab'ix chee rumal ri utaat.
11. Na utz taj we kinchakuuj.
12. Kaq'i'taj le achi chee le kuub'ij le ralk'u'aal.

ENGLISH TO K'ICHEE'

1. This man cured me a long time ago.
2. It is good that which you said to the people in the city hall the day before yesterday.
3. The man who spoke to you yesterday will come today in the afternoon.
4. The horse that you sold me is sick now.
5. The children obeyed that which their father said to them.
6. That boy who left the day before yesterday works here.
7. The father of my wife died a long time ago.
8. Has your older brother still not arrived from town?
9. It is necessary that the man who gave me this horse go with us to the courthouse.
10. The child whom you cured a long time ago is sick again.

USEFUL EXPRESSIONS

1. La maaj k'ax chaawee?
   Is there nothing wrong with you?

   Maaj.
   Nothing.

2. Jas k'ax chaawee?
   What's wrong with you?

3. K'ax nujoloom.
   My head hurts.

   K'ax nuwach.
   My eye(s) hurt.

   K'ax nuxkin.
   My ear(s) hurt.

   K'ax nuware.
   My tooth aches.

   K'ax nuqul.
   My throat hurts.

   K'ax nupaam.
   My stomach hurts.

4. K'o pamaaj chwee.
   I have diarrhea.

   K'o kaqa pamaaj chwee.
   I have dysentery (bloody diarrhea).

   K'o kumatz chwee.
   I have rheumatism.

   Maaj nuchuq'aab'.
   I don't have any strength.

5. Na karaj ta nuwaa.
   I don't have an appetite.

6. La akunam awiib'?
   Have you cured yourself (taken medicine)?

The Demonstrative Pronouns: *wa′*, *la′*, *ri′*

We have already seen such sentences as:

    Chikop wa′. This is an animal.

    Me′s la′.   That (one there) is a cat.

Wa′ in the above example means "this"; *la′* in the above example means "that (one there)."

There is a third one of these demonstratives that completes the set of three, namely, *ri′* "that" (not present).

wa′ "this"	The demonstrative pronoun used for somebody or something very close to the speaker; the companion of the demonstrative article we, which we saw in the last lesson
la′ "that" (one there)	The demonstrative pronoun used for somebody or something visible to the speaker or spoken of as if it were; the companion of the demonstrative article le, which we saw in the last lesson
ri′ "that"	The demonstrative pronoun used for somebody or something not visible to the speaker, or some aspect done in the past time or not yet done; the companion of the demonstrative article ri, which we saw in the last lesson

SOME COMMON USES OF *WA*', *LA*', AND *RI*'

USED ALONE AS "THIS" OR "THAT" AS SUBSTITUTES FOR THE NAMES OF PERSONS, THINGS, OR ASPECTS

wa'

WITH PERSONS	Ajchaak we ala.	This boy is a worker.
	Ajchaak wa'.	This is a worker.
WITH THINGS	Niim we ab'aj.	This rock is big.
	Niim wa'.	This is big.
WITH ACTIONS	Utz we kinchakuuj.	This which I am working at is good.
	Utz wa'.	This is good.

la'

WITH PERSONS	Xkoos le achi.	That man got tired
	Xkoos la'	That (one) got tired
WITH THINGS	K'a'n le tz'i'.	That dog is mean.
	K'a'n la'.	That (one) is mean.
WITH ACTIONS	Utz le xuub'ij le achi.	That which the man said is good.
	Utz la'.	That is good.

ri'

WITH PERSONS	Jachin ri achi?	Who is that man?
	Jachin ri'?	Who is that?
WITH THINGS	Xpax ri b'oj.	That pot broke.
	Xpax ri'.	That broke.
WITH ACTIONS	K'ax ri kach'awik.	That way in which he talks is harsh.
	K'ax ri'.	That is harsh.

USED WITH THEIR COMPANION DEMONSTRATIVE ARTICLES, *WE*, *LE*, AND *RI*, TO INTENSIFY THE DEMONSTRATIVES

wa' + we wa' we achi   this man here
la' + le   la' le achi   that man there
ri' + ri   ri' ri achi   that very man
    (Intensifies the object spoken of even though not present.)
    NOTE: As above, these three can also be used with persons, things, or actions.

USED WITH *ARE*' (*AREE*) "HE/SHE/IT" OR WITH *A'RE*' (*A'REE*) "THEY" (FOR LIVING THINGS).

are' + wa'	Aree wa' nuwuuj. or Aree nuwuuj wa'.
this is	This is (it) my book.

a're' + wa'	A'ree wa' raal. or A'ree raal wa'.
these are	These are (they) her children.
are' + la'	Aree la' kuuchakuuj. or Aree kuuchakuj la'.
that is	That is what he labors over.
a're' + la'	A'ree la' le waal. or A'ree le waal la'.
those are	Those are my children.
are' + ri'	Aree ri' ko'ch. or Aree ko'ch ri'.
that is (not present)	That (not present) is their house.
a're' + ri'	A're ri'ajk'ayiib'. or A're ajk'ayiib' ri'.
those are (not present)	Those (not present) are sellers.

NOTE: These forms can be used as substitutes for persons, things, or actions.

*The words *are'* and *a're'* lose the final glottal stop and the final *e* becomes *ee* if these words are immediately followed by another word beginning with a consonant.

USED WITH *JE'* TO INDICATE MANNER OR DIRECTION. *JE'* IS APPROXIMATELY TRANSLATED AS "THIS (THAT) WAY"

jee wa'	manner	Jee wa' ri nukeej in.
	"like this"	My horse is like this.
	direction	Jee wa' katpeetik.
	"this way"	Come this way.
jee la'	manner	Jee la' xuub'ij le achi chwee.
	"like that, there"	Like that, there, he said it to me.
	direction	Xeeb'ee le winaq jee la'.
	"that way"	The people went that way.
jee ri'	manner	Jee ri' kachakun ri achi.
	"like that"	Like that the man works.
	direction	This form will not be treated for the present.

NOTE: In this lesson and in lesson 24 we have studied in some detail some of the demonstratives and their uses in K'ichee'. Much remains to be said about this peculiarity of the language, but the treatment of such complex grammatical problems is beyond the scope of this grammar.

VOCABULARY

| wa' | (DEM PRO) | this, this one (very close to the speaker) |
| la' | (DEM PRO) | that there, that one there (visible to the speaker, or spoken of as if it were) |

ri'	(DEM PRO)	that one, that very one (not present to the speaker; a future, past, or hypothetical event)
wa' we	(DEM PRO)	this very, this here
la' le	(DEM PRO)	that there
ri' ri	(DEM PRO)	that very (intensifies the object spoken of even though not present)
are' (*aree)	(PER PRO)	he/she/it
a're' (*a'ree)	(PER PRO)	they
aree wa'	(DEM)	this is it, this is
a'ree wa'	(DEM)	these are they, these are − −
aree la'	(DEM)	that there is it, that there is − −
a'ree la'	(DEM)	those there are they, those there are − −
aree ri'	(DEM)	that is it, that is − −
a'ree ri'	(DEM)	those are they, those are − −
jee wa'	(MANNER, DIR)	this way, like this
jee la'	(MANNER, DIR)	like that there, that way there
jee ri'	(MANNER, DIR)	like that

* This form loses the glottal stop (') when it is not the final word in the phrase.

K'ICHEE' TO ENGLISH

1. Nima chaak wa' we kaqachakuuj.
2. Jachin la'?
3. Kapee chi na ri' chwe'q.
4. La' xojuuch'aab'ej iwir.
5. Jas chee na kiisipaj ta wa' chqee?
6. Chajij alaq ronojel la' le ximb'ij cheech alaq.
7. Aree ri' nutz'ii' ri xink'ayij chee ri achi.
8. La aree la' ri tinamit ri kab'ee wi na la?
9. Aree wa' xuub'ij ri intaat chwee aretaq ximb'ee ruk' pa chaak.
10. A'ree la' raal le ixoq le xeech'aw quk' iwir.
11. Jee la' kel le b'e kab'ee pa tinamit.
12. Jee ri' kach'aw le watz.
13. Kixok'owa jee wa'.
14. Xo'k'ow ri' ri winaq.
15. K'ax xuub'ij ri' ri achi chwee.
16. Utz jee la' kab'ij la.
17. Kanuum chi la' le ala.
18. La aree wa' awatz'iaaq?

ENGLISH TO K'ICHEE'

1. This one is sick.
2. This man here will go with us tomorrow.
3. That man there gave us the land as a gift.
4. These are the man's horses.
5. That is our house there.
6. Those (not present) are good children.
7. My house is like that one there.
8. The sick one was cured over there.
9. The boy's clothes are like these.
10. That one died yesterday.
11. That one (visible) will come again.
12. That book there is new.
13. Enter (*alaq*) over there.
14. The market in my town is like that one (not present).
15. This which I am saying is good.
16. You (*at*) close the door of the house like this.

USEFUL EXPRESSIONS

1. Utz kaakunaj awiib'.
   You should cure yourself (take medicine).

2. Janipaa chi umajim le yaab'iil chaawee?
   How long have you been sick?

3. Wemna katkunax aninaq, katnimatajik.
   If you don't get medical attention quickly, you'll get worse.

4. La k'o kunab'al katajin kaatijo?
   Are you taking medicine?

5. Chaatijaa oxib' pastiya pa jun q'iij: jun nimaq'ab', jun b'enaq'iij, jun chaaq'ab'.
   Take three pills a day: one in the morning, one in the afternoon, and one in the night.

LESSON

26

Radical Transitive Verbs in Active Voice
in Incomplete and Completed Aspects and
Intensification of Adjectives with –*alaj*

TRANSITIVE VERBS

In lessons 15–23 we studied Derived Transitive Verbs in all five voices in incomplete and completed aspects as well as in the impertive mood. Derived Intransitive Verbs, we saw, are those whose roots end with vowels. We will now begin with the study of Radical Transitive Verbs. Radical Transitive Verbs are those whose roots are monosyllabic and end in either consonants or glottal stops.

Radical Transitive Verbs, like Derived Transitive Verbs, are conjugated in the five voices in the incomplete and completed aspects as well as in the imperative mood. The voices and the aspects for Radical Transitive Verbs have the same identical meanings that they have for Derived Transitive Verbs. The only difference between the two classes is the slight difference in their formation, which we will see below.

TWO SUBCLASSES OF RADICAL TRANSITIVE VERBS

Subclass A: Roots that end in consonants, other than glottal stops:

k'ut "show"   b'an "do" or "make"

Subclass B: Roots that end in glottal stops:
    su' "wipe"   ya' "give"   to' "help"

Generally, these two subclasses are conjugated identically except in rare instances that will be pointed out when encountered.

MEANING OF ACTIVE VOICE

In K'ichee' we have five voices for transitive verbs. Each of these five voices is a way of placing emphasis or focus on one or more of the main elements of the clause with the transitive verb: subject, verb, or object.

Active voice, with which we are dealing in this lesson, places equal emphasis on all three of the elements: subject, verb, and object, as we saw in lesson 15.

MEANING OF INCOMPLETE AND COMPLETED ASPECT

In the K'ichee' verbs it is better to talk of aspects of an action rather than of time or tense (see lessons 9 and 10). The aspect markers we have seen so far in the verb indicates whether the action is incomplete (marked by *k-* or *ka-*) or whether it is completed (marked by *x-*).

FORMULA

+ ASPECT	+ OBJECT	+ SUBJECT	+ ROOT	± TERMINATION
Incomplete	in	in (w)		u if vowel in root
k- (ka-)	at	aa (aaw)		is u
[OR]	∅	uu (r)		
	la	la la		[OR]
Completed	oj	qa (q)		o if vowel in root is
x-	ix	ii (iiw)		other than u
	ee	ki (k)		
	alaq	alaq alaq		

In the formula it should be noted that the only difference between Radical Transitive Verbs and Derived Transitive Verbs appears in the termination marker. In Derived Transitive Verbs we saw that the termination in Active Voice was *-j* immediately following the root (e.g., *kinwesaaj* "I take it out") or *-a'*, as we saw in lesson 23 (e.g., *kinch'aqab'a'* "I wet it").

In Radical Transitive Verbs, the termination marker for Active Voice is the termination *-u* or *-o*. The termination marker *-u* is used for a verb whose root vowel is *u*; otherwise *o* is used for roots whose vowels are either *a, e, i,* or *o*. This active voice termination marker, unlike the *-j* active voice marker for Derived Transitive Verbs, only occurs if the verb is the final word in an utterance.

MODEL CONJUGATION OF FOUR RADICAL TRANSITIVE VERBS

Two verbs in subclass A are conjugated below, one whose root vowel is *u* and the other whose root vowel is not *u*; also conjugated are two verbs in subclass B, one whose root vowel is *u* and the other whose root vowel is not *u*, in Active Voice and in incomplete and completed aspects (here the object will always be third person singular).

SUBCLASS A: ROOT VOWEL U (K'UT "SHOW")

Incomplete Aspect

Kink'utu.	I show it.	Kaqak'utu.	We show it.
Kaak'utu.	You show it.	Kiik'utu.	You show it.
Kuuk'utu.	He shows it.	Kakik'utu.	They show it.
Kak'ut la.	You show it.	Kak'ut alaq.	You show it.

Completed Aspect

Xink'utu.	I showed it.	Xqak'utu.	We showed it.
Xaak'utu.	You showed it.	Xiik'utu.	You showed it.
Xuuk'utu.	He showed it.	Xkik'utu.	They showed it.
Xk'ut la.	You showed it.	Xk'ut alaq.	You showed it.

SUBCLASS A: ROOT VOWEL OTHER THAN U (B'AN "MAKE" OR "DO")

Incomplete Aspect

Kimb'ano.	I do it.	Kaqab'ano.	We do it.
Kaab'ano.	You do it.	Kiib'ano.	You do it.
Kuub'ano.	He does it.	Kakib'ano.	They do it.
Kab'an la.	You do it.	Kab'an alaq.	You do it.

Completed Aspect

Ximb'ano.	I did it.	Xqab'ano.	We did it.
Xaab'ano.	You did it.	Xiib'ano.	You did it.
Xuub'ano.	He did it.	Xkib'ano.	They did it.
Xb'an la.	You did it.	Xb'an alaq.	You did it.

NOTE: Radical Transitive Verbs always have a short vowel in the root in active voice.

SUBCLASS B: ROOT VOWEL U (SU' "WIPE")

Incomplete Aspect

Kinsu'u.	I wipe it.	Kaqasu'u.	We wipe it.
Kaasu'u.	You wipe it.	Kiisu'u.	You wipe it.
Kuusu'u.	He wipes it.	Kakisu'u.	They wipe it.
Kasu' la.	You wipe it.	Kasu' alaq.	You wipe it.

Completed Aspect

Xinsu'u.	I wiped it.	Xqasu'u.	We wiped it.
Xaasu'u.	You wiped it.	Xiisu'u.	You wiped it.
Xuusu'u.	He wiped it.	Xkisu'u.	They wiped it.
Xsu' la.	You wiped it.	Xsu' alaq.	You wiped it.

SUBCLASS B: ROOT VOWEL OTHER THAN U (TO' "HELP")

Incomplete Aspect

Kinto'o.	I help him.	Kaqato'o.	We help him.
Kaato'o.	You help him.	Kiito'o.	You help him.
Kuuto'o.	He helps him.	Kakito'o.	They help him.
Kato' la.	You help him.	Kato' alaq.	You help him.

Completed Aspect

Xinto'o.	I helped him.	Xqato'o.	We helped him.
Xaato'o.	You helped him.	Xiito'o.	You helped him.
Xuuto'o.	He helped him.	Xkito'o.	They helped him.
Xto' la.	You helped him.	Xto' alaq.	You helped him.

In the four model verbs conjugated above, if the verb is not final in an utterance, the -*u* and -*o* termination ordinarily disappears.

Kink'utu.	I show it.	Kink'ut le chaak.	I show the work.
Kimb'ano.	I do it.	Kimb'an le chaak.	I do the work.
Kinsu'u.	I wipe it.	Kinsu' le watz'iaaq.	I wipe my clothes.
Kinto'o.	I help him.	Kinto' le achi.	I help the man.

▄ INTENSIFICATION OF ADJECTIVES WITH -*ALAJ*

In lesson 4 we saw that the adjectives can be intensified with the use of the adverb *sib'alaj* (*b'alaj*), which means "very."

niim	big
sib'alaj niim	very big

Another way to intensify adjectives, which also gives the meaning of "very," is to attach -*alaj* to the end of the adjective.

niim	big	nimalaj	very big
k'a'n	mean	k'a'nalaj	very mean
utz	good	utzalaj	very good
itzel	evil	itzelalaj	very evil
k'ax	difficult	k'axalaj	very difficult

The difference in usage between (1) *sib'alaj* + adjective and (2) adjective + *alaj*:

(1) is used when the adjective is equated with the noun:
   Sib'alaj niim le tz'i'.   The dog is very big.
   Sib'alaj saq le ja'.   The water is very clear.

(2) is used when the adjective modifies the noun:
   nimalaj tz'i'   very big dog
   saqalaj ja'   very clear water

VOCABULARY

b'an	(TVR)*	to make, do
k'ut	(TVR)	to show
to'	(TVR)	to help
su'	(TVR)	to wipe
loq'	(TVR)	to buy
ya'	(TVR)	to give, place/put (yaa when not final)
ketzal	(N)	Guatemalan monetary unit
jun	(NUM)	one
ke'eb'	(NUM)	two (keb' when not final)
oxib'	(NUM)	three
kajib'	(NUM)	four
jo'ob'	(NUM)	five (job' when not final)
jee . . . jasa		so . . . as (e.g., jee kib'an ix jasa ri kimb'an in "so do as I do")
ch-wach	(PREP)	before, in front of
chuwa ja		in front of the house, home
Kimb'e chuwa ja.		I am going home.
chnuwach		in front of me
chaawach		in front of you
chuwach (chuwa)		in front of him, her
chwach la		in front of you
chqawach		in front of us
chiiwach		in front of you
chikiwach		in front of them
chwach alaq		in front of you

* From now on in the lesson vocabularies all Radical Transitive Verbs will be labeled (TVR), and all Derived Transitive Verbs will be labeled (TVD).

MODEL SENTENCES

1. Ronojel q'iij le keb' achijaab' kakib'an le k'axalaj kichaak pa juyub'.
   (every day the two men   they do it the very hard their work
     in hills)
   Every day the two men do their very hard work in the hills.

2. Le ixoq xuuk'ut le k'aak' atz'iak chuwach le raal ali.
   (the woman she showed the new clothes to her child-daughter)
   The woman showed her new clothing to her daughter.

3. Ri utzalaj ala kojuuto' chee ri chaak.
   (the very good boy he helps us with the work)
   The very good boy helps us with the work.

K'ICHEE' TO ENGLISH

1. Xaa kaab'an k'ax chkeech le oxib' awalk'u'aal rumal ri katq'ab'arik.
2. Xinkito' le winaq aretaq xojb'ee pa k'ayib'al.
3. Jee kab'an alaq, jasa wa' we kimb'ano.
4. Xqayaa job' ketzal chiiweech, rajiil le k'isik' xqaloq' chiiweech.
5. Xsu' la uchii le b'oj chee le atz'iaq.
6. Le ajchakiib' keekiloq' na ee kajib' chomalaj taq keej.
7. Kiik'ut le rajaaw le nimalaj ulew chqawach.
8. La chwach alaq xuub'an wi ri ch'a'ooj ri ala?
9. Jawi kaqato' wi qiib' chuwach le jun k'ax?
10. Ri qanaan karesaj na puk'olib'al ri pwaq ri xuuyaa ri qataat cheech.
11. Chiib'iij jasa le xkik'ut le imaystr chiiwach.
12. Le kitaat kinaan le a'k'alaab' kakik'ut ri utzalaj taq chaak chkiwach le
    kalk'u'aal.
13. Iwir xinloq' la' le q'analaj me's chee jun achi ri kachakun wuuk'.
14. Jachin kato' alaq pa k'ayib'al?
15. Aree wa' xyaa la chwee iwir.
16. Kojb'ee na chuwa ja. Rajawaxik kaqato' qataat jee la'.

ENGLISH TO K'ICHEE'

1. Tomorrow the men are going to show me the very difficult work.
2. This which I give you (laal) is very good.
3. You (ix) helped us two days with the work.
4. We wipe the bottle with the very white cloth.
5. The three very good children are going home. It is necessary that
   they make their father's firewood there.

6. Did the diviner help you (*at*) in the face of the very big difficulty?
7. So help one another (*ix*) as I help you.
8. You (*alaq*) bought the very big tree from its owner.
9. These are the very white flowers the woman gave us.
10. The thieves do a lot of harm in their lives.
11. So show the very good works to your children as your parents showed them to you a long time ago.
12. I am going home. I have to make my father's tortillas in order that he go to work.
13. That man there is the one we helped with the work.
14. Slowly the children showed themselves to us first, and after that they spoke to us.
15. What do you (*laal*) do every day when you go to town?

USEFUL EXPRESSIONS

1. Jas uwach kunab'al katajin kaatijo?
   What kind of pills are you taking?

2. La k'o q'aaq' chaawiij?
   Do you have a temperature?

   K'olik.
   I have.

   Maaj.
   I haven't.

3. Chaab'anaa jachike ri kuub'ij le doctor chaawee.
   Do whatever the doctor tells you.

4. Maach'it awiib'.
   Don't do anything to make yourself worse.

27

The Imperatives of Radical Transitive Verbs in Active Voice and Use of the Progressive Aspect Marker *katajinik*

▌ IMPERATIVES

The imperatives for Radical Transitive Verbs in Active Voice are formed according to the following formula:

Imperative Marker*	Object†	Subject†	Root	Termination‡
ch-	in	in (w)		
(k-)	at	aa (aaw)		
	∅	uu (r)		
	la	la		
	oj	ka (k)		
	ix	ii (iiw)		
	ee	ki (k)		
	alaq	alaq		

* The imperative marker can be either *ch-*, which is the more acceptable or common form, or simply the *k-* sound. With the first person plural and with the *laal* and *alaq* forms, the *ch-* does not occur when the object is third person singular (him, her, it). In the *laal* and *alaq* forms, the imperative marker is used only if the verb root should begin with a vowel (*chilaa la* "see it!"). If the object is other than third person singular, then the *ch-* (*k-*) is always used (see model conjugations below).

† The *laal* or *alaq* forms of the verbs, either as subject or object, always appear immediately after the verb and are never found in the place where the other six subject and six object pronouns occur.

‡ See below for a detailed discussion of the terminations for the imperatives for Radical Transitive Verbs in Active Voice.

We saw that the termination for Derived Transitive Verbs in Active Voice is always -*j*, even with the imperatives. The termination for Radical Transitive Imperatives in Active Voice is determined by the vowel occurring in the root of the verb as follows:

Root Vowel	Imperative Termination
a	a' (aa-)
b'an	b'ana'
e	a' (aa-)
mes	mesa'
i	a'
tij	tija'
o	o' (oo-)
loq'	loq'o'
u	u' (uu-)
k'ut	k'utu'

We will now take examples for roots containing each of the five vowels, five for subclass A and five for subclass B, and conjugate them in the imperative in Active Voice, always using the third person singular object for simplicity.

NOTE: When the imperative is not utterance-final, the glottal stop is retained if the following sound is a vowel, but the glottal stop is lost if the next sound is a consonant. Whenever the glottal stop is lost, the vowel of the imperative suffix becomes long (e.g., *b'anaa la*).

SUBCLASS A

1. Root vowel *a*: *b'an* "do, make"

		qab'ana'	let's do it
chaab'ana'	do it	chiib'ana'	do it
chuub'ana'	let him do it	chkib'ana'	let them do it
b'anaa la	do it	ban a'laq	do it

2. Root vowel *e*: *mes* "sweep"

		qamesa'	let's sweep it
chaamesa'	sweep it	chiimesa'	sweep it
chuumesa'	let him sweep it	chkimesa'	let them sweep it
mesaa la	sweep it	mes a'laq	sweep it

3. Root vowel *i*: *il* "see"

The root of this verb begins with a vowel and is conjugated exactly like Simple Passive Verbs whose roots begin with vowels (see lesson 17).

		qila′	let's see it
chaawila′	see it	chiiwila′	see it
chirila′ (rila′)	let him see it	chkila′	let them see it
chilaa la	see it	chil a′laq	see it

4. Root vowel *o*: *loq′* "buy"

		qaloq′o′	let's buy it
chaaloq′o′	buy it	chiiloq′o′	buy it
chuuloq′o′	let him buy it	chkiloq′o′	let them buy it
loq′oo la	buy it	loq′o′ alaq	buy it

5. Root vowel *u*: *k′ut* "show"

		qak′utu′	let's show it
chaak′utu′	show it	chiik′utu′	show it
chuuk′utu′	let him show it	chkik′utu′	let them show it
k′utuu la	show it	k′utu′ alaq	show it

Subclass B

1. Root vowel *a*: *ya′* "give"

		qaya′a′	let's give it
chaaya′a′	give it	chiiya′a′	give it
chuuya′a′	let him give it	chkiya′a′	let them give it
ya′aa la	give it	ya′a′ alaq	give it
		(ya′ alaq)	

2. Root vowel *e*: no example found

3. Root vowel *i*: *j′i′* "massage"

		qaji′a′	let's massage it
chaaj′i′a′	massage it	chiiji′a′	massage it
chuuji′a′	let him mas-sage it	chkiji′a′	let them mas-sage it
ji′aa la	massage it	ji′a′ alaq	massage it

4. Root vowel *o*: *to′* "help"

		qato′o′	let's help him
chaato′o′	help him	chiito′o′	help him
chuuto′o′	let him help him	chkito′o′	let them help him
to′oo la	help him	to′o′ alaq	help him

5. Root vowel *u*: *su'* "wipe"

chaasu'u'	wipe it	qasu'u'	let's wipe it
chuusu'u'	let him wipe it	chiisu'u'	wipe it
su'uu la	wipe it	chkisu'u'	let them wipe it
		su'u' alaq	wipe it

■ PROGRESSIVE ASPECT MARKER *KATAJINIK* (*TAJIN*)

MEANING

In English we express progressive aspect (aspect going on at the time spoken of) with the verb "to be" + the "-ing" form of the main verb: "The man is working" in present time or "The man was working" in past time. In K'ichee' this same idea is expressed with the progressive aspect word *katajin(ik)*, followed by a Transitive or Simple Intransitive Verb in its proper person and always in the incomplete aspect because of the progressive nature of the action.

USE

The progressive aspect is used in several ways:

a. To express progressive aspect in present time, *katajin* + *verb* in incomplete aspect is used. The context tells that the aspect is progressing in present time.

Katajin ku'l le winaq chaaniim.
The people are arriving now.

b. To express progressive aspect in past time, *katajin* + *verb* in incomplete aspect is used, but the context shows that it is in the past time.

Katajin kajosq'ix le ulew aretaq xinoopan chila'.
The land was being cleared when I arrived over there.

The completed aspect *x-* in *xinopanik* indicates that *katajin kajosq'ix* is in the past time.

c. To express progressive aspect in future time, *katajin* + *verb* in incomplete aspect is used, but the context shows that it is future time.

Katajin keewa' le winaq aretaq kojok pa ja.
The people will be eating when we enter the house.

d. At times *katajin* may be used without other verbs:
Katajin jab'.   It's raining.
Katajin le q'ojoom.   The marimba is playing.

NOTE: *katajinik* can be used with Simple Intransitive and Transitive Verbs in all five voices:

1. With Simple Intransitive Verbs:
   Katajin kojwa'ik.   We are eating.

2. With Transitive Verbs in Active Voice:
   Katajin kixuukunaj le itaat.   You father is curing you.

3. With Transitive Verbs in Simple Passive Voice:
   Katajin kinkunax waraal.   I am being cured here.

4. With Transitive Verbs in Completed Passive Voice:
   Katajin keekunataj le ee yawab'iib'.   The sick ones are getting cured.

5. With Transitive Verbs in Absolutive Antipassive Voice:
   La katajin kakunan le ajq'iij chee la?   Is the diviner curing you?

6. With Transitive Verbs in Agent-Focus Antipassive Voice:
   Laal katajin kakunan la le ak'aal.   You yourself are curing the child.

VOCABULARY

mes	(TVR)	to sweep
il	(TVR)	to see, look after
tij	(TVR)	to eat
q'i'	(TVR)	to bear, withstand
aj'iik'	(N)	maid, servant, worker paid by the month
aj'ik'aab'	(N)	maids, servants
pruta	(N)	fruit
paam	(N)	stomach, inside
waaqiib'	(NUM)	six
wuquub'	(NUM)	seven
wajxaqiib'	(NUM)	eight
b'elejeb'	(NUM)	nine
lajuuj	(NUM)	ten
upa ja		inside of a house, household
ch-pam	(PREP)	inside of

chnupaam	inside of me	chqapaam	inside of us
chaapaam	inside of you	chiipaam	inside of you
chuupaam	inside of him	chkipaam	inside of them
chpaam la	inside of you	chpaam alaq	inside of you

MODEL SENTENCES

1. Tijaa le wa la taat, ya hora chik kojb'eek.
   (eat it the food   you sir   now time   we go)
   Eat your food, sir; it is now time for us to go.

2. Katajin kuumes upa le ja le aj'iik' aretaq xojok chuupaam.
   (she is sweeping inside the house   the maid   when we
      entered   inside it)
   The maid was sweeping inside the house when we entered it.

K'ICHEE' TO ENGLISH

1. Chaawila' upaam le waaqiib' pruta, we utz.
2. Katajin kakiq'i' k'ax le ee b'elejeb' achijaab' rumal ri keqa'n.
3. Qamesaa na upa le ja, k'atee k'u ri' kojb'ee pa nimaq'iij.
4. Chi'la la la' le ee wajxaqiib' winaq le katajin keeb'iin jee la'.
5. Ri taat, naan, rajawaxik chkik'utuu ri utza taq chaak chkiwach le ee
   kalk'u'aal.
6. Xwilo chi le ee lajuuj chikop katajin kakitij le pruta pa le wulew aretaq xinoopan pa chaak.
7. Chiitijaa le iwaa areechi kiiq'i' le b'ee.
8. Chi'wilaa le ak'alaab' pa ja, ix aj'ik'aab'.
9. Cheeloq'o' alaq ri ee wuquub' karne'l ri katajin keek'ayix jee la'.
10. Chuuk'utuu na le chaak chkiwach le aj'ik'aab' le achi, k'atee k'u ri'
    kaqayaa uwaa.
11. Chinaato'oo chee le eqa'n.
12. B'anaa b'a alaq jasa ri xb'ix cheech alaq iwir.
13. Ya'aa la ri pruta chkee le chikop areechi ku'x choma'q.
14. Qato'oo qiib' pa qak'aslemaal.
15. Chaaya'a' uwaa le achi, kanuum chik.

ENGLISH TO K'ICHEE'

1. Show yourself (*laal*) to the doctor in order that he cure you.
2. Wipe (*at*) the inside of the cooking pot so that I can put (give) the
   food (*riki'l*) in it.
3. Help one another (*alaq*) with the very hard work.
4. Let the man show the road to the eight boys who are passing in front
   of his house.
5. Eat your (*laal*) food first and then we'll help you.
6. See (*ix*) those ten men there; they are working with me.
7. Let's do the work that our fathers gave us yesterday.

8. Let those eight men buy their tortillas in the market.
9. Give (*at*) us the six machetes that are necessary for us.
10. Let them help us nine days in the work.
11. We were making our firewood when the shepherds arrived there with us.
12. We aren't going to go yet; we are helping our father.
13. Why are the women making the tortillas at night?
14. The girl was sweeping the inside of the house when she was called by her mother.
15. The boys are buying clothes in the market.

USEFUL EXPRESSIONS

1. La xaq jee' ub'anom le yaab'il chaawee?
   Are you getting along alright? (asked of a sick person)

2. La kuuyaa chi aweech?
   Are you feeling better now?

3. La xtani' le yaab'il chaawee?
   Has your sickness passed?

4. Kulnutaa chi atzijool chwe'q.
   I'll come to visit you again tomorrow.

5. Chaatija' awaa arechi kapee achuq'ab'.
   Eat your food so that you will get your strength back.

Radical Transitive Verbs in Simple Passive Voice

MEANING OF SIMPLE PASSIVE VOICE

We have already seen that "voice" in K'ichee' is a way of spotlighting one or more of the three main elements of the verb phrase: subject, verb, or object. Simple Passive Voice is used when one wishes to place emphasis on the object of the verb phrase. It is somewhat similar to the passive voice in English.

FORMATION

We saw that the marker for the Simple Passive Voice in Derived Transitive Verbs is -x(ik) attached to the verb root. Radical Transitive Verbs have no such marker attached to the root, but are conjugated exactly as Simple Intransitive Verbs in incomplete and completed aspects:

+ Aspect	+ Person	+ Root	± ik
Incomplete	in		
k- (ka-)	at		
	Ø		
[OR]	la		
Completed	oj		
x-	ix		
	ee		
	alaq		

In incomplete and completed aspects both subclasses A and B are conjugated identically.

Incomplete

SUBCLASS A		SUBCLASS B	
Kinch'aayik.	I am hit.	Kinto'ik.	I am helped.
Katch'aayik.	You are hit.	Katto'ik.	You are helped.
Kach'aayik.	He is hit.	Kato'ik.	He is helped.
Kach'aay la.	You are hit.	Kato' la.	You are helped.
Kojch'aayik.	We are hit.	Kojto'ik.	We are helped.
Kixch'aayik.	You are hit.	Kixto'ik.	You are helped.
Keech'aayik.	They are hit.	Keeto'ik.	They are helped.
Kach'aay alaq.	You are hit.	Kato' alaq.	You are helped.

Completed

SUBCLASS A		SUBCLASS B	
Xinch'aayik.	I was hit.	Xinto'ik.	I was helped.
Xatch'aayik.	You were hit.	Xatto'ik.	You were helped.
Xch'aayik.	He was hit.	Xto'ik.	He was helped.
Xch'aay la.	You were hit.	Xto' la.	You were helped.
Xojch'aayik.	We were hit.	Xojto'ik.	We were helped.
Xixch'aayik.	You were hit.	Xixto'ik.	You were helped.
Xeech'aayik.	They were hit.	Xeeto'ik.	They were helped.
Xch'aay alaq.	You were hit.	Xto' alaq.	You were helped.

NOTE: Notice that in the subclass A verbs, the root vowel gets lengthened in both the incomplete and completed aspects in the Simple Passive Voice (e.g., *b'an* "to do" becomes *b'aan* in the Simple Passive Voice in incomplete and completed aspects).

IMPERATIVE

In the imperatives, the formation of the two subclasses varies slightly, but only from the root onward.

Subclass A is formed exactly like imperatives of Simple Intransitive Verbs.

		kojch'aayoq	let us be hit
katch'aayoq	be hit	kixch'aayoq	be hit
ch'aayoq	let him be hit	cheech'aayoq	let them be hit
ch'aaya la	be hit	ch'aay a'laq	be hit

In subclass B the formation of the Simple Passive Voice imperatives is best shown simply by giving two examples each for the roots having each of the five vowels. In the first example in each case, the verb will be utterance-final. In the second example the verb will not be utterance-final. Vowel length is not regular for the root vowels in this subclass.

ROOT VOWEL A: YA' "TO GIVE"

Utterance-Final

		kojyo'oq	let us be given
katyo'oq	be given	kixyo'oq	be given
yo'oq	let it be given	cheeyo'oq	let them be given
yo'qa la	be given	yo'q a'laq	be given

Not Utterance-Final

		kojyo'qa chee	let us be given to him
katyo'qa chee	be given to him	kixyo'qa chee	be given to him
yo'qa chee	let it be given to him	cheeyo'qa chee	let them be given to him
yo'qa la chee	be given to him	yo'q a'laq chee	be given to him

ROOT VOWEL E: NO EXAMPLE FOUND

ROOT VOWEL I: TI' "TO BE BITTEN"

Utterance-Final

		kojti'oq	let us be bitten
katti'oq	be bitten	kixti'oq	be bitten
ti'oq	let him be bitten	cheeti'oq	let them be bitten
tiyo'qa la	be bitten	tiyo'q a'laq	be bitten

Not Utterance-Final

kattiyo'qa rumaal	be bitten by him
tiyo'qa rumaal	let him be bitten by him
tiyo'qa la rumaal	be bitten by him
kojtiyo'qa rumaal	let us be bitten by him
kixtiyo'qa rumaal	be bitten by him
cheetiyo'qa rumaal	let them be bitten by him
tioyo'q a'laq rumaal	be bitten by him

ROOT VOWEL *O*: *TO'* "TO HELP"
7

		kojto'oq	let us be helped
katto'oq	be helped	kixto'oq	be helped y'all
to'oq	let him be helped	cheeto'oq	let them be helped
to'qa la	be helped	to'q a'laq	be helped

Not Utterance-Final

katto'qa rumaal	be helped by him
to'qa rumaal	let him be helped by him
to'qa la rumaal	be helped by him
kojto'qa rumaal	let us be helped by him
kixto'qa rumaal	be helped by him
cheeto'qa rumaal	let them be helped by him
to'q a'laq rumaal	be helped by him

ROOT VOWEL *U*: *SU'* "TO WIPE"

Utterance-Final

		kojsu'oq	let us be wiped
katsu'oq	be wiped	kixsu'oq	be wiped y'all
su'oq	let it be wiped	cheesu'oq	let them be wiped
su'qa la	be wiped	su'q a'laq	be wiped

Not Utterance-Final

katsu'qa rumaal	be wiped by him
su'qa rumaal	let it be wiped by him
su'qa la rumaal	be wiped by him
kojsu'qa rumaal	let us be wiped by him
kixsu'qa rumaal	be wiped by him
cheesu'qa rumaal	let them be wiped by him
su'q a'laq rumaal	be wiped by him

VOCABULARY

ch'ayik	(TVR)	to be hit
b'a'ik	(TVR)	to be chewed
ch'ajik	(TVR)	to be washed
ti'ik	(TVR)	to be bitten (by animals)
chapik	(TVR)	to be taken hold of, to be caught, to be begun
q'ab' (q'ab'aaj)	(PN)	hand, hands

xa'n	(N)	mosquito
ti'iij	(N)	meat (ti' when possessed by eater; e.g., nuti' "my meat to eat")
chíla b'aa'	(COMMON EXPRESSION)	well, look

NOTE: From now on all Radical Transitive Verbs will be listed in Simple Passive Voice - *ik* form:

e.g., ch'ayik   (TVR)   to be hit

MODEL SENTENCES

1. Xch'aaj le atz'iaq kumal le ixoqiib' pa ja'.
   (it was washed   the clothes   by them   the women   in the river)
   The clothes were washed in the river by the women.

2. Cheechaapa ri a'chijaab; xaq keekich'ay ri kixoqiil.
   (let them be grabbed   the men   just they hit them   the [their] wives)
   Let the men be detained; they just hit their wives.

K'ICHEE' TO ENGLISH

1. Xeeti' le ak'alaab' kumal le xa'n.
2. Ronojel q'iij cheech'aaja le ak'alaab' kumal le kinaan.
3. Kixch'aaya kumal le itaat wee kiib'an k'ax chkee le ichaaq'.
4. Xojchaap chee qaq'ab' rumal qanaan aretaq xojb'ee pa k'ayib'al.
5. Rajawaxik kab'a' ri ti'iij aretaq katiijik.
6. Utz ka'il la (kiil la) rumal le doctor chwe'q, xa laal yawaab'.
7. Chíla b'aa', na kimb'ee taj.
8. Keech'aay le o'xib' alaj taq ak'alaab' rumal le kitaat we keeb'ee pa nimaq'iij.
9. Na kixti' ta kumal xa'n we kiiq'u'j le k'uul chaaq'ab'.
10. La xto' alaq kumal le alk'u'al alaq pa le chaak?

ENGLISH TO K'ICHEE'

1. We'll be helped with the load by our older brother.
2. Was the money given to the workers by the owner of the work?
3. I am taken by the hand by my mother when I go with her to the market.
4. The clothes are being washed by the little girls in the river.
5. If the meat is chewed, it won't do one harm (harm to one).
6. Did the mosquitoes bite you (*alaq*) when you bathed in the river?

7. The doctor cured the man who was bitten by the dog.
8. If the boys rob at the fiesta, they will be caught.
9. The inside of the house was being swept when its owner arrived there.
10. Who was hit by the child on the road?

USEFUL EXPRESSIONS

1. Jas ub'i wa'?
   What is this called?

2. Jas ub'ixiik wa' pa ich'ab'al?
   How do you say this in your language?

3. Jas uwach wa'?
   What is this?

4. Jas upataan wa'?
   What is this used for?

5. Na weta'm ta mas ich'ab'al. or Na kintaa ta mas ich'ab'al.
   I don't understand your language very well.

Radical Transitive Verbs in Completed Passive and Absolutive Antipassive Voices

COMPLETED PASSIVE VOICE

Completed Passive Voice, like Simple Passive Voice, has the spotlight focused on the object of the verb phrase. However, Completed Passive Voice emphasizes the condition or state of the object, resulting from the action done to it (see lesson 20).

FORMATION

Incomplete and completed aspects

ASPECT	PERSON	ROOT	VOWEL*	TAJ	IK
Incomplete	in				
k- (ka-)	at				
[OR]	Ø				
	oj				
Completed	ix				
x-	ee				
	alaq				

POSITIONAL ASPECT

PERSON	ROOT	VOWEL*	TAL	IK
Same markers (see above)				

IMPERATIVE MOOD

ASPECT	PERSON	ROOT	VOWEL*	TAJ	OQ
k-, ch- except in 3rd person sing., laal, alaq where it is ∅	same markers (see above)				

* The vowel in the formulas is present between the root and the *taj* with some
subclass A roots to facilitate pronunciation (e.g., *kak'ututajik* "It will become
shown"). With others it is not needed (e.g., *kab'antajik* "It will get done"). Roots
that take this vowel must be memorized. There appears to be no simple fixed
rule to predict its occurrence. With subclass B roots, the vowel is never added
(e.g., *xto'tajik* "He got helped"; *xsu'tajik* "It got wiped").

CONJUGATION OF COMPLETED PASSIVE VOICE

Two model verbs are conjugated in Completed Passive Voice: *ilik* (subclass
A) "to be seen" and *to'ik* (subclass B) "to be helped":

Subclass A: ilik "to be seen"   Subclass B: *to'ik* "to be helped"

Incomplete Aspect

Kinilitajik.	I will become seen.	Kinto'tajik.	I will get helped.
Katilitajik.	You will become seen.	Katto'tajik.	You will get helped.
Kilitajik.	He will become seen.	Kato'tajik.	He will get helped.
Kilitaj la.	You will become seen.	Kato'taj la.	You will get helped.
Kojilitajik.	We will become seen.	Kojto'tajik.	We will get helped.
Kixilitajik.	You will become seen.	Kixto'tajik.	You will get helped.
Ki'litajik.	They will become seen.	Keeto'tajik.	They will get helped.
Kilitaj alaq.	You will become seen.	Kato'taj alaq.	You will get helped.

Completed Aspect

Xinilitajik.	I became seen.	Xinto'tajik.	I became helped.
Xatilitajik.	You became seen.	Xatto'tajik.	You became helped.
Xilitajik.	He became seen.	Xto'tajik.	He became helped.
Xilitaj la.	You became seen.	Xto'taj la.	You became helped.
Xojilitajik.	We became seen.	Xojto'tajik.	We became helped.
Xixilitajik.	You became seen.	Xixto'tajik.	You became helped.
Xi'litajik.	They became seen.	Xeeto'tajik.	They became helped.
Xilitaj alaq.	You became seen.	Xto'taj alaq.	You became helped.

Positional Aspect

In ilitalik.	I am seen.	In to'talik.	I am helped.
At ilitalik.	You are seen.	At to'talik.	You are helped.
Ilitalik.	He is seen.	To'talik.	He is helped.
Ilital la.	You are seen.	To'tal la.	You are helped.
Oj ilitalik.	We are seen.	Oj to'talik.	We are helped.
Ix ilitalik.	You are seen.	Ix to'talik.	You are helped.
I'litalik.	They are seen.	Ee to'talik.	They are helped.
Ilital alaq.	You are seen.	To'tal alaq.	You are helped.

Imperative Mood

Chinilitajoq.	Let me become seen.	Chinto'tajoq.	Let me become helped.
katilitajoq	become seen	katto'tajoq	become helped
Chilitajoq.	Let me become seen.	To'tajoq.	Let him become helped.
chilitaja la	become seen	to'taja la	become helped
Kojilitajoq.	Let us become seen.	Kojto'tajoq.	Let us become helped.
kixilitajoq	become seen	kixto'tajoq	become helped
Chi'litajoq.	Let them become seen.	Cheeto'tajoq.	Let them become helped.
chilitaj a'laq	become seen	to'taj a'laq	become helped

ABSOLUTIVE ANTIPASSIVE VOICE

Absolutive Antipassive Voice is used when one wishes to place the emphasis on the action of the verb clause with only secondary emphasis given to the actor and with no direct object present (see lesson 21).

Formation

Incomplete and completed aspects:

ASPECT	PERSON	ROOT	VOWEL*	IK
Incomplete	in	I		
k- (ka-)	at	you		
	∅	he/she/it		
[OR]	la	you		
Completed	oj	we		
x-	ix	you		
	ee	they		
	alaq	you		

Imperative Mood

Imp. Prefix	Person	Root	Vowel*	Oq
k-, ch except in third person singular, laal, alaq where it is ∅	same markers (see above_			

* With subclass A roots, the vowel is always present (e.g., *kinsub'unik* "I deceive"). When the root vowel is *u*, the vowel is also *u*. If the root vowel is *a*, the vowel is also *a* (e.g., *kach'ayanik* "he hits") If the root vowel is *e, i,* or *o*, the vowel is *o* (e.g., *kamesonik* "he sweeps"). With subclass B roots, the vowel is not necessary (e.g., *Kalu'n le aaq* "The pig roots").

CONJUGATION OF ABSOLUTIVE ANTIPASSIVE VOICE

Subclass A: mesik (TVR) "to be swept"   *Subclass B: su'ik* (TVR) "to be wiped"

Incomplete Aspect

Kimmesonik.	I sweep.	Kinsu'nik.	I wipe.
Katmesonik.	You sweep.	Katsu'nik.	You wipe.
Kamesonik.	He sweeps.	Kasu'nik.	He wipes.
Kameson la.	You sweep.	Kasu'n la.	You wipe.
Kojmesonik.	We sweep.	Kojsu'nik.	We wipe.
Kixmesonik.	You sweep.	Kixsu'nik.	You wipe.
Keemesonik.	They sweep.	Keesu'nik.	They wipe.
Kameson alaq.	You sweep.	Kasu'n alaq.	You wipe.

Completed Aspect

Ximmesonik.	I swept.	Xinsu'nik.	I wiped.
Xatmesonik.	You swept.	Xatsu'nik.	You wiped.
Xmesonik.	He swept.	Xsu'nik.	He wiped.
Xmeson la.	You swept.	Xsu'n la.	You wiped.
Xojmesonik.	We swept.	Xojsu'nik.	We wiped.
Xixmesonik.	You swept.	Xixsu'nik.	You wiped.
Xeemesonik.	They swept.	Xeesu'nik.	They wiped.
Xmeson alaq.	You swept.	Xsu'n alaq.	You wiped.

Imperative Mood

Katmesonoq	sweep	Katsu'noq	wipe
Mesonoq.	let her sweep.	Su'noq.	Let her wipe.
Mesona la	sweep	Su'na la	wipe
Kojmesonoq.	let us sweep.	Kojsu'noq.	Let us wipe.
Kixmesonoq	sweep	Kixsu'noq	wipe
Cheemesonoq.	let them sweep.	Cheesu'noq.	Let them wipe.
Meson a'laq	sweep	Su'n a'laq	wipe

NOTE: Just as we saw for Derived Transitive Verbs (lesson 21), there are also many Radical Transitive Verbs that can theoretically be formed in Absolutive Antipassive Voice but are not used because they make no sense to the native speaker.

VOCABULARY

riqik	(TVR)	to be found, to be encountered, to be met
kuuriq tyeempo		the time will arrive
xuuriq tyeempo		the time arrived
to'ik	(TVR)	to be helped (Absolutive Antipassive Voice irregular: tob'ik or tob'anik)
ti'ik	(TVR)	to be bitten (by an animal), (Absolutive Antipassive Voice irregular: tiyo'nik)
ch'ajik	(TVR)	to be washed (two forms in Abolutive Antipassive Voice—irregular: ch'ajo'manik "to do laundry"; regular: ch'ajanik "to wash oneself")
tikik	(TVR)	to be planted (two forms in Absolutive Antipassive Voice: tikonik, tiko'nijik)
loq'ik	(TVR)	to be bought (Absolutive Antipassive Voice irregular: loq'o'manik)
q'olik	(TVR)	to be picked (as coffee, beans, etc.) (Absolutive Antipassive Voice irregular: q'olowik)
kape	(N)	coffee
kinaq'	(N)	beans
ab'iix	(N)	corn plant
aweex	(N)	corn planting
ya mero	(ADV-SPAN)	almost, nearly
naqaaj	(ADV)	near, nearby, close by (timewise), recently
ch-naqaaj	(PREP)	near

chnunaqaaj	near me	chqanaqaaj	near us
chaanaqaaj	near you	chiinaqaaj	near you
chuunaqaaj	near him	chkinaqaaj	near them
chnaqaj la	near you	chnaqaj alaq	near you

MODEL SENTENCES

1. Xtikitaj ri abiix pa juyub' kumal le achijaab'.
   (it got planted   the corn   in hills   by them   the men)
   The corn became planted by the men in the hills.

2. Le alab'oom keetob'an na chee le aweex aretaq kuuriq tyeempo cheech.
   (the boys   they will help later   with the corn planting   when it meets time)
   The boys will help with the corn planting when the time arrives for it.

K'ICHEE' TO ENGLISH

1. Ku'xlan na keeb' oxib' q'iij le a'chijaab' aretaq kab'antaj le jach' kumaal.
2. Katajin keeq'olow ri i'xoqiib' chuunaqaaj le tinamit.
3. K'ax keetiyo'n le tz'i'.
4. Kojtob'ana chkee le qataat.
5. Xtikitaj le kinaq' pulew ruk' le ab'iix.
6. Le laj ali katajin kameson chqanaqaaj.
7. Q'olotaja le kape aninaq; ya mero kapee jab'.
8. La xb'antaj le chaak umal alaq?
9. Jachin chiiweech xriqitaj pa nimaq'iij.
10. Xaq kixq'i'tajik we kixb'ee pa aweex quuk'.
11. Ya mero kuurik tyeempo kojb'ee pa jach'.
12. In kintiko'nij kuk' le a'chijaab' aretaq kakib'an aweex chqanaqaaj.
13. Na ya'tal ta chiiweech kixwa' kuk' nimaq taq winaq.

ENGLISH TO K'ICHEE'

1. When the people finished eating (when the food got eaten by the people), they went to work again.
2. Let's help with the harvest when the time arrives for it.
3. The girls pick near their mothers.
4. The corn will become planted by the workers near our house.
5. It's almost time for the corn planting; the rain is near now.
6. Did your (at) father hit you when you became found at the fiesta by him?
7. It's not for you (ix) (it's not given to you) to hit your wives when you become drunk.
8. Why were you buying in the market at night when we arrived there?
9. The women do laundry near the big rock in the river.

10. We don't pass before that man's house; his dog bites.
11. These are the beans that got picked yesterday near the town.
12. When the beans were bought by us, we gave them to our servants.

USEFUL EXPRESSIONS

1. Sib'alaj q'aaq' kamik.
   It's very hot today.

2. Sib'alaj teew kamik.
   It's very cold today.

3. Kapee jab'.
   It's going to rain.

4. Kimb'ee nimaq'ab'.
   I'm going in the morning.

   Kimb'ee pa q'iij.
   I'm going at noon.

   Kimb'ee b'enaq'iij.
   I'm going in the afternoon.

   Kimb'ee chaaq'ab'.
   I'm going at night.

LESSON

30

Radical Transitive Verbs in Agent-Focus Antipassive Voice and Uses of *b'anik* with Spanish Verbs

RADICAL TRANSITIVE VERBS IN AGENT-FOCUS ANTIPASSIVE VOICE

Agent-Focus Antipassive Voice places the emphasis on the subject or agent of the verb phrase. In English we would express this idea like this: "I myself do it" or "I am the one who does it" (see lesson 22).

We saw in lesson 22 that the marker for Derived Transitive Verbs in Agent-Focus Antipassive Voice is *-n* immediately following the root. In Radical Transitive Verbs the marker for Agent-Focus Antipassive Voice is *-w* or *vowel + w* immediately following the root. The formula for Agent-Focus Antipassive Voice in incomplete and completed aspect is as follows.

Incomplete Aspect

SEPARATED SUBJECT PRONOUN	+ ASPECT	+ OBJECT*	+ SUBJECT*	+ ROOT[†]	± VOWEL[‡]	+ W	± IK
in	k- (ka-)	in	in				
at	k- (ka-)	at	at				
are'	k- (ka-)	∅	∅	laal		la	la
oj	k- (ka-)	oj	oj				
ix	k- (ka-)	ix	ix				
a're'	k- (ka-)	ee	ee				
alaq	k- (ka-)	alaq	alaq				

Completed Aspect

SEPARATED SUBJECT PRONOUN	+ ASPECT	+ OBJECT*	+ SUBJECT*	+ ROOT†	± VOWEL‡	+ W	± IK
in	x-	in	in				
at	x-	at	at				
are'	x-	∅	∅	laal		la	la
oj	x-	oj	oj				
ix	x-	ix	ix				
a're'	x-	ee	ee				
alaq	x-	alaq	alaq				

* Either subject or object must be the third person or *laal* or *alaq*, as we saw in detail in lesson 22.

† In subclass B the root in Agent-Focus Antipassive Voice takes the following forms:

Root vowel a	-o'w (ik)	ya'	yo'w (ik)
Root vowel e	no example found		
Root vowel i	-i'ow (ik)	q'i'	q'i'ow (ik)
		ji'	ji'ow (ik)
Root vowel o	-o'w (ik)	to'	to'w (ik)
Root vowel u	-u'w (ik)	su'	su'w (ik)

‡ This vowel is to aid pronunciation and is only found following subclass A roots.

If the root vowel is *u*, the vowel is *u*:

k'ut, k'utuwik

If the root vowel is other than *u* (*a, e, i, o*), the vowel is *o*:

b'an, b'anowik tik, tikowik
b'ey, b'eyowik loq', loq'owik

MODEL VERB

For simplicity the object will always be third person singular, ∅. See lesson 22 for a complete description of all of the possible subject-object combinations for verbs in the Agent-Focus Antipassive Voice.

Incomplete Aspect

SUBCLASS A: K'UTIK "TO BE SHOWN"

In kink'utuwik.	I am the one who shows it.
At katk'utuwik.	You are the one who shows it.
Aree kak'utuwik.	He is the one who shows it.
Laal kak'utuw la.	You are the one who shows it.
Oj kojk'utuwik.	We are the ones who show it.

SUBCLASS A: K'UTIK "TO BE SHOWN"

Ix kixk'utuwik.	You are the ones who show it.
A'ree keek'utuwik.	They are the ones who show it.
Alaq kak'utuw alaq.	You are the ones who show it.

SUBCLASS B: YA'IK "TO BE GIVEN"

In kinyo'wik.	I am the one who gives it.
At katyo'wik.	You are the one who gives it.
Aree kayo'wik.	He is the one who gives it.
Laal kayo'w la.	You are the one who gives it.
Oj kojyo'wik.	We are the ones who give it.
Ix kixyo'wik.	You are the ones who give it.
A'ree keeyo'wik.	They are the ones who give it.
Alaq kayo'w alaq.	You are the ones who give it.

Completed Aspect

SUBCLASS A: K'UTIK "TO BE SHOWN"

In xink'utuwik.	I am the one who showed it.
At xatk'utuwik.	You are the one who showed it.
Aree xk'utuwik.	He is the one who showed it.
Laal xk'utuw la.	You are the one who showed it.
Oj xojk'utuwik.	We are the ones who showed it.
Ix xixk'utuwik.	You are the ones who showed it.
A'ree xeek'utuwik.	They are the ones who showed it.
Alaq xk'utuw alaq.	You are the ones who showed it.

SUBCLASS B: YA'IK "TO BE GIVEN"

In xinyo'wik.	I am the one who gave it.
At xatyo'wik.	You are the one who gave it.
Aree xyo'wik.	He is the one who gave it.
Laal xyo'w la.	You are the one who gave it.
Oj xojyo'wik.	We are the ones who gave it.
Ix xixyo'wik.	You are the ones who gave it.
A'ree xeeyo'wik.	They are the ones who gave it.
Alaq xyo'w alaq.	You are the ones who gave it.

IMPERATIVE MOOD

We are not going to conjugate the Radical Transitive Verb in Agent-Focus Antipassive Voice in the imperative mood since it is so rarely used.

◼ USE OF *B'ANIK* WITH SPANISH VERBS

As K'ichee' speakers come more and more in contact with Spanish, they begin to adopt many Spanish words into their own language. When a Spanish verb is taken into K'ichee' and still used as a verb, it is done by using the K'ichee' verb *b'anik* "to be done, made" in the desired voice, aspect, and person, followed by the infinitive of the borrowed Spanish verb. (*B'anik* is one of the most commonly used verbs in the language.)

Examples of *b'anik* with a Spanish loan verb:

Active Voice
Ximb'an engañar le achi.   I deceived the man.

Simple Passive Voice
Ximb'aan engañar rumal le achi.   I was deceived by the man.

Completed Passive Voice
Ximb'antaj engañar rumal le achi.   I got deceived by the man.

Absolutive Antipassive Voice
not used with this Spanish loan word

Agent-Focus Antipassive Voice
Le achi ximb'anow engañar.   The man is the one who deceived me.

VOCABULARY

b'eyik	(TVR)	to be delayed
muqik	(TVR)	to be buried
tojik	(TVR)	to be paid, to be paid for
na'ik	(TVR)	to be felt
cha'ik	(TVR)	to be chosen, to be selected
engañar, b'anik	(TVR)	to be deceived
kaminaq	(N, ADJ)	dead one; dead
kaminaqiib'	(N)	dead ones
maataam	(ADV)	late
tayik	(TVR)	to be heard, to be asked (IRREGULAR)

Active Voice
Xinto. (utterance-final)   I heard it.
Xintaa ri'. (not utterance-final)   I heard that.

Simple Passive Voice, Incomplete and Completed Aspects
    Xtayik. (utterance-final)   It was heard.
    Xtaa le q'ojoom. (not utterance-final)   The merimba was heard.

Imperative Mood
    Chaataa'! (utterance-final)   Hear it!
    Chaataa ri'! (not utterance-final)   Hear that!

Completed Passive Voice
    Xtaatajik.   It got heard.

Absolutive Antipassive Voice
    Kintaanik. (rare)   I hear.

Agent Focus Antipassive Voice
    In kintoowik.   I'm the one who hears it.

MODEL SENTENCES

1. Aree le qanaan xtoow chqeech we maataam kojpee pa k'ayib'al.
   (it is the our mother   she herself   asked it to us   if late   we
       come   from market)
   It was our mother who asked us if we would come back late from
   market.

2. K'ax kakib'an le winaq we xaq kakib'an engañar kiib'.
   (bad they do it   the people   if just they deceive one another)
   The people do bad if they deceive one another.

K'ICHEE' TO ENGLISH

1. Maataam xixulik, jachin xixb'eyow pa b'e?
2. In xinyo'w le kotz'i'j chee le ak'aal.
3. Xeecha' oxib' chkee le keej areechi kakeqaj kijastaaq le winaq.
4. Jachin katowik jasa le kimb'ij chiiwee?
5. We ne keeniman le ak'alaab' wee alaq kak'utuw alaq le utz
   chkiwach.
6. Xojb'aan engañar aretaq xb'ix chqech chi kojtooj aninaq.
7. Jachin chiiwech keetojow le a'chijaab'?
8. A'ree le a'chijaab' keemuquw le kaminaq.
9. Oj xojno'wik aretaq xul le xib'ineel chaaq'ab'.
10. Laal kato'w la le achi chwe'q.

ENGLISH TO K'ICHEE'

1. Are you (*ix*) the ones who are going to give me the money so that I can pay for the food?
2. Shall we work with the man who selected us?
3. We came late. It was our father who delayed us.
4. You (*at*) were the one who deceived us when you gave us the money.
5. Who will bury the dead ones?
6. Who selected you (*alaq*) for the work in the courthouse?
7. I am the one who gave the money to the sick woman.
8. Who wiped the inside of this pot with a rag?
9. The people became delayed when they heard that there was no one to pay them.
10. We are the ones who washed the clothes of the dead person when he was buried.

DRILL

Conjugate the verb *tayik* in all eight persons in the incomplete and completed aspects, and in the imperative mood in the five voices and give the English translation for each.

USEFUL EXPRESSIONS

1. Xtik'i' le q'iij.
   It's noontime.

2. Xook umooy.
   It's dusk.

3. Je'l saq'iij kamik.
   It's a lovely sunny day today.

4. Xel saq'iij.
   The dry season is over.

5. Xok q'alaj.
   The rainy season has begun.

LESSON

31

The Negative Imperative and Other Negative Forms

THE NEGATIVE IMPERATIVE

We have seen the imperative forms for the Simple Intransitive Verbs and the two classes of transitive verbs in the various voices. Now we shall study the negative imperative for these same verbs.

MEANING

The negative imperative in English can be translated in the following manner: "let me not," "do not," "don't," "let him not," etc.

FORMATION

The marker for the negative imperative is *m-*. In order to form the negative imperative with any verb in any voice or person, the incomplete aspect marker *k-* or *ka-* is exchanged for *m-* or *ma-* (*ma-* is used where *ka-* is used in the incomplete aspect; here, as in the incomplete aspect, it is used to facilitate pronunciation). This is the only change that occurs. Otherwise, the verbs are conjugated as we have seen in the incomplete aspect.

CONJUGATION OF A MODEL SIMPLE INTRANSITIVE VERB

q'ab'ar "to get drunk"

Minq'ab'arik.	Let me not get drunk.	Mojq'ab'arik.	Let's not get drunk.
Matq'ab'arik.	Don't get drunk.	Mixq'ab'arik.	Don't get drunk.
Maq'ab'arik.	Let him not get drunk.	Meeq'ab'arik.	Let them not get drunk.
Maq'ab'ar la.	Don't get drunk.	Maq'ab'ar alaq.	Don't get drunk.

CONJUGATION OF A MODEL RADICAL TRANSITIVE VERB IN THE ACTIVE, SIMPLE PASSIVE, COMPLETED PASSIVE, AND ABSOLUTIVE ANTIPASSIVE VOICES

ch'ayik "to be hit"

Active Voice

Minch'ayo.	Let me not hit him.	Maqach'ayo.	Let's not hit him.
Maach'ayo.	Don't hit him.	Miich'ayo.	Don't hit him.
Muuch'ayo.	Let him not hit him.	Makich'ayo.	Let them not hit him.
Mach'ay la.	Don't hit him.	Mach'ay alaq.	Don't hit him.

Simple Passive Voice

Minch'aayik.	Let me not be hit.	Mojch'aayik.	Let's not be hit.
Match'aayik.	Don't be hit.	Mixch'aayik.	Don't be hit.
Mach'aayik.	Let him not be hit.	Meech'aayik.	Let them not be hit.
Mach'aay la.	Don't be hit.	Mach'aay alaq.	Don't be hit.

Completed Passive Voice

Minch'ayatajik.	Let me not get hit.	Mojch'ayatajik.	Let's not get hit.
Match'ayatajik.	Don't get hit.	Mixch'ayatajik.	Don't get hit.
Mach'ayatajik.	Let him not get hit.	Meech'ayatajik.	Let them not get hit.
Mach'ayataj la.	Don't get hit.	Mach'ayataj alaq.	Don't get hit.

Absolutive Antipassive Voice

Minch'ayanik.	Let me not hit.	Mojch'ayanik.	Let's not hit.
Match'ayanik.	Don't hit.	Mixch'ayanik.	Don't hit.
Mach'ayanik.	Let him not hit.	Meech'ayanik.	Let them not hit.
Mach'ayan la.	Don't hit.	Mach'ayan alaq.	Don't hit.

CONJUGATION OF MODEL DERIVED TRANSITIVE VERB IN ACTIVE, SIMPLE PASSIVE, COMPLETED PASSIVE, AND ABSOLUTIVE ANTIPASSIVE VOICES

elaq'axik "to be stolen, to be robbed"

Active Voice

Mawelaq'aaj (minwelaq'aaj).	Let me not steal it.	Maqelaq'aaj.	Let's not steal it.
Maawelaq'aaj.	Don't steal it.	Miiwelaq'aaj.	Don't steal it.
Marelaq'aaj.	Let him not steal it.	Makelaq'aaj.	Let them not steal it.
Melaq'aj la.	Don't steal it.	Melaq'aj alaq.	Don't steal it.

Simple Passive Voice

Minelaq'axik.	Let me not be robbed.	Mojelaq'axik.	Let's not be robbed.
Matelaq'axik.	Don't be robbed.	Mixelaq'axik.	Don't be robbed.
Melaq'axik.	Let him not be robbed.	Me'laq'axik.	Let them not be robbed.
Melaq'ax la.	Don't be robbed.	Melaq'ax alaq.	Don't be robbed.

Completed Passive Voice

Minelaq'atajik.	Let me not get robbed.	Mojelaq'atajik.	Let's not get robbed.
Matelaq'atajik.	Don't get robbed.	Mixelaq'atajik.	Don't get robbed.
Melaq'atajik.	Let him not get robbed.	Me'laq'atajik.	Let them not get robbed.
Melaq'ataj la.	Don't get robbed.	Melaq'ataj alaq.	Don't get robbed.

Absolutive Antipassive Voice (irregular in this voice: elaq'ik)

Minelaq'ik.	Let me not steal.	Mojelaq'ik.	Let us not steal.
Matelaq'ik.	Don't steal.	Mixelaq'ik.	Don't steal.
Melaq'ik.	Let him not steal.	Me'laq'ik.	Let them not steal.
Meelaq' la.	Don't steal.	Melaq' alaq.	Don't steal.

▍ OTHER NEGATIVE FORMS

As we saw in lesson 6, in K'ichee' in order to form a simple question that expects a "yes" or "no" answer, the interrogative word *la* is placed as the first word in the sentence (e.g., *La katb'ee wuuk'?* "Are you going with me?").

To form a negative question, the negative question word *lamna* is placed at the beginning of the sentence.

Lamna: negative question word

Lamna katb'ee wuuk'?	Aren't you going with me?
Lamna xuuyaa le wuuj chaawee?	Did he not give you the paper?

Other negative words are formed by adding -*mna* to their positive counterparts. For example, *wemna* "if not" is the negative form of *we* "if"; *we nemna* "perhaps not" is the negative form of *we ne* "perhaps"; *pinemna* "even though . . . not" is the negative form of *pine* "even though."

Wemna: "if not" is the negative form of *we* "if"

Wemna kaqab'an le chaak, kojuuch'ay qataat.	If we don't do the work, our father will hit us.
Wemna kojb'eek, kab'ison ri qanaan.	If we don't go, our mother will be sad.

We nemna: "perhaps not" is the negative form of *we ne* "perhaps"

We nemna kojkito' le winaq.	Perhaps the people won't help us.
We kakam le achi, we nemna kakimuq le winaq pa utinamiit.	If the man dies, perhaps the people won't bury him in his town.

Pinemna: "even though . . . not" is the negative form of *pine* "even though"

Kinyaa wa' we ch'iich' chaawee, pinemna utz.	I'll give you this machete, even though it is not good.
Pinemna kab'ee le watz, kimb'ee in pa k'ayib'al.	Even though my older brother doesn't go, I'm going to the market.

Jas chemna: "why not" (this is also said with *jas chee* + *na . . . taj*)

Jas chemna keewar le winaq waraal? (Jas chee na keewar ta le winaq waraal?)	Why don't the people sleep here?
Jas chemna xuub'an le rikiil le laj ali? (Jas chee na xuub'an ta le rikiil le laj ali?)	Why didn't the little girl make the meal?

There are other negative words which are formed in the same way, but only these five will be introduced here.

MODEL SENTENCES

1. Jee miib'an ix jasa kakib'an le ee nik'aj chi winaq.
   (in the manner don't you do it what they do the rest of the people)
   Don't you do what the rest of the people do.

2. Wemna katpee aataam, na katwiye'j taj.
   (if not you come early, not I'll wait for you)
   If you don't come early, I won't wait for you.

VOCABULARY

kojik	(TVR)	to be put, believed, put on
k'amik	(TVR)	to be received, gotten
teew	(N)	cold
nik'aj	(N, ADJ)	half
nik'aj chik		rest of, remainder
aataam	(ADV)	early
we nemna	(ADV)	perhaps not
wemna	(CONJ)	if not
pine	(CONJ)	even though, although
pinemna	(CONJ)	even though . . . not; although . . . not
jas chee	(INTER)	why?
jas chemna	(INTER)	why . . . not
lamna	(INTER)	negative question word

K'ICHEE' TO ENGLISH

1. Na kinchakun ta in, wemna kojto'ik.
2. Jas chemna kuuk'am le pwaq le ala ri xsipax chee rumal ri utaat?
3. Wemna kul ri achi aataam, kojwarik.
4. Lamna utz kaawil wa' we keej? (utz + ilik "to like")
5. Wemna kaaq'i' le eeqa'n, kaab'ij chee le awatz, areechi katuuto' chee.
6. Lamna xiimes upa le ja iwir?
7. Wemna kakoj atz'iaq la, teew kana' la.
8. Wemna kojto'taj chee le chaak, we nemna kojb'ee iwuk' pa nimaq'iij.
9. Pinemna kinwa' in iwuk' chwe'q, kawa' ri intaat.
10. Jas chee na katob'an ta alaq chkee le winaq aretaq kakiriq kiib' pa q'atb'al tziij?

ENGLISH TO K'ICHEE'

1. Even though we fought over the land a long time ago, we still love one another.
2. Why don't you (laal) buy that firewood there?
3. Aren't you (ix) going to eat your beans?
4. If we don't give him the money, our father will hit us.
5. Don't place (at) the bottle near the rock.
6. Let's not work tomorrow.
7. Let the man not do harm to his wife.
8. Let us not do what the rest of the people do when they fight.
9. Don't cover up (laal) with the blanket yet if you aren't going to sleep.
10. Don't hit one another, children.

DRILL

Convert the imperatives in the following sentences into negative imperatives and then rewrite the sentences and translate them into English.

1. War a'laq pa ja kamik.
2. Chaakojoo le k'aak' atz'iyaq.
3. Chiiya'aa le nik'aj chi riki'l pa le bo'j.
4. Chaatijaa le awaa chaaniim.
5. Chinto'oo la chee le chak.
6. Chuuchapaa le ak' le ak'aal.
7. Cheechaa la la' le oxib' achijaab'
8. Katchakuna pa wulew chwe'q.

USEFUL EXPRESSIONS

1. Kana'taj chwee.
   I remember it (it is remembered to me).

2. Kasachan chwee.
   I forget it (it is forgotten to me).

3. Laatz' nuwach.
   I am busy.

4. Tolon nuwach.
   I am free (not busy).

5. Kasaach nuk'u'x.
   I become upset.

LESSON

32

Perfect Aspect of Radical and Derived Transitive Verbs in Active and Simple Passive Voices and the Special Case of *eta'maxik*

▌ MEANING OF PERFECT ASPECT

A verb in Perfect Aspect indicates that the action was begun in some past time and the action itself, or the effects of the action, continue up to the present time. The perfect in K'ichee' is somewhat similar to the perfect tense in English.

FORMATION OF RADICAL AND DERIVED TRANSITIVE
VERBS IN ACTIVE AND SIMPLE PASSIVE VOICES
The voice marker in these cases is the termination -*m*.

Active Voice places emphasis in all three of the main elements of the verb phrase: subject, verb, and object (see lesson 15). Simple Passive Voice places emphasis on the object of the verb phrase (see lesson 19).

Object	Subject	Root	Vowel*	m
in	nu (w)			
at	aa (aaw)			
∅	uu (r)			
la	la			
oj	qa (q)			
ix	ii (iiw)			

Object	Subject	Root	Vowel*	m
ee	ki (k)			
alaq	alaq			

* With Radical Transitive Verbs this vowel is *o* unless the vowel in the root is *u*, and then this vowel becomes *u*. Derived Transitive Verbs do not require this vowel since their roots end in vowels. If the verb is the last word in the uttrance, this vowel is lengthened. Otherwise, it is short.

MODEL CONJUGATIONS OF VERBS IN PERFECT ASPECT

For the sake of simplicity, we shall use only first person singular and second person singular (familiar) forms as objects.

Radical Transitive Verb

Subclass A: ilik "to be seen"

At wiloom.	I have seen you.
In aawiloom.	You have seen me.
At riloom.	He has seen you.
In ilom la.	You have seen me.
At qiloom.	We have seen you.
In iiwiloom.	You have seen me.
At kiloom.	They have seen you.
In ilom alaq.	You have seen me.

Derived Transitive Verb

tzukuxik "to be searched for"

At nutzukuum.	I have searched for you.
In aatzukuum.	You have searched for me.
At uutzukuum.	He has searched for you.
In tzukum la.	You have searched for me.
At qatzukuum.	We have searched for you.
In iitzukuum.	You have searched for me.
At kitzukuum.	They have searched for you.
In tzukum alaq.	You have searched for me.

Subclass B: to'ik "to be helped"

At nuto'oom.	(at nuto'm − −)	I have helped you.
In aato'oom.	(in aato'm − −)	You have helped me.
At uuto'oom.	(at uuto'm − −)	He has helped you.
In to'm la.		You have helped me.
At qato'oom.	(at qato'm − −)	We have helped you.
In iito'oom.	(in iito'm − −)	You have helped me.
At kito'oom.	(at kito'm − −)	They have helped you.
In to'm alaq.		You have helped me.

SIMPLE PASSIVE VOICE
Places emphasis on the object of the verb phrase.

FORMULA

Person	Root	Vowel*
in		
at		
∅		
la		
oj		
ix		
ee (')		
alaq		

* With Radical Transitive Verbs this vowel is *o* unless the vowel in the root is *u;* then this vowel becomes *u.* Derived Transitive Verbs do not require this vowel.

Radical Transitive Verb
SUBLASS A: ILIK "TO BE SEEN"

In iloom.	I have been seen.
At iloom.	You have been seen.
Iloom.	He has been seen.
Ilom la.	You have been seen.
Oj iloom.	We have been seen.
Ix iloom.	You have been seen.
I'loom.	They have been seen.
Ilom alaq.	You have been seen.

Derived Transitive Verb
TZUKUXIK "TO BE SEARCHED FOR"

In tzukuum.	I have been searched for.
At tzukuum.	You have been searched for.
Tzukuum.	He has been searched for.
Tzukum la.	You have been searched for.
Oj tzukuum.	We have been searched for.
Ix tzukuum.	You have been searched for.
Ee tzukuum.	They have been searched for.
Tzukum alaq.	You have been searched for.

SUBCLASS B: TO'IK "TO BE HELPED"

In to'oom.	(in to'm — —)	I have been helped.
At to'oom.	(at to'm — —)	You have been helped.
To'oom.	(to'm — —)	He has been helped.
To'm la.		You have been helped.
Oj to'oom.	(oj to'm — —)	We have been helped.

SUBCLASS B: TO'IK "TO BE HELPED"

Ix to'oom.	(ix to'm − −)	You have been helped.
Ee to'oom.	(ee to'm − −)	They have been helped.
To'm alaq.		You have been helped.

NOTE: In lesson 23 we saw a special type of Derived Transitive Verb that terminates in Active Voicewith the following ending: vowel + glottal stop + vowel + -*j*. In the perfect aspect in Active and Simple PassiveVoices these types of Derived Transitive Verbs are conjugated as follows:

terne'xik   (tvd)   to be followed

Active Voice

Nuterne'eem.	I have followed him.
(nuterne'm−)	(if not utterance-final)

Simple Passive Voice

In terne'eem.	I have been followed.
(in terne'm−)	(if not utterance final)

SOME FURTHER USES OF THE PERFECT ASPECT

1. Continued Aspect

In K'ichee' many verbs, when used in the Perfect Aspect, can express the idea of an action begun in past time and continuing into the present. This use of the Perfect Aspect is generally translated into English as an "-ing" form of the verb:

Le achi uuchapom uch'iich' aretaq xok pa ja.	The man was holding his machete when he entered into the house.
Qeeqam le kape aretaq xojb'ee pa kayib'al.	We were carrying the coffee on our backs when we went to the market.

2. Verbal Adjective

At times the verb in the Perfect Aspect is used as an adjective or a noun:

Tzakom saqmo'l.	Boiled egg.
Elaq'am pwaq.	Stolen money.

3. Pluperfect Aspect

The Perfect Aspect is translated as the Pluperfect ("had") when it is used in a sentence accompanied by a second verb phrase whose verb is in the Completed Aspect:

| Kib'anom chi kichaak le achi-jaab' aretaq xeeqach'aab'eej. | The men had already done their work when we spoke to them. |
| Qaloq'om chi le ja aretaq xaataa chee rajaaw. | We had already bought the house when you asked its owner for it. |

4. Future Perfect Aspect

The Perfect Aspect is translated as the Future Perfect ("will have") when it is used in a sentence accompanied by a second verb phrase whose verb is in the Incomplete Aspect:

| Wee nee majim chi le chomaal aretaq kojoopanik. | Perhaps the meeting will have already begun when we arrive. |
| Ee qamulim chi le ak'alab' pa ja aretaq ku'l le kinaan. | We will have already gathered the children in the house when their mothers arrive. |

■ THE SPECIAL CASE OF ETA'MAXIK "TO BE LEARNED"

The verb eta'maxik is a derived transitive verb whose root begins with a vowel, and as such, it is conjugated like all verbs of this class:

ACTIVE VOICE (SEE LESSONS 15–18)

Kinweta'maaj "I will learn it"	Kaqeta'maaj "We will learn it"
Kaaweta'maaj "You will learn it"	Kiiweta'maaj "You will learn it"
Kareta'maaj "He/she will learn it"	Kaketa'maaj "They will learn it"
Keta'maj la "You (formal) will learn it"	Keta'maj alaq "You (formal) will learn it"

SIMPLE PASSIVE VOICE (SEE LESSON 19)

Xeta'maxik   "It was learned"

COMPLETED PASSIVE VOICE (SEE LESSON 20)

Xeta'matajik   "It got finished being learned"

ABSOLUTIVE ANTIPASSIVE VOICE (SEE LESSON 21)

Eta'maxik   does not appear to be used in this voice.

AGENT FOCUS ANTIPASSIVE VOICE (SEE LESSON 22)

In xineta'manik	"I'm the one who learned it"
At xateta'manik	"You're the one who learned it"
Aree xeta'manik	"He/she is the one who learned it"
Laal xeta'man la	"You are (formal) the one who learned it"
Oj xojeta'manik	"We are the ones who learned it."
Ix Xixeta'manik	"You are the ones who learned it"
A'ree xe'ta'manik	"They are the ones who learned it"
Alaq xeta'man alaq	"You (formal) are the ones who learned it"

However, with this verb there is an additional aspect, very similar in construction to the Perfect Aspect, and indicates that the subject is in the state of having learned something, or knows something. This Positional Aspect is conjugated as follows:

weta'aam	(weta'm — —)	I know it
aaweta'aam	(aweta'm — —)	you know it
reta'aam	(reta'm — —)	he knows it
eta'm la		you know it
qeta'aam	(qeta'm — —)	we know it
iiweta'aam	(iweta'm — —)	you know it
keta'aam	(keta'm — —)	they know it
eta'm alaq		you know it

MODEL SENTENCES

1. Ojer chi nuloq'om wa' we nutz'ii'.
   It's been a long time since I've bought this dog of mine.

2. Le nujii' ruk'a'm le chiim aretaq xoopan chuwa wo'ch.
   My son-in-law was carrying the bag when we arrived at my house.

3. Le nub'aluuk uuk'ayim chi ri ulew aretaq xqak'ulub'aa le wanaab' ruuk'.
   My brother-in-law had already sold the land when we married my sister to him.

VOCABULARY

b'olik	(TVR)	to be roasted in fire
tzakik	(TVR)	to be cooked by boiling or cooked by steam
saq'uul	(N)	plantain
chomaal	(N)	meeting, plan, intention
achalaal	(PN)	sibling, near relative
jii'	(PN)	son-in-law
b'aluuk	(PN)	brother-in-law (male's)
anaab'	(PN)	sister (male's)
xib'aal	(PN)	brother (female's)
ojer	(ADJ)	a long time ago
ojer chik		its been a long time since — —
janipa'	(INTER)	how many? how much? when?
naab'e	(NUM, ADV)	first, at first
k'imuul	(ADV)	many times

K'ICHEE' TO ENGLISH

1. Qatijom tzakom saq'uul pa k'ayib'al.
2. Le nub'aluuk u'chajim le ralk'u'aal pa ja aretaq xqach'aab'eej.
3. B'anom chi le sii' rumal le uxib'aal le ali aretaq kuutij uwaa.
4. Le laj ala reqam uwaa aretaq xb'ee pa chaak.
5. Oj kiye'm chi le ee qachalaal aretaq xojok pa nimaq'iij.
6. Kamik kojki'kotik rumal ri qariqom qiib' kuk' wa' we qachalaal.
7. Ojeer chi uuriqom yaab'iil le qanaan.
8. Le nujii' uk'ayim ri ujastaaq rumaal ri kaq'ab'arik.
9. Naab'e sib'alaj kakito' kiib le winaq; kamik chik na kito'm ta chi kiib'.
10. Le wanaab' uutzakom wa' we saq'uul chqeech.
11. Janipaa chi relesam rib' le ak'aal pa chaak?
12. Janipaa chi aayo'm ri uwaa le ala?

ENGLISH TO K'ICHEE'

1. Who are you (at) waiting for (PERFECT)"
2. The dead man is buried (PERFECT) near the big tree.
3. The man was carrying (PERFECT) the money when he went to the meeting at night.
4. I don't know the road that goes to town.
5. The door of the house was tied when we saw it.
6. I have helped you many times with the corn planting.

7. Why have you (*laal*) not done your work?
8. It has been a long time since the people have spoken to their relatives in town.
9. I was waiting for my friends in front of the house when its owner came.
10. The meeting had already begun when the men spoke to each other.
11. You (*laal*) were taking care of us (PERFECT) when our father went to work.
12. How long has it been since you (*laal*) have spoken to us?

SPECIAL DRILL

Conjugate the following verbs in the Perfect Aspect in Active Voice (using all the possible subject-object combinations) and Simple Passive Voice.

1. loq'oxik   (tvd)   to be loved
2. to'ik   (tvr)   to be helped
3. tijoxik   (tvd)   to be instructed
4. ilik   (tvr)   to be seen
5. terne'xik (tvd)   to be followed

USEFUL EXPRESSIONS

1. Xk'aj nuwach.
   I learned a hard lesson (won't do it again).

2. Kinok iil chee.
   I fuss over him.

3. Keb' uk'u'x kuub'ano.
   He does it unwillingly.

4. Ruk' uk'u'x kuub'ano.
   He does it willingly (with all his heart).

5. Keel nuk'u'x chee.
   My heart goes out to him.

Perfect Aspect of Simple Intransitive Verbs
and Radical and Derived Transitive Verbs in
Completed Passive, Absolutive Antipassive,
and Agent-Focus Antipassive Voices

MEANING OF PERFECT ASPECT

As we saw in lesson 32, a verb in the Perfect Aspect indicates that the action was begun at some past time and the action itself, or the effects of the action, continue up to the present time. The Perfect Aspect in K'ichee' is somewhat similar to the Perfect Tense in English.

FORMATION OF THE PERFECT ASPECT
Perfect Aspect of Simple Intransitive Verbs

Person	Root	i*	naq
in			
at			
Ø			
la			
oj			
ix			
ee			
alaq			

* With some verbs this *i* is used to facilitate pronunciation.

MODEL CONJUGATION OF SIMPLE INTRANSITIVE VERBS

In aatinnaq.	I have bathed.	Oj aatinnaq.	We have bathed.
At aatinnaq.	You have bathed.	Ix aatinnaq.	You have bathed.
Aatinnaq.	He has bathed.	A'tinnaq.	They have bathed.
Aatinnaq la.	You have bathed.	Aatinnaq alaq.	You have bathed.

Perfect Aspect of Radical and Derived Transitive Verbs in the
Completed Passive and Absolutive Antipassive Voices

The Completed Passive Voice places emphasis on the state of the object (see lesson 20). The Absolutive Antipassive Voice places emphasis on the action of the verb phrase (see lesson 21).

PERSON	ROOT	VOWEL*	VOICE MARKER	NAQ
in		a, e, i, o, or u	taj	
at			(Completed Passive Voice)	
Ø				
la				
oj		n		
ix			(Absolutive Antipassive Voice)	
ee				
alaq				

* At times this vowel is present following Radical roots to help facilitate pronunciation. This vowel is always identical to the vowel in the verb root: for example, *b'an, b'anatajik; k'ut, k'ututaj.*

MODEL CONJUGATION OF VERBS IN COMPLETED PASSIVE VOICE

Radical Transitive Verbs

SUBCLASS A: ILIK "TO BE SEEN"

In ilitajnaq.	I have become seen.
At ilitajnaq.	You have become seen.
Ilitajnaq.	He has become seen.
Ilitajnaq la.	You have become seen.
Oj ilitajnaq.	We have become seen.
Ix ilitajnaq.	You have become seen.
I'litajnaq.	They have become seen.
Ilitajnaq alaq.	You have become seen.

SUBCLASS B: TO'IK "TO BE HELPED"

In to'tajnaq.	I have become helped.
At to'tajnaq.	You have become helped.
To'tajnaq.	He has become helped.
To'tajnaq la.	You have become helped.
Oj to'tajnaq.	We have become helped.
Ix to'tajnaq.	You have become helped.
Ee to'tajnaq.	They have become helped.
To'tajnaq alaq.	You have become helped.

Derived Transitive Verbs

KUNAXIK "TO BE CURED"

In kunatajnaq.	I have become cured.
At kunatajnaq.	You have become cured.
Kunatajnaq.	He has become cured.
Kunatajnaq la.	You have become cured.
Oj kunatajnaq.	We have become cured.
Ix kunatajnaq.	You have become cured.
Ee kunatajnaq.	They have become cured.
Kunatajnaq alaq.	You have become cured.

MODEL CONJUGATION OF VERBS IN ABSOLUTIVE ANTIPASSIVE VOICE

Radical Transitive Verbs

SUBCLASS A: CH'AYIK "TO BE HIT"

In ch'ayannaq.	I have hit.
At ch'ayannaq.	You have hit.
Ch'ayannaq.	He has hit.
Ch'ayannaq la.	You have hit.
Oj ch'ayannaq.	We have hit.
Ix ch'ayannaq.	You have hit.
Ee ch'ayannaq.	They have hit.
Ch'ayannaq alaq.	You have hit.

Derived Transitive Verbs

KUNAXIK "TO BE CURED"

In kunannaq.	I have cured.
At kunannaq.	You have cured.
Kunannaq.	He has cured.
Kunannaq la.	You have cured.
Oj kunannaq.	We have cured.
Ix kunannaq.	You have cured.

Derived Transitive Verbs

KUNAXIK "TO BE CURED"

Ee kunannaq.	They have cured.
Kunannaq alaq.	You have cured.

SUBCLASS B: SU'IK "TO BE WIPED"

In su'nnaq.	I have wiped.
At su'nnaq.	You have wiped.
Su'nnaq.	He has wiped.
Su'nnaq la.	You have wiped.
Oj su'nnaq.	We have wiped.
Ix su'nnaq.	You have wiped.
Ee su'nnaq.	They have wiped.
Su'nnaq alaq.	You have wiped.

Perfect Aspect of Radical and Derived Transitive
Verbs in Agent Focus Antipassive Voice

Agent-Focus Antipassive Voice places emphasis on the subject of the verb phrase. With Agent-Focus Antipassive Voice the subject, verb, and object must all be present in the verb phrase (see lesson 22).

SEPARATED SUBJECT PRONOUN	OBJECT*	SUBJECT*	ROOT	VOWEL[†]	MARKER	VOICE	I[‡]	NAQ
in	in	in		o, u		w		
at	at	at				(Radical Transitive Verb)		
are'	∅	∅						
laal	la	la				n		
oj	oj	oj				(Derived Transitive Verb)		
ix	ix	ix						
a're'	ee	ee						
alaq	alaq	alaq						

* In this voice either the subject or object must be third person (singular or plural) or *laal* or *alaq* (see lesson 22).

† This vowel is often present following Radical roots to facilitate pronunciation (see lesson 30). If the root vowel is *a, e, i,* or *o,* this vowel is *o.* If the root vowel is *u,* this vowel is *u.*

‡ This *i* always follows the Agent-Focus Antipassive Voice marker *w* for Radical Transitive Verbs (*-winaq*), but it is not used following the Agent-Focus Antipassive Voice marker *n* for Derived Transitive Verbs (*-nnaq*).

MODEL CONJUGATIONS OF RADICAL AND DERIVED VERBS IN AGENT FOCUS ANTIPASSIVE VOICE

For the sake of simplicity the object will always be third person singular.

Radical Transitive Verbs
Subclass A: *ch'ayik* "to be hit"

In in ch'ayowinaq.	I am the one who has hit him.
At at ch'ayowinaq.	You are the one who has hit him.
Aree ch'ayowinaq.	He is the one who has hit him.
Laal ch'ayowinaq la.	You are the one who has hit him.
Oj oj ch'ayowinaq.	We are the ones who have hit him.
Ix ix ch'ayowinaq.	You are the ones who have hit him.
A're' ee ch'ayowinaq.	They are the ones who have hit him.
Alaq ch'ayowinaq alaq.	You are the ones who have hit him.

Subclass B: *to'ik* "to be helped"

In in to'winaq.	I am the one who has helped him.
At at to'winaq.	You are the one who has helped him.
Aree to'winaq.	He is the one who has has helped him.
Laal to'winaq la.	You are the one who has helped him.
Oj oj to'winaq.	We are the ones who have helped him.
Ix ix to'winaq.	You are the ones who have helped him.
A're' ee to'winaq.	They are the ones who have helped him.
Alaq to'winaq alaq.	You are the ones who have helped him.

Derived Transitive Verbs
kunaxik "to be cured"

In in kunannaq.	I am the one who has cured him.
At at kunannaq.	You are the one who has cured him.
Aree kunannaq.	He is the one who has cured him.
Laal kunannaq la.	You are the one who has cured him.
Oj oj kunannaq.	We are the ones who have cured him.
Ix ix kunannaq.	You are the ones who have cured him.
A're' ee kunannaq.	They are the ones who have cured him.
Alaq kunannaq alaq.	You are the ones who have cured him.

NOTE: We saw in lesson 23 a special type of Derived Transitive Verb that terminates in Active Voice with the following ending: vowel + glottal stop + vowel + -*j*. In the Perfect Aspect in Agent-Focus Antipassive Voice these types of Derived Transitive Verbs are conjugated as follows:

AGENT-FOCUS ANTIPASSIVE VOICE

uk'a'xik (TVD) "to be carried, to be possessed"

In in uk'a'nnaq.	I am the one who has carried it.
At at uk'a'nnaq.	You are the one who has carried it.
Are' uk'a'nnaq.	He is the one who has carried it.
Laal uk'a'nnaq la.	You are the one who has carried it.
Oj oj uk'a'nnaq.	We are the ones who have carried it.
Ix ix uk'a'nnaq.	Y'all are the ones who have carried it.
A're' u'k'a'nnaq.	They are the ones who have carried it.
Alaq uk'a'nnaq alaq.	You are the ones who have carried it.

This type of Derived Transitive Verb can also be conjugated in Completed and Absolutive Antipassive Voices in the Perfect Aspect, but these forms are so rarely used that they will not be included in this grammar.

Some Further Uses of the Perfect Aspect

1. Continued Action or State

    In K'ichee' many verbs, when used in the Perfect Aspect, can express the idea of an action begun in past time and continued into the present. This use of the Perfect is generally translated into English as an "-ing" form of the verb:

k'atinaq le k'ache'laj.	The forest is still burning.
Warnaq le ak'aal.	The child is sleeping.
We ne peetnaq ri achi chaaniim.	Maybe the man is coming now.

2. Verbal Adjective

    At times the verb in the Perfect Aspect is used as an adjective:

kaminaq tz'i'	dead dog
saachinaq achi	lost man

3. Pluperfect Aspect

    The Perfect Aspect is translated as the Pluperfect ("had") when it is used in a sentence accompanied by a second verb phrase whose verb is in the completed aspect:

Kaminaq chi ri achi aretaq xojoopan pa ro'ch.	The man had already died when we arrived at his house.
Oj aatinnaq chik aretaq xojiiwil pa b'e.	We had already bathed when you saw us on the road.

4. Future Perfect Aspect

The Perfect Aspect is translated as the Future Perfect ("will have") when it is used in a sentence accompanied by a second verb phrase whose verb is in the incomplete aspect:

O'kinaq chi le i'xoqiib' pa k'ayib'al aretaq keeqil chwe'q.	The women will have already entered the market when we see them tomorrow.
Rajawaxik ix ulinaq chik aretaq kojb'ee oj.	It's necessary that you will have already arrived when we go.

MODEL SENTENCES

1. K'imuul oj ok'owinaq waraal.
   We have passed by here many times.

2. Aretaq b'antajnaq chi le chaak kumal le a'chijaab', xu'xlanik.
   When the work had become done by the men, they rested.

3. Jachin eqannaq la' le sii'?
   Who's backpacking that firewood there?

VOCABULARY

aj	(N)	fresh corn
chiim	(N)	woven bag
chomaal	(N)	meeting, plan
q'aaq'	(N)	fire, light, heat
taq'aaj	(N)	Pacific coastal lowlands
achi'iil	(PN)	companion, friend
myeer	(ADV)	earlier in the day
-muul	(ADV)	times
jumuul		one time
kaamuul		two times
oxmuul		three times
k'imuul		many times
janipaa muul?	(INTER)	how many times?
ma	(CONJ)	because
xa k'u jee ri'	(CONJ)	and for that reason

K'ICHEE' TO ENGLISH

1. Aree wanaab' tzakowinaq we saq'uul chqeech.
2. Oxmuul in ch'awinaq ruk' le achi pa taq'aaj.

3. Jachin yo'winaq le b'oloom aj chiweech?
4. La myeer ulinaq alaq?
5. Nab'ee sib'alaj keechakun le alab'oom; kamik chik na ee chakunnaq ta chik.
6. Paxnaq taq le saqmo'l; xa k'u jee ri' na xinloq' taj.
7. Oj tob'annaq cheech alaq. Xa k'u jee ri' rajawaxik kojto' alaq kamik.
8. Iye'b'naq chi ri qachi'iil aretaq xojoopan pa ro'ch.
9. Aretaq ya'tajnaq chi le aj pa le q'aaq' rumal le ixoq, xuutij uwaa.
10. B'antajnaq chi le chomaal aretaq xkiyaj kiib' le winaq.
11. Warnaq le ak'aal chaaniim ma xa yawaab'.
12. La k'imuul ix peetnaq waraal?

ENGLISH TO K'ICHEE'

1. How many times has your (ix) companion come here?
2. The child was sleeping (PERFECT) when the thief entered the house, and for this reason he did not hear him.
3. Three times I have helped on the coast with the corn planting.
4. Who knows the road that goes to town?
5. The money had already been placed in the bag because it was to be given (INCOMPLETE ASPECT) to the man.
6. Which one of you (ix) was carrying (PERFECT) the light when you went to town at night?
7. I have worked many times on the coast.
8. Were you (laal) resting (PERFECT) when your friend called you?
9. The child has fallen three times here.
10. It's been a long time since I have passed by here.
11. The boys are sick, and for that reason they have not played recently (chik).
12. Are you the one (at) who has tied the dog in front of the house?

SPECIAL DRILL

Convert the verbs in the following sentences into Perfect Aspect.

1. Xinchakun chila'.
2. Xeepee le a'jchakiib' pa taq'aaj.
3. Kixwar jeela' pa ja.
4. Kakam le yawaab'.
5. Kok la pa kayib'al.

6. Xojto'taj kumal le qachalaal.
7. Kilitaj alaq kumal le alk'u'aal alaq.
8. Kasik'itaj le achi rumal rachi'iil.
9. Xtzukutaj le pwaq qumaal.
10. Kab'antaj ri chaak iwumaal.
11. Keeloq'o'man le ixoq'iib' pa kayib'al.
12. Tob'an a'laq chkee le yawab'iib'.
13. Xojq'olow kuk' le winaq.
14. Xeetojon le winaq cheech alaq.
15. Jas chee xixch'o'jin kuk' le iwachalaal?
16. Jachin xk'ayin la' le ulew chee la?
17. La ix kixloq'ow le kape chee le ak'aal.
18. Oj xojilow le pwaq pa b'e.
19. La alaq kayo'w alaq kiwaa le winaq?
20. Jachin chkeech le winaq xixto'w chee le chaak?
21. La ix xixtow le chomaal pa q'atb'al tziij?

USEFUL EXPRESSIONS

1. Kak'aman chwee.
   I get accustomed to it.

2. Kuuk'am uwach chwiij.
   He gets used to me.

3. Chaawach k'o wi.
   It's up to you.

4. Maaj wee chawee.
   What you do is none of my business.

5. Maaj awee chwee.
   What I do is none of your business.

LESSON

34

Positional Intransitive Verbs in Incomplete, Completed, Perfect, and Positional Aspects and in the Imperative Mood

MEANING OF THE POSITIONAL INTRANSITIVE VERB

We have already studied Simple Intransitive Verbs in lessons 9, 10, 11, 12, and 33. We shall now study another type of Intransitive Verb. This new type we shall call Positional Intransitive Verbs. What is the difference between the Simple Intransitive Verb we have already seen and the Positional Intransitive Verb?

First it should be noted that two types of verbs are alike in the fact that they express only a subject and the action done by it and do not express any direct object. The difference is that the Simple Intransitive Verb expresses an action of a subject (I walk; i.e., I do the action of walking), while the Positional Intransitive Verb expresses the state, condition, or position the subject is in (I'm seated; i.e., I am in a seated state) or the action that brings or brought the subject into that state, condition, or position (I sat down; i.e., I got into a seated state).

The stuctural difference between the two classes of Intransitive Verbs can be seen in the slightly distinct ways in which they are conjugated. We shall now see in detail the conjugation of the Positional Intransitive Verb.

CONJUGATION OF INCOMPLETE AND COMPLETED ASPECTS OF POSITIONAL VERBS

As we have seen, in K'ichee' it is better to talk of the aspects of an action rather than of time (see lessons 9 and 10). The Incomplete Aspect indicates that the action is incomplete relative to the time being spoken about. The Completed Aspect indicates that the action is completed relative to the time spoken about.

The Positional Intransitive Verb in the Incomplete Aspect expresses the action that brings a subject into a certain state (I sit down; i.e., I get into a seated state). The Positional Intransitive Verb in the Completed Aspect expresses the action that brought a subject into a certain state (I sat down; i.e., I got into a seated state).

The Positional Intransitive Verbs, when conjugated in these two aspects, use what we shall call the Active Root of Positional Verbs, which is easily recognized by the fact that it always ends in -i' (k) (-k, like the -ik termination in Simple Intransitive Verbs, disappears when the verb is not utterance-final; however, the -i' is always retained since it is part of the root).

In some dialects, the termination is -e'(ik), with the -ik termination dropping off if the verb is not the last word in the utterance: e.g., kint'uye'ik "I sit down," kint'uye' pa ja "I sit down in the house."

Some examples of Active Roots of Positional Intransitive Verbs are:

t'uyi'	to sit
tak'i'	to stand
q'oyi'	to lie down
k'uli'	to marry
k'asi'	to live

Using the Active Root, the Positional Intransitive Verb in Incomplete and Completed Aspects is conjugated exactly like the Simple Intransitive Verb in these aspects (see lessons 9 and 10).

MODEL CONJUGATION OF POSITIONAL VERBS: T'UYI', "SIT"

Incomplete Aspect

Kint'uyi'k.	I sit.	Kojt'uyik.	We sit.
Katt'uyi'k.	You sit.	Kixt'uyi'k.	You sit.
Kat'uyi'k.	He sits.	Keet'uyi'k.	They sit.
Kat'uyi' la.	You sit.	Kat'uyi' alaq.	You sit.

Completed Aspect

Xint'uyi'k.	I sat.	Xojt'uyik.	We sat.
Xatt'uyi'k.	You sat.	Xixt'uyi'k.	You sat.
Xt'uyi'k.	He sat.	Xeet'uyi'k.	They sat.
Xt'uyi' la.	You sat.	Xt'uyi' alaq.	You sat.

In Perfect and Positional Aspects and Imperative Mood, Positional Intransitive Verbs use a second root that we shall call the Positional Root of the Positional Intransitive Verb.

The great majority of Positional Intransitive Verbs have Active Roots in one of the following two forms:

consonant + vowel + consonant + *i'* (CVC+i'): e.g., *t'uyi'* "sit"
consonant + vowel + glottal stop (') + *i'* (CV'+i'): e.g., *ku'i'* "sit"

The Positional Roots are formed from these Active Root types in the following ways:

Active Root	*Positional Root*	*Active Root*	*Positional Root*
CVC+i'	CV*C+V*+l	CV'+i'	CV'+l
tak'i'	tak'al, stand	q'a'i'	q'a'l, lean
peni'	penel, coat thickly	q'e'i'	q'e'l, turn lengthwise
q'oyi'	q'oyol, lie down	cho'i'	cho'l, loosen
t'uyi'	t'uyul, sit	ku'i'	ku'l, sit

* The second vowel of the Positional Root is always the same as the first vowel of this root (e.g., t<u>a</u>k'al, t'<u>uyu</u>l). We see that *l* marks the Positional Root in each of the above examples, (tak'a<u>l</u>, pene<u>l</u>). However, if the consonants *l* or *r* occur as one of the consonants in the root, then vowel + *n* almost always takes the place of the usual vowel + *l* as the marker for the Positional Root:

k'uli'	k'ulan, marry
choli'	cholan, line up
teri'	teren, follow
kori'	koron, loosen

CONJUGATION OF POSITIONAL VERBS IN IMPERATIVE MOOD

The Imperative Mood for the Positional Intransitive Verb is formed exactly like the Imperative for the Simple Intransitive Verb (see lesson 12), only now the Positional Root is used:

Chinq'oyoloq.	Let me lie down.	Kojq'oyoloq.	Let's lie down.
Katq'oyoloq.	Lie down.	Kixq'oyoloq.	Lie down.
Q'oyoloq.	Let him lie down.	Cheeq'oyoloq.	Let them lie down.
Q'oyola la.	Lie down.	Q'oyol a'laq.	Lie down.

CONJUGATION OF POSITIONAL VERBS
IN THE PERFECT ASPECT

This aspect refers to some aspect begun in past time (relative to the time spoken of) and the aspect or the effects of the aspect continue up to the present (see lesson 32).

This aspect of the Positional Verb is conjugated exactly like the Simple Intransitive Verb in the Perfect Aspect (lesson 32), only now the Positional Root is used.

In t'uyulinaq.	I have sat.	Oj t'uyulinaq.	We have sat.
At t'uyulinaq.	You have sat.	Ix t'uyulinaq.	You have sat.
T'uyulinaq.	He has sat.	Ee t'uyulinaq.	They have sat.
T'uyulinaq la.	You have sat.	T'uyulinaq alaq.	You have sat.

POSITIONAL ASPECT OF POSITIONAL INTRANSITIVE VERBS

Unlike the Simple Intransitive Verbs, every Positional Intransitive Verb has a Positional Aspect that is identical in meaning to the Completed Passive Voice Positional Aspect of Transitive Verbs ending in *tal(ik)* (see lesson 20). This Positional Aspect indicates that the subject of the verb phrase is in some condition or state (hence the name Positional Verb).

SCHEMA FOR THE POSITIONAL ASPECT OF POSITIONAL INTRANSITIVE VERBS

Person	*Positional Root*	*ik**
in		
at		
Ø		
la†		
oj		
ix		
ee		
alaq†		

* The *-ik* ordinarily disappears if the verb is not utterance-final.

† The *la* and *alaq* forms ordinarily follow the verb (see model conjugation below).

MODEL CONJUGATION

In t'uyulik.	I am seated.	Oj t'uyulik.	We are seated.
At t'uyulik.	You are seated.	Ix t'uyulik.	You are seated.
T'uyulik.	He is seated.	Ee t'uyulik.	They are seated.
T'uyul la.	You are seated.	T'uyul alaq.	You are seated.

In the Positional Aspect the four plural forms (*oj, ix, ee,* and *alaq*) can generally have an alternate construction, having the same meaning as the plural forms we saw above (*oj t'uyulik* "we are seated," etc.).

Formation of Alternate Plural Form

Root Type CVC+i'		Root Type CV'+i'	
Standard Plural Form	Alternate Plural Form	Standard Plural Form	Alternate Plural Form
t'uyulik	t'uyut'uj	q'a'lik	q'a'q'oj
tak'alik	tak'atoj	q'e'lik	q'e'q'oj
q'oyolik	q'oyoq'oj	cho'lik	cho'choj
mulanik	mulumul	ku'lik	ku'kuj
k'ulanik	k'uluk'uj		

THE MEANING AND CONJUGATION OF THE POSITIONAL INTRANSITIVE VERB *K'OJI'*

K'oji' is one of the most important and frequently used verbs in K'ichee'. It has several translations: "to be (in place)," "to exist," "there is (are)," "to have." Since this verb is so frequently used and because it is somewhat irregular, we shall conjugate it in all of the forms that we have so far studied.

Incomplete Aspect

kink'oji'k	I will be	kojk'oji'k	we will be
katk'oji'k	you will be	kixk'oji'k	you will be
kak'oji'k	he will be	keek'oji'k	they will be
kak'oji' la	you will be	kak'oji' alaq	you will be

Completed Aspect

xink'oji'k	I was	xojk'oji'k	we were
xatk'oji'k	you were	xixk'oji'k	you were
xk'oji'k	he was	xeek'oji'k	they were
xk'oji' la	you were	xk'oji' alaq	you were

Impertive Mood

chink'oloq	let me be	kojk'oloq	let us be
katk'oloq	be	kixk'oloq	be
k'oloq	let him be	chek'oloq	let them be
k'ola la	be	k'ol a'laq	be

Perfect Aspect

in k'olinaq	I have been	oj k'olinaq	we have been
at k'olinaq	you have been	ix k'olinaq	you have been
k'olinaq	he has been	ee k'olinaq	they have been
k'olinaq la	you have been	k'olinaq alaq	you have been

Positional Aspect (Utterance-Final)

in k'olik	I am	oj k'olik	we are
at k'olik	you are	ix k'olik	you are
k'olik	he is	ee k'olik	they are
k'o la (laal k'olik)	you are	k'o alaq (alaq k'oolik)	you are

Positional Aspect (Not Utterance-Final)

In k'o waraal.	I am here.	Oj k'o waraal.	We are here.
At k'o waraal.	You are here.	Ix k'o waraal.	You are here.
K'o waraal.	He is here.	Ee k'o waraal.	They are here.
K'o la waraal (laal k'o waraal).	You are here.	K'o alaq waraal (alaq k'o waraal).	You are here.

Positional Aspect of the Negative Form maaj

in maaj	(na in k'o taj)	I am not
at maaj	(na at k'o taj)	you are not
maaj	(na k'o taj)	he is not
maaj la	(laal maaj) (na k'o ta la)	you are not
oj maaj	(na oj k'o taj)	we are not
ix maaj	(na ix k'o taj)	you are not
ee maaj	(na ee k'o taj)	they are not
maaj alaq	(alaq maaj) (na k'o ta alaq)	you are not

The following examples show some uses of the positional verb 'k'oji':

K'o ri achi pa ja.	The man is at home.
Na in k'o ta pa chaak aretaq xpee jab'.	I was not at work when it rained.
Oj k'olinaq chila' pa tinamit.	We have been there in town.
Ee maaj qachalaal aretaq xojoopan pa ko'ch.	Our relatives were not there when we arrived at their home.

In K'ichee' there is no verb meaning "to have." This idea is expressed in K'ichee' using the verb *k'oji'*, as illustrated in the following examples:

Kak'oji' na arajiil we katchakunik.	You will have money if you work. (There will be later your money if you work.)
Maaj nuwaa.	I have no food.
La ee maaj iwachi'iil?	Don't you have any companions?
La k'o k'ax chaawee?	Do you have any pain?
Maaj (k'ax chwee).	I don't (have pain).

MODEL SENTENCES

1. Janipaa chi ix k'ulanik?
   For how long now are you married?

2. K'ola na la. Na ka'ee ta la chaaniim.
   Stay a while more. Don't go now.

3. Jawii katb'ee wi? Maaj kimb'ee wi.
   Where are you going? I'm not going anywhere.

4. La k'ax at k'olik?
   Are you in pain?

5. Q'ala ik'u'x chwiij chi kixinto'o.
   Have confidence in me that I will help you.

VOCABULARY

t'uyi'	(IVP)	to sit
tak'i'	(IVP)	to stand
q'oyi'	(IVP)	to lie
k'uli'	(IVP)	to marry
k'oji'	(IVP)	to be (in place), to exist, there is (are), have (see model conjugation above)
maaj	(IVP)	there is not (negative form of Positional Aspect of k'oji')
ku'i'	(IVP)	to sit
choli'	(IVP)	to line up
xuli'	(IVP)	to go down
paqi'	(IVP)	to go up
kori'	(IVP)	to loosen
cho'i'	(IVP)	to loosen
q'e'i'	(IVP)	to turn lengthwise
muli'	(IVP)	to gather together
q'a'i'	(IVP)	to lean
q'a'i k'u'x		to be consoled, confide (literally, "heart leans")
naj	(ADV)	far, a long time
k'asi'	(IVP)	to live, be awake

irregular forms of k'asi':
Imperative Mood: *katk'asloq* "live!"
Positional Aspect: *at k'aslik (at k'as–)*

Dyoos	(N-SPAN)	God

FIGURE 34.1. *Ee t'uyul le achijaab'* (the men are sitting). Photograph by John Edvalson.

aq'ab'	(N)	night, early morning
Xaq	(ADV)	only, just (no more than)
xewi (xeu–)	(ADV)	only (of all possibilities, only this)

K'ICHEE' TO ENGLISH

1. Naj xojk'oji' pa tinamit aretak xojb'ee pa nimaq'iij.
2. Ee k'o b'elejee' ukarne'lab' ri kitaat ri qachalaal.
3. B'iis ee k'o le ak'alaab' rumaal ri xkam ri kitaat.
4. Rajawaxik kaq'a'i qak'u'x chriij Dyoos; xeu ri are' kojto'wik.
5. T'uyul a'laq, Taat. Kojch'aw juch'iin uk' alaq.
6. Ee sib'alaj winaq ee mulan pa kayib'al; katajin keeloq'o'man chila'.
7. La ee k'ask'oj le taat, naan alaq?
8. Kixq'oyoloq, ak'alaab'; ya hora chik kojwarik.
9. Chwe'q konojel ri a'chijaab' keexuli' pa taq'aaj. K'o jach' kakib'an chila'.
10. Q'e'l le nima chee' pa le b'e; xaa k'u jee ri' na xojok'ow ta jee la'.
11. Naj k'o wi le tinamit chee le wo'ch.
12. Cholan le nimaq taq chee' chrij le ja.

13. Jun aq'ab' xk'asi' le ixoq ruk' le yawaab'.
14. Xkori' le eqa'n chriij le achi; na ko ta jat'iim.
15. Xaq ee tak'atoj le alab'oom chuwach le ko'ch aretaq xok'ow le kanaab'.

ENGLISH TO K'ICHEE'

1. Why don't you lie down, Mother, if you are tired?
2. The woman was consoled when she saw her husband alive.
3. Is your father home, children?
4. Are you married to (*ruk'*) the man to whom you were talking yesterday?
5. There is no one in the house.
6. Have you (*alaq*) been in the town behind that mountain there?
7. Sit down, children; there is something (*k'o*) I am going to show you.
8. The drunks sat a long time in front of the marimba.
9. We were the only ones (*xeu ri oj*) who stood up when we were called.
10. All of the men were gathered in the courthouse when we sat down.
11. The man stayed awake all night when he married off his daughter.
12. Did no one speak when you asked who did it?

USEFUL EXPRESSIONS

1. Saq qawach chee.
   He/she/it is well known to us.

2. Janiik'.
   I don't know. (answer to a question when reply not known)

3. Yaatal chwee, kinch'awik.
   I am worthy to speak (it is given to me to speak).

4. Yupul uwachiil jachin xb'anowik.
   It is not known who did it.

5. Saq uwachiil jachin xb'anowik.
   It is known who did it.

35

Nominalized Forms of Simple and Positional Intransitive Verbs and of Radical and Derived Transitive Verbs in Simple Passive and Absolutive Antipassive Voices

In K'iche verbs both intransitive and transitive can be nominalized; that is, they can be changed into nouns and then behave as nouns (can be possessed, can be subjects or objects of verb phrases, or can be objects of prepositions). These nominalized verb forms are ordinarily translated into English as gerunds ("-ing" forms) or as infinitives. In this lesson we shall see some of these nominalized forms along with some of their more common uses.

NOMINALIZED FORMS OF SIMPLE AND POSITIONAL INTRANSITIVE VERBS

FORMATION

Possessive Pronoun	*Verb* Root*	*Vowel -m† Termination*
nu (w)		
a (aw)		
u (r)		
la		
qa (q)		
i (iw)		
ki (k)		
alaq		

* For Positional Verbs the Positional Root is used (lesson 33).

† This vowel is ordinarily *ee*, but ocassionally it is *aa* or *ii*.

MODELS

SIMPLE INTRANSITIVE

Verb Root	Nominalized Form in Vowel -m
wa' "eat"	wa'iim "act of eating"
war "sleep"	waraam "act of sleeping"
b'iin "walk"	b'iineem "act of walking"
ka'y "look"	ka'yeem "act of looking"
b'ee "go"	b'eenaam "act of walking"
peet "come"	peeteem "act of coming"

POSITIONAL INTRANSITIVE

Verb Root	Nominalized Form in Vowel -m
t'uyul "sit"	t'uyuleem "act of sitting"
tak'al "stand"	tak'aleem "act of standing"
q'oyol "lie down"	q'oyoleem "act of lying down"
ku'l "sit"	ku'leem "act of sitting"
k'ulan "marry"	k'ulaneem "act of marrying"

USES

OBJECT OF PREPOSITIONS

With pa "to, for"

Kojb'ee pa wa'iim.	We are going to eat (for the act of eating).
Xeeb'ee le winaq pa ka'yeem.	The people went to look (for the act of looking)
La kixb'ee quk' pa etz'aneem?	Are you going with us to play (for the act of playing).
Xb'ee le ali pa k'ulaneem.	The girl went to get married (for the act of marrying).

With chee "from, to, for"

Xinq'i'taj chee le b'ineem.	I became bored from walking (from the act of walking).
Xeekoos le achijaab' chee le tak'aleem.	The men became tired from standing (from the act of standing).

SUBJECT OF VERBS

Xpee nuwaraam.	I'm sleepy (my sleepiness came).
Le paqaleem kuub'an k'ax chqeech.	The climb (act of going up) does us harm.

OBJECT OF TRANSITIVE VERBS

Peeteem kuub'an le ala chaaniim.	The boy is coming (does the act of coming) right now.
Xqamajij paqaleem chuwa le juyub'.	We began going up (the act of going up) on the face of the mountain.

NOUN PHRASES IN NONVERBAL SENTENCES

K'ax b'ineem chaaq'ab'.	Walking (act of walking) is hard at night.
Na utz ta ka'yeem pa taq nimaq'iij.	Watching (the act of watching) at fiestas is not good.

Nominalized Forms of Radical and Derived Transitive Verbs in Simple Passive Voice Formation:

Possessive Pronoun	Verb Root	Termination*
nu (w)		
a (aw)		ik
u (r)		(Radical)
la		
qa (q)		xik
i (iw)		(Derived)
ki (k)		
alaq		

* The *-ik* suffix becomes *-iik* when possessed. The long *ii* may subsequently be shortened by regular phonological rules.

MODELS

RADICAL TRANSITIVE VERBS

Verb Root	*Nominalized Form in -ik*
b'an "do"	b'anik "to be done (being done)"
ya' "give"	ya'ik "to be given (being given)"

DERIVED TRANSITIVE VERBS

Verb Root	*Nominalized Form in -xik*
tzuku "look for"	tzukuxik "to be searched for (being search for)"
uk'a' "carry"	uk'a'xik "to be carried (being carried)"

USES

OBJECT OF PREPOSITIONS

With pa, "to, for"

Kimb'ee pa kunaxik chwe'q pa tinamit.	I'm going to be cured (for being cured) tomorrow in town.
Le tz'i' xaa kuuyaa rib' pa kamisaxik.	The dog just gives himself to be killed (for being killed).

With chee, "to, for"

NOTE: If the possessive pronoun immediately following *chee* is a consonant, *chee* is pronounced *chi* (e.g., *chiriye'xiik* "to wait for him," *chiqach'aab'exiik* "to speak to us"). If the possessive pronoun immediately following *chee* is *a, aw, u, i,* or *iw,* the following forms are used:

chee + achajixiik	chachajixiik	to take care of you
chee + uloq'iik	chuloq'iik	to buy it
chee + iwiye'xiik	chiwiye'xiik	to wait for you

If the possessive pronouns are either *la* or *alaq,* the following forms are used:

chee + to'ik la	chto'ik la	to help you
chee + iye'xik alaq	chiye'xik alaq	to wait for you

Examples:

Kojb'ee chuloq'iik qawaa.	We go to buy (for it to be bought) our food.
T'uyul le achi chila' chireye'xiik ri rixoqiil.	The man is seated over there to wait for (her to be waited for) his wife.
Xk'oji' le ak'aal chuwa ja chuchajixiik uchaaq'.	The child stayed in front of the house to take care of (for his to be cared for) his younger sibling."
Xeepee le qachalaal chiqach'aab'exiik.	Our relatives came to speak to us (for our being spoken to).
La kixb'ee pa kayib'al chkik'ayixiik le ikarne'l?	Are you going to market to sell (for them to be sold) your sheep?
Xeepaqi' le achijaab' chuwi' le juyub' chkeqaxiik le yawab'iib'.	The men went up on top of the mountain to carry (for them to be carried) the sick ones.
Kinkowin chub'aniik ri chaak.	I am able to do the work.

Object of Transitive Verbs

Rajawaxik kaqab'an utza-laj kiloq'oxiik le qataat qanaan.	It is necessary that we love our father and mother very much (we do very good the act of their being loved).
Le achi xuuchap uya'iik le pwaq chkec le ajchakiib'.	The man began to give (the act of its being given) the money to the workers.

Noun Phrases in Nonverbal Sentences

Utz riliik la' le juyub'.	That mountain there is nice to look at (good its being seen).
K'ax ub'aniik le chaak pa taq juyub'.	It is difficult to do (it to be done) the work in the hills.
Na k'ax ta kichajixiik le ak'alaab'.	It is not difficult to take care of (their to be taken care of) the children.

NOMINALIZED FORMS OF RADICAL AND DERIVED TRANSITIVE VERBS IN ABSOLUTIVE ANTIPASSIVE VOICE

Formation

Verb Root   *Termination -nik*

MODELS

Verb Root   *Nominalized Form in -nik*
Radical

toj "pay"	tojonik* "act of paying"
ch'aj "wash"	ch'ajanik "act of washing"

Derived

k'ayi "sell"	k'ayinik "act of selling"
kuna "cure"	kunanik "act of curing"

  * With Radical verbs in subclass A a vowel is placed between the root and *-nik* to facilitate pronunciation (e.g., *tojonik, ch'ajanik*).

USES

Objects of Prepositions

With pa "to, for"

Kab'ee le achi pa kunanik.	The man goes to cure (for the act of curing).
Ee b'eenaq le ixoqiib' pa k'ayinik.	The women have gone to sell (for the act of selling).

With chee "for, from"

Xq'i'taj le ala chee ri tob'anik.	The boy got bored with helping (from act of helping).
Le ajq'iij kakowin chee le kunanik. [kowin (itv) to be able]	The diviner is able to cure (for the act of curing).

OBJECTS OF TRANSITIVE VERBS

Wa' we achijaab' kakib'an k'ayinik pa taq tinamit.	These men here do selling (act of selling) in the towns.
Le ali majaa kareta'maj ri uchapaniik.	The girl still has not learned her work (her act of grasping with hands).
Kaqamajij chomanik pa k'atb'al tziij chwe'q.	We will begin planning (act of planning) in the courthouse tomorrow.

NOUN PHRASE IN NONVERBAL SENTENCE

K'ax le tzukunik pa taq juyub'.	Searching (hunting) is difficult in the mountains.
Na utz ta le kamisanik.	Killing (act of killing) is not good.

NOTES

1. Many Transitive verbs in Antipassive Voice and a few Simple Intransitive Verbs have irregular nominalized forms:

Intransitive

Verb Root	Nominalized Form
oq' "cry"	oq'eej "act of crying"

Transitive

Verb Root	Nominalized Form
loq' "buy"	loq'ooj "act of buying"
ch'aj "wash"	ch'ajo'n "act of washing"
eqa "backpack"	eqa'n "act of packing (load)"
yaj "scold"	yaaj "act of scolding"
elaq'a "rob"	elaq' "act of robbing (robbery)"
chaku "work"	chaak "act of working (work)"

2. Radical and Derived Transitive Verbs also have nominalized forms in Active and Completed Passive Voices. However, these forms will not be studied in this preliminary grammar.

3. Simple and Positional Intransitive Verbs have an additional nominal-ized form that terminates in *-ik* instead of vowel + *-m*. Those forms will not be included in this grammar. However, it should be kept in mind that many Simple Intransitive Verbs have both of these forms (*peteem, peetik*), while others only have one or the other of the two (*wa'iim* "act of eating"; *q'ab'arik* "act of getting drunk").

4.   From now on all Simple and Positional Intransitive verbs will be listed in the vocabulary under the nominalized *-ik* form.

VOCABULARY

q'inomarik	(IVS)	to become rich
tanalik	(IVP)	to stop, cease
keemik	(TVR)	to be woven
ch'aakik	(TVR)	to be won, earned
piilik	(TVR)	to be butchered
paajik	(TVR)	to be weighed
ajk'aay	(N)	seller
ajk'ayiib'	(N)	sellers
q'inoom	(ADJ, N)	rich, rich one
q'inomaab'	(N)	rich ones
po't	(N)	woven blouse
waakax	(N)	cow, bull
ixiim	(N)	dry, shelled corn
lej	(N)	tortilla
rajiil	(N)	its price, money
kapaqi' rajiil		its price goes up
kaqaaj rajiil		its price goes down

K'ICHEE' TO ENGLISH

1. Xuuchap paqaleem rajiil le ixiim pa k'ayib'al.
2. Niimaq'ab' le ajchakiib' kakichap uleem pa k'ayib'al.
3. Xinkoosik; kimb'ee na pa waraam.
4. Noojimaal le ala xuub'ij k'ulaneem chee le ali.
5. Maja' katani' le k'ayinik pa le k'ayib'al.
6. Le q'inoom a'chi xq'inomar chee le k'ayinik.
7. Le nima waakax na kuuyaa ta rib' pa pilik.
8. Jasa ora kab'ee alaq chwe'q chkiloq'iik le ee aaq?
9. Jampaa katpee chi chqach'aab'exiik?
10. K'ax upajiik le ixiim.

FIGURE 35.1. *Kakemen le ixoq* (the woman weaves). Photograph by Winston Scott.

11. Ronojel q'iij le achi kab'ee pa tzukunik pa taq juyub'.
12. Majaa kuuchap b'iineem le ak'aal.
13. Kapee na le qachi'iil chkunaxik alaq.
14. Xa xyojtaj le qach'iich' (automobile). Chwe'q kaqayaa pa suk'umaxik.
15. Na kuub'an ta chi qaajeem rajiil le wa.
16. Chaab'ana' utzalaj ukeemiik le po't.
17. Na kojtani' ta chee le b'iineem.
18. Le q'ab'areel ojer chi umajim ub'aniik k'ax cheech urajiil.
19. Chaab'ana' utzalaj ujosq'ixiik le ulew.

ENGLISH TO K'ICHEE'

1. The girls have gone to bathe in the river.
2. Weigh the corn well (do very good its act of being weighed the corn).
3. The children began walking in the hills.
4. The girls go to market to help their mothers.
5. Tomorrow our father is going to be cured.
6. Yesterday the rich man began to butcher cows in front of the market.
7. At what time is there entrance in the market (act of entering is made)?
8. The sellers get bored from (*chee*) their being in markets.

9. Yesterday the price of the dry shelled corn began going down.
10. I was not able to buy the blouse.
11. When will you (*ix*) go to see the men?
12. The rich ones do not stop gathering their money (they do not stop for the its being gathered their money).
13. We have come to speak to you (*alaq*).
14. Stay (be) (*at*) here to sell your tortillas.
15. I haven't started to sell in the market yet.
16. It is necessary that you (*alaq*) go to eat with the men.
17. The women began to backpack their children.

USEFUL EXPRESSIONS

1. Kintij nuchuq'aab' chub'aniik.
   I'll do my best to do it.

2. Kink'is nuk'u'x chub'aniik.
   I'll try one last time to do it.

3. K'o upataan chwee.
   It is useful to me.

4. Maaj upataan chwee.
   It is not useful to me.

5. Xaq wee wi chi in k'a'n.
   I am ill-tempered by nature (it is just the way I am, that I am ill-tempered).

Formation of Person Agents with Simple Intransitive
Verbs and with Radical and Derived Transitive Verbs
in the Absolutive Antipassive Voice and the Use of
Familiar Prefixes *a-* and *al-* with Proper Names

◼ FORMATION OF PERSON AGENTS

Person agents can be formed from a good majority of the Simple Intransitive
and Transitive Verbs in K'ichee'. This phenomenon is very much like what
we have in English whereby a person agent can be formed by suffixing *-er*
to the verb:

Verb	*Person Agent*
walk	walker
watch	watcher
sleep	sleeper
help	helper
kill	killer

The general rule in K'ichee' for the formation of person agents is the suffixing of *-l* or *-vowel + l* to the verb root. We shall now examine in more
detail the formation and use of these person agents.

PERSON AGENTS FOR SIMPLE INTRANSITIVE VERBS
FORMATION
Root + *eel*

Root		Person agent	
b'iin	travel	b'iineel	traveler
ka'y	look, watch	ka'yeel	watcher
kam	die	kameel	one who dies
ok'ow	pass by	ok'oweel	passerby
q'ab'ar	get drunk	q'ab'areel	drunk

USES

1. Functions as a noun

Nimalaj q'ab'areel le achi.	The man is a big drunk.
Xa in ka'yeel ximpee pa nimaq'iij.	I came to the fiesta just as a watcher.
Xa oj kameel, xa oj ok'oweel pa we uwach ulew.	We are just ones who die (mortal), we are just passersby (transitory) in this world. (a common saying among the people)

2. Functions as an adjective (not as common as no. 1 above)

b'ineel ja'   moving water (rivers or streams)

PERSON AGENTS FOR RADICAL AND DERIVED TRANSITIVE VERBS IN ABSOLUTIVE ANTIPASSIVE VOICE

FORMATION

+ ROOT	± VOWEL*	+ VOICE MARKER N	+ EEL

* At times this vowel is here after Radical subclass A roots to aid pronunciation (see lesson 29).

MODELS

Radical

Root		Person Agent	
ch'ay	hit	ch'ayaneel	hitter
sub'	deceive	sub'uneel	deceiver
kol	save, defend	koloneel	savior, defender

Derived

Root		Person Agent	
kamisa	kill	kamisaneel	killer
eqa	backpack	eqaneel	backpacker
q'alu	hold in arms	q'aluneel	one who holds in arms (godparent at a baptism)

NOTE: Almost any Radical or Derived Transitive Verb that can be conjugated in Absolutive Antipassive Voice will also have Person Agent forms in this voice.

Uses

1. Functions as a noun

Rajawaxik kaqasik'ij jun eqaneel chee le eqa'n.	We must call a backpacker for the load.
K'o jun koloneel pa q'atb'al tziij.	There is a defender in the courthouse.

2. Functions as an adjective (not as common as no. 1)

ch'ayaneel a'chi	pugnacious man
kamisaneel tz'i'	killer dog

NOTES

1. There are some Simple Intransitive Verbs and many Transitive Verbs in Absolutive Antipassive Voice that form the Person Agent in ways distinct from the one we just saw above:

INTRANSITIVE

Root		Person Agent	
xojow	dance	ajxojoloob'*	dancer

TRANSITIVE

Root		Person Agent	
chaku	work	ajchaak*	worker
elaq'a	rob	elaq'oom	thief
yuq'u	herd	ajyuuq'*	shepherd

* The *aj-* prefix indicates origin or occupation, e.g.:

ajchaak	worker
ajyuuq'	shepherd
ajNiwala'	from Nahuala
ajwaraal	from here

2. Most Person Agents form plurals with the suffix -*aab'*:

Singular		*Plural*	
q'ab'areel	drunkard	q'ab'arelaab'	drunkards
ch'ayaneel	hitter	ch'ayanelaab'	hitters

3. It should be noted that Radical and Derived Transitive Verbs in Active Voice also have Person Agent forms, but they will not be presented in this preliminary grammar.

USE OF THE FAMILIAR PREFIXES *A-* AND *AL-* WITH PROPER NAMES

PROPER NAMES IN GENERAL

First names used in K'ichee' for both sexes are generally Spanish first names adapted to the K'ichee' sound system.

Males		*Females*	
SPANISH NAME	K'ICHEE' NAME	SPANISH NAME	K'ICHEE' NAME
Manuel	Weel	Manuela	We'l
Juan	Xwaan	Juana	Xwa'n
Pedro	Luu'	Micaela	Mike'l
Tomás	Maax	Francisca	Sika'
Diego (Santiago)	Te'k	Magdalena	Ma't
Miguel	Mikeel	Catarina	Taliin
Francisco	Si's	Dominga	Ramuux
Antonio	Tuun	Pascuala	Ku'l
		Isabela	Xe'p

FAMILIAR VERSUS FORMAL CONTRAST IN NAMING

We have seen that in K'ichee' there are two ways of addressing a person: with the familiar *at* form or the formal *laal* form. This familiar-formal contrast is also employed when using people's names, either directly in addressing them or indirectly when speaking about them.

USE OF THE PREFIXES *A-* AND *AL-* ON PEOPLE'S NAMES TO INDICATE FAMILIARITY.

For boys or men: To use male names on a familiar basis, *a-* is prefixed to the desired name. This prefix *a-* is a shortened form of *ala* "boy." Examples of names with this familiar *a-* prefix are as follows:

aWeel	Manuel	aLuu'	Pedro
aXwaan	Juan	aMaax	Tomás

For girls or women: To use female names on a familiar basis, *al-* is prefixed to the desired name. The *-al* prefix is a shortened form of *ali* "girl." In some towns (Samayac) the completed form, *ali*, is used in place of the shorter *al-* (e.g., *ali We'l* "Manuela"). This familiar form with the *al-* prefix is shown below:

alWe'l	Manuela	alMari'y	Maria
alTaliin	Catarina	alRamuux	Dominga

If speaker A speaks to B using the familiar *at* form, he will also prefix *a-* or *al-* to Speaker B's name. Furthermore, if Speaker A is speaking to another person about B, in those intances speaker A will continue to prefix the *a-* or *al-* to speaker B's name.

La katb'ee wuuk', aWeel?	Are you going with me, Manuel?
Kab'ee le alWe'l wuuk'.	Manuela is going with me.

Using *taat* or *naan* and the Formal Pronoun (*laal*) with Names

The use of the *taat* "Mister" and *naan* "Ms." immediately before a person A's first name when A is spoken to or about indicates that A is a person of stature in the community and should be addressed with the respectful *laal* pronoun.

Examples of the use of *taat* or *naan* as signs of respect with people's names:

(taat) Weel	Manuel	(taat) Luu'	Pedro
(taat) Xwaan	Juan	(taat) Maax	Tomás
(naan) We'l	Manuela	(naan) Mari'y	Maria
(naan) Taliin	Catarina	(naan) Ramuux	Dominga

MODEL SENTENCES

1. Ronojel q'iij keeb'ee le chajinelaab' chuchajixiik le kab'iix.
   Every day the guards go to guard their corn.

2. Xaq wa'kateel le achi; maaj kuuchakuuj.
   The man is just a wanderer; he doesn't work at anything.

3. La aweech wa' we ja, aWeel?
   Is this house yours, Manuel?

4. Jampaa chi kapee la, Naan We'l?
   When will you come again, Manuela?

VOCABULARY

jampa'	(ADV)	when
uwach ulew	(N)	world
b'iineel	(N)	traveler
ka'yeel	(N)	watcher
kameel	(N)	one who dies
ok'oweel	(N)	passerby
wa'kateel	(N)	wanderer
q'ab'areel	(N)	drunkard

ch'ayaneel	(N)	hitter
sub'uneel	(N)	deceiver
koloneel	(N)	defender, savior
eqaneel	(N)	backpacker
q'aluneel	(N)	one who holds in arms (godparent at a baptism)
kamisaneel	(N)	killer
ajxojoloob'	(N)	dancer
Weel	(N)	Manuel
Xwaan	(N)	Juan
Luu'	(N)	Pedro
Maax	(N)	Tomás
Te'k	(N)	Diego, Santiago
Si's	(N)	Francisco
Tuun	(N)	Antonio
We'l	(N)	Manuela
Sika'	(N)	Francisca
Ma't	(N)	Magdalena
Taliin	(N)	Catarina
Ramuux	(N)	Dominga
Xe'p	(N)	Isabela
ee (ch)	(POSS PRO)	

wee (ch)	mine	qee (ch)	ours
awee (ch)	yours	iwee (ch)	yours
ree (ch)	his, hers, its	kee (ch)	theirs
ee (ch) la	yours	ee (ch) alaq	yours

K'ICHEE' TO ENGLISH

1. Le achi k'o jastaq reech; ma xa elaq'oom.
2. Oj ka'yelaab' xojpee pa nimaq'iij.
3. Chaachajij awiib' chwach le kamisaneel tz'i'.
4. Sib'alaj kakiq'i' eqa'n le eqanelaab'.
5. Aretaq xtzaaq le q'ab'areel pa jun b'iineel ja', xkamik.
6. La eech la we wuuj, taat Maax?
7. Aree qeech wa', alTaliin.
8. Xa oj ok'oweel pa we uwach ulew; na naj ta kojk'oji'k.
9. La' le alRamuux xa ch'ayaneel; kuuch'ay le uchaaq'.
10. Le alSica', aree q'aluneel chkee le ak'alaab'.
11. Reech alXe'p wa' we ja.

ENGLISH TO K'ICHEE'

1. That woven bag there is Francisco's (FAMILIAR).
2. Is that yours, Magdalena (*laal*)?
3. Let Juan (FAMILIAR) be grabbed (detained); he's just a hitter.
4. I saw the curer; his name is Diego (FORM).
5. Are these things here yours, Pedro (*laal*)?
6. The dancers are just big drunkards.
7. The men came as backpackers (see "K'ichee' to English," no. 2).
8. Don't go to the fiesta, Antonio; there are hitters there.
9. The killer will pay his (offenses) in jail.
10. There are many wanderers in this world.

USEFUL EXPRESSIONS

1. Toq'ob' uwach.
   He is to be pitied (poor guy).

2. Chaab'anaa jun toq'ob' chwee, — —.
   Do me a favor, — —.

3. Chaakuyuu numaak.
   Pardon me. (used frequently when one begins speaking or asks a
   favor)

   Chaasachaa numaak.
   Pardon me.

4. Raj ximpeetik.
   I almost came.

5. Maaj raj ximpeetik.
   I almost did not come.

LESSON

37

Formation of Nouns from Adjectives and Unpossessed Forms of Obligatorily Possessed Nouns

FORMATION OF NOUNS FROM ADJECTIVES

In English many adjectives can be transformed into abstract nouns by adding the suffix "-ness" to them (e.g., good, goodness; big, bigness; white, whiteness).

In K'ichee', in a very like manner, adjectives can be transformed into abstract nouns by adding the suffix -vowel + *l*:

Adjective		Noun	
utz	good	utziil	goodness, peace
niim	big	nimaal	bigness, size, greatness
choom	fat	chomaal	fatness
yawaab'	sick	yaab'iil	sickness
saq	white, clear	saqiil	whiteness, clearness
k'a'n	mean	k'a'naal	meanness

NOTES

1. It cannot be predicted what vowel will occur in the -vowel + *l* suffix. It seems that -*aa* and -*ii* are the most commonly occuring vowels, though -*ee*, -*oo*, and -*uu* are also used.

2. The -vowel + *l* termination can also be suffixed to nouns to indicate intimate possession: e.g., *ixoq* "woman," *wixoqiil* "my wife" (the woman I possess intimately). This use of the -vowel + *l* suffix with nouns will not be treated in this preliminary grammar.

UNPOSSESSED FORMS OF OBLIGATORILY POSSESSED NOUNS

In the vocabularies of the past lessons we have found a few nouns that were labeled "pn" (obligatorily possessed noun), such as the following:

chii'	(pn)	mouth, edge, opening, door
paam	(pn)	stomach, inside, diarrhea
alk'u'aal	(pn)	child (man's or couple's)
k'ajool	(pn)	son (man's)

When we say that these nouns are obligatorily possessed, it is to be understood that this class of nouns has one form when accompanied by possessive pronouns (my, your, etc.) and a distinct form (ordinarily) when not possessed.

The above four examples of obligatorily possessed nouns fall into two categories:

1. Body parts
   chii'   mouth
   paam   stomach

2. Kinship terms
   alk'u'aal   child
   k'ajool   son (man's)

Most nouns in category 1 and some nouns in category 2, when used without possessive pronouns (my, your, etc.), are terminated with a generalizing suffix to indicate that the possessor is not expressed.

GENERALIZING SUFFIX -AAJ FOR BODY PARTS

Most nouns that fit in this category when used without possessive pronouns are generally terminated with the generalizing suffix -*aaj*:

Possessed Form		Unpossessed Form	
nuchii'*	my mouth	chi'iij (chi'aaj)	mouth
nupaam	my stomach	pamaaj	stomach
nujoloom	my head	jolomaaj	head
nupalaj	my face	palajaaj	face
nuwi'	my hair	wi'aaj	hair

Possessed Form		Unpossessed Form	
nuwach	my face, my eyes	wachaaj	face, eyes, eye infection
waqan	my foot (feet)	aqanaaj	foot (feet)
nub'i'	my name	b'i'aaj	name

*Here the termination is either -aaj or -iij.

GENERALIZING SUFFIX -XEEL FOR KINSHIP TERMS

Some nouns of this category, when used without possessive pronouns, are terminated with the generalizing suffix -xeel:

Possessed Form		Unpossessed Form	
nuk'ajool	my son (man's)	k'ajolaxeel	son (man's)
inchaaq'	my younger sibling	chaq'ixeel	younger sibling
walk'u'aal	my child	alk'wa'laxeel	child
intaat	my father	tataxeel	father
nunaan	my mother	nanaxeel	mother
nujii'	my son-in-law	jiya'xeel	son-in-law

NOTES

1. In the above examples we can see that a vowel is added between the noun and the -xeel suffix to aid pronunciation.

2. The unpossessed -xeel form of obligatorily possessed nouns is pluralized with the termination -xelaab':

Singular		Plural	
k'ajolaxeel	son	k'ajolaxelaab'	sons
alk'wa'laxeel	child	alk'wa'laxelaab'	children

3. There are a few nouns that receive the -xeel termination even when possessed (e.g., tijoxeel "student"; nutijoxeel "my student").

4. There are at least two commonly used nouns of the kinship category whose unpossessed forms are terminated in the suffix -oom:

Possessed Form		Unpossessed Form	
wixoqiil	my wife	ixoqiloom	wife
wachajiil	my husband	achajiloom	husband

MODEL SENTENCES

1. Sib'alaj keech'o'jin la' le winaq; na kakaj ta utziil.
   Those people there fight alot; they don't want peace.

2. Kawaj jun nub'o'j, je' unimaal la'.
   I want a clay pot that size (like that its size).

3. K'ax kuub'an le q'oxoom jolomaaj chqeech.
   Headaches (head colds) harm us.

4. Na utz taj wemna keetob'an le alk'wa'laxelab' chkee ri kitaat, kinaan.
   It is not good if the children don't help their parents.

VOCABULARY

utziil	(N)	goodness, peace
nimaal	(N)	bigness, size
chomaal	(N)	fatness
yab'iil	(N)	sickness
saqiil	(N)	whiteness, clearness
k'a'naal	(N)	meanness
chi'iij (chi'aaj)	(PN)	mouth, opening, door, edge
pamaaj	(PN)	stomach, inside, excrement, diarrhea
jolomaaj	(PN)	head
palajaaj	(PN)	face
wi'aaj	(PN)	hair
wachaaj	(PN)	face, eyes, eye infection
aqanaaj	(PN)	foot, feet
b'i'aaj	(PN)	name
k'ajolaxeel	(PN)	son (man's)
k'ajolaxelaab'	(PL)	sons
alk'wa'laxeel	(PN)	child (man's or couple's)
alk'wa'laxelaab'	(PL)	children
chaq'ixeel	(PN)	younger sibling
chaq'ixelaab'	(PL)	younger siblings
jiya'xeel	(PN)	son-in-law
jiya'xelaab'	(PL) (-jii' = POS-SESSED FORM)	sons-in-law
tataxeel	(PN)	father
tataxelaab'	(PL)	fathers
nanaxeel	(PN)	mother
nanaxelaab'	(PL)	mothers
achajiloom	(PN)	husband
ixoqiloom	(PN)	wife
tijoxeel	(N)	student, disciple
tijoxelaab'	(PL)	students, disciples

ajtiij	(N)	teacher
ajtijaab'	(PL)	teachers
kunab'al	(N)	medicine
q'oxoom	(N)	pain, soreness
q'oxoom jolomaaj		headache
q'oxoom pamaaj		stomachache, etc. (for other parts of the body)
junaam	(ADJ, ADV)	equal, same
junaam ruk'		equal with it, same as it

K'ICHEE' TO ENGLISH

1. Aree la' kuukunaj le q'oxoom jolomaaj.
2. La k'o kunab'al rech wachaaj uk' la?
3. Le q'aaq' pa taq'aaj kuuyaa pamaaj chkee le ajchakiib'.
4. Rajawaxik kasik'ix le b'i'aaj pa q'atb'al tziij.
5. La aariqom le q'oxoom pamaaj?
6. Wa' we ala, utzalaj k'ajolaxeel.
7. Ri achajiloom rajawaxik kakiloq'oj kiib' ruk' ri rixoqiil.
8. Ri nanaxeel ku'ch'aj le ee raal ronojel nimaq'ab'.
9. Le jiya'xelaab' katajin keekito' le kitaat.
10. Xa junaam ri kik'a'nal ri ala ruk' ri ratz.

ENGLISH TO K'ICHE

1. It is the man's meanness that does him harm.
2. The people become discouraged (bored) with the sickness.
3. The whiteness of the two clothes is just the same.
4. This medicine here cures diarrhea.
5. There is a big face on the front of the rock.
6. It is necessary that all the children (alk'wa'laxelaab') be loved equally (equal their being loved).
7. The husband must love and take care of his wife.
8. The students are not equal with their teacher.
9. The younger sibling is helped by his older sibling.
10. It is the fight that gave the headache to me.

SPECIAL DRILLS

A. Change the following adjectives into nouns and give the translations in English.

1. q'eq, black
2. q'or, lazy
3. sak'aaj, industrious
4. q'an, yellow
5. rax, green
6. joron, cold

B. Change the names of the following body parts from the given possessed forms into unpossessed forms.

1. nuxkiin, my ear
2. nutza'm, my nose
3. nuware, my tooth (teeth)
4. nuqul, my throat
5. nuk'u'x, my heart
6. nuch'u'k. my elbow

USEFUL EXPRESSIONS

1. Xaq chub'aniik kuub'ano kojuuyajo.
   Just to be mean he scolds us.

2. Katiyo'w kuuna' chwee.
   He is envious and hateful of me.

3. Xpee royowaal.
   He became angry.

4. Xqaaj royowaal.
   He calmed down.

5. Naj uwi' chwee.
   He stares at me.

Directional and Locational Adverbs *loq, b'iik,* and *kanoq*
and Conjugation of Irregular Derived Transitive Verb
ajawaxik and Use of Auxiliary Verbs *kowinem* and *ajawaxik*

DIRECTIONAL AND LOCATIONAL ADVERBS

In K'iche there are seven adverbs that indicate either the direction in which
an object is moving or its current location. In this lesson we are going to
study briefly three of these adverbs: *loq, b'iik,* and *kanoq.*

DIRECTIONAL-LOCATIONAL ADVERB *LOQ*

MEANING
The adverb *loq* "here" (i.e., in this direction, toward the speaker) is derived
from the Simple Intransitive Verb *ul* "arrive here."

USES
This particle is used in a great number of ways. Here we shall see only a few
of its uses with Simple Intransitive and Transitive Verbs.

With Simple Intransitive Verbs
    Le achi xka'y loq.   The man looked here.
    Iwir xintzalij loq.   Yesterday I returned here.

With Transitive Verbs

We k'o arajiil chaak'amaa loq. (k'amik "to be received" + loq = "to be brought here")	If you have money, bring it here.
Le achi xa tak'al puwi' le laj juyub' aretaq xojril loq.	The man was just standing on top of the small hill when he saw us here."

ALTERNATE FORM OF *LOQ*

Loq has the form *la* when it is not utterance-final:

Iwir xojtzalij la pa kayib'al.	Yesterday we returned here from market.
We k'o arajiil, chaak'amaa la chwe'q.	If you have money, bring it here tomorrow.

Loq (la) combines with certain words that precede it in the form *u'loq (u'la)*. (See note in lesson 2 regarding words that end in vowels immediately followed by words beginning in vowels.)

With the adverb *na* "later, afterward, first"

na + loq > nu'loq
(na + la; nu'la – –)

Chwe'q kink'am nu'loq.
(Kink'am nu'la chwe'q.)
Tomorrow I will bring it here.

With the formal pronoun *la* "you":

la + loq > lu'loq
(la + la; lu'la – –)

La aninaq katzalij lu'loq?
La katzalij lu'la aninaq?
Will you return here quickly?

With the adverb *wi*, which indicates direction in general:

wi + loq > wu'loq
(wi + la; wu'la – –)

La' le atz'iyaq; jawi' xaak'am wu'loq?
(Jawi' xaak'am wu'la la' le atz'iyaq?)
Where did you bring that clothing from?

With the adverb *chi* "again, now"

chi + loq > chu'loq
(chi + la; chu'la − −)

Le achi xka'y chu'loq.
(Xka'y chu'la le achi.)
The man looked this way again.

With the negative *na . . . taj*

na . . . ta + loq > na . . . tu'loq
(na . . . ta + la > na . . . tu'la − −)

Ri' na nuk'amom tu'loq.
(Na nuk'amom tu'la ri'.)
I have not brought that here.

DIRECTIONAL-LOCATIONAL ADVERB *B'IIK*

MEANING
The adverb *b'iik*, meaning "away from here," "out from here" (in a direction away from the speaker), is derived from the Simple Intransitive Verb *b'e* "go."

USES
This particle is used in a great number of ways. Here we shall see only a few of its uses with Simple Intransitive and Transitive Verbs.

With Simple Intransitive Verbs

Le ali xel b'iik.	The girl went out away from here.
Le achijaab' xeeq'ab'ar b'iik.	The men got drunk before going away from here.

With Transitive Verbs

Chaak'amaa b'iik. (k'amik "to be received" + b'ik = to be taken away)	Take it away from here.
Xojch'aay b'iik.	We were beaten away from here.

ALTERNATE FORMS OF *B'IIK*
B'iik has the form *b'i* when it is not utterance-final:

Le ali xel b'i pa ja.	The girl went out of the house away from here.
Chaak'amaa b'i ach'iich'.	Take your machete away from here.

B'iik (b'i) combines with certain words that precede it in the form *u'b'iik* (*u'b'i–*).

With the adverb *na* "later, afterward, first":

> *na + b'iik > nu'b'iik*
> (*na + b'ii > – nu'bi–*)

Chwe'q kink'am nu'b'iik.
(Kink'am nu'b'i chwe'q.)
Tomorrow, afterward, I'll take it away from here.

With the formal pronoun *la* "you":

> *la + b'iik > lu'b'iik*
> (*la + b'i – lu'b'i–*)

La kamik kak'am lu'b'ik?
(La kak'am lu'b'i kamik?)
Are you taking it away from here today?

With the adverb *wi*, indicating direction in general:

> *wi + b'iik > wu'b'iik*
> (*wi + b'i > wu'b'i–*)

Le pwaq pa ja xelaq'ax wu'b'iik.
(Pa ja xelaq'ax wu'b'i le pwaq.)
The money was stolen away from inside the house.

With the adverb *chi* "again, now":

> *chi + b'iik > chu'b'iik*
> (*chi + b'i > chu'b'i–*)

Le ak'alaab' xeek'aam chu'b'ik.
(Xeek'am chu'b'i le ak'alaab'.)
The children were taken away again.

With the negative *na . . . taj*:

> *na . . . ta + b'iik > na . . . tu'b'iik*
> (*na . . . ta + b'i > na . . . tu'b'i–*)

Kamik na kaqak'am tu'b'iik.
(Na kaqak'am tu'b'i kamik.)
We will not take it away today.

DIRECTIONAL-LOCATIONAL ADVERB *KANOQ*

MEANING

The adverb *kanoq* "behind" (i.e., remaining behind) is derived from the Simple Intransitive Verb *kanajik* "remain."

USES

This particle is used in a great number of ways. Here we shall see only a few of its uses with Simple Intransitive and Transitive Verbs.

With Simple Intransitive Verbs

Na xpee ta ri qachi'iil, xa warnaq kanoq.	Our companion did not come, he just remained behind sleeping.
Le ajchakiib' xeekanaj kanoq.	The workers remained behind.

With Transitive Verbs

Xqayaa kanoq. (ya'ik "to be given" + kanoq = "to be left behind")	We left it behind.
Le qataat xuub'ij kanoq chi kapee chi na.	Our father said before he left that he would come again later. (he's gone but his words remain behind)

Alternate Forms of *kanoq:*

Kanoq has the form *kan* when it is not utterance-final:

Xeekaanaj kan le ajchakiib'.	The workers remained behind.
Xinyaa kan le nuchiim pa k'ayib'al.	I left my woven bag behind in the market.

Kanoq, unlike *loq* and *b'iik*, undergoes no changes when it precedes such words as *na*, *la*, *wi*, and *chik*:

Kayaa na kan le pwaq.	The money will be left behind.

CONJUGATION OF IRREGULAR DERIVED TRANSITIVE VERB *AJAWAXIK*

Since *ajawaxik* "to be wanted, to be loved" is one of the most commonly used verbs in the language, we shall conjugate it here in the four voices in which it is used: Active, Simple Passive, Completed Passive, and Agent-Focus Antipassive. The root for the Active Voice conjugation is simply *aa*. The root for the conjugation of the other three voices is *ajawa*.

Active Voice

For simplicity the object will always be third person singular.

Incomplete Aspect

Kawaaj.	I want it.	Kaqaaj.	We want it.
Kaawaaj.	You want it.	Kiiwaaj.	You want it.
Karaaj.	He wants it.	Kakaaj.	They want it.
Kaj la.	You want it.	Kaj alaq.	You want it.

Completed Aspect

Xwaaj.	I wanted it.	Xqaaj.	We wanted it.
Xaawaaj.	You wanted it.	Xiiwaaj.	You wanted it.
Xraaj.	He wanted it.	Xkaaj.	They wanted it.
Xaj la.	You wanted it.	Xaj alaq.	You wanted it.

Imperative Mood

chaawaaj	want it	chiiwaaj	want it
chiraaj.	Let him want it.	Chikaaj.	Let them want it.
chaj la	want it	chaj alaq	want it

NOTE: Perfect Aspect is rarely used.

Simple Passive Voice

Incomplete Aspect

Kinajawaxik.	I am wanted.	Kojajawaxik.	We are wanted.
Katajawaxik.	You are wanted.	Kixajawaxik.	You are wanted.
Kajawaxik.	He is wanted.	Ka'jawaxik.	They are wanted.
Kajawax la.	You are wanted.	Kajawax alaq.	You are wanted.

NOTE: From the nominalized form of this voice we get the commonly used form that we have already used: *rajawaxik* "it is necessary" ("it is to be wanted").

Completed Aspect

Xinajawaxik.	I was wanted.	Xojajawaxik.	We were wanted.
Xatajawaxik.	You were wanted.	Xixajawaxik.	You were wanted.
Xajawaxik.	He was wanted.	Xa'jawaxik.	They were wanted.
Xajawax la.	You were wanted.	Xajawax alaq.	You were wanted.

NOTE: Imperative Mood and Perfect Aspect are rarely used.

COMPLETED PASSIVE VOICE

Incomplete Aspect

Kinajawatajik.	I am becoming wanted.	Kojajawatajik.	We are becoming wanted.
Katajawatajik.	You are becoming wanted.	Kixajawatajik.	You are becoming wanted.
Kajawatajik.	He is becoming wanted.	ka'jawatajik.	They are becoming wanted.
Kajawataj la.	You are becoming wanted.	Kajawataj alaq.	You are becoming wanted.

Completed Aspect

Xinajawatajik.	I was becoming wanted.	Xojajawatajik.	We were becoming wanted.
Xatajawatajik.	You were becoming wanted.	Xixajawatajik.	You were becoming wanted.
Xajawatajik.	He was becoming wanted.	Xa'jawatajik.	They were becoming wanted.
Xajawataj la.	You were becoming wanted.	Xajawataj alaq.	You were becoming wanted.

NOTE: Imperative Mood and Perfect Aspect are rarely used.

Positional Aspect

In ajawatalik.	I am wanted.	Oj ajawatalik.	We are wanted.
At ajawatalik.	You are wanted.	Ix ajawatalik.	You are wanted.
Are' ajawatalik.	He is wanted.	A're' a'jawatalik.	They are wanted.
Ajawatal la.	You are wanted.	Ajawatal alaq.	You are wanted.

NOTE: This verb is not used in Antipassive Voice.

AGENT-FOCUS ANTIPASSIVE VOICE

For simplicity the object will always be third person singular.

Incomplete Aspect

In kinajawanik.	I am the one who wanted it.	Oj kojajawanik.	We are the ones who want it.
At katajawanik.	You are the one wants it.	Ix kixajawanik.	You are the one who want it.
Aree kajawanik.	He is the one wants it.	A'ree ka'jawanik.	They are ones who want it.
Laal kajawan la.	You are the one who wants it.	Alaq kajawan alaq.	You are the ones want it.

Completed Aspect

In xina-jawanik.	I am the one who wanted it.	Oj xojajawanik.	We are the ones who wanted it.
At xatajawanik.	You are the one who wanted it.	Ix xixajawanik.	You are the ones who wanted it.
Aree xajawanik.	He is the one who wanted it.	A'ree xa'jawanik.	They are the ones who wanted it.
Laal xajawan la.	You are the one wanted it.	Alaq xajawan alaq.	You are the ones who wanted it.

NOTE: Imperative Mood is rarely used.

Perfect Aspect

In in ajawannaq.	I am the one who has wanted it.
At at ajawannaq.	You are the one who has wanted it.
Are' ajawannaq.	He is the one who has wanted it.
Laal ajawannaq la.	You are the one who wanted it.
Oj oj ajawannaq.	We are the ones who have wanted it.
Ix ix ajawannaq.	You are the ones who have wanted it.
A're' a'jawannaq.	They are the ones who have wanted it.
Alaq ajawannaq alaq.	You are the ones who have wanted it.

ONE USE OF AUXILIARY VERBS *KOWINEEM* AND *AJAWAXIK*

In English auxiliary verbs like "to be able" and "to want" are used together with the infinitive form of the main verb of the clause: "I am able to work" or "I want to go." In lesson 35 we saw some ways to form main verbs with their auxiliaries in K'ichee'.

If the auxiliary verb is intransitive:

Kinkowin chub'aniik le chaak.   I am able to do the work.

If the auxiliary verb is transitive:

Xuumajij ub'aniik le chaak.   He began to do the work.

Another way to form main verbs with their auxiliaries is to use the auxiliary verb (Simple Intransitive or Transitive) in the desired person and aspect, followed by the main verb, which must agree with it in person and aspect (ordinarily).

Two of the auxiliary verbs most commonly used in this way are *kowineem* (IVS) "to be able" and *ajawaxik* (TVD) "to be wanted."

Incomplete Aspect

Kinkowinik kimb'eek.	I am able to go. (I am able, I go.)
Kawaaj kimb'eek.	I want to go. (I want it, I go.)

Completed Aspect

Xatkowinik xaab'ano.	You were able to do it. (You were able, you did it.)
Xaawaaj xaab'ano.	You wanted to do it. (You wanted, you did it.)

Note that some auxiliaries cannot be used in this parallel auxiliary–main verb type of construction. For example, the verb *majixik* (TVD) "to be begun" does not admit usage in this type of parallel construction. When this type of verb is used as an auxiliary to the main verb, it must be with the main verb in a nominalized form, as we saw in lesson 35:

Xuumajij nuyajiik.   He began to scold me. (He began my being scolded.)

MODEL SENTENCES

1. Kinkowinik kink'am b'i le pwaq we karaj ri intaat.
   I can take the money away if my father wants me to.

2. La kaj la kojtzalij la aninaq?
   Do you want us to return here quickly.

3. Oj xojajawanik xyaa kan le wa kumal le ajk'ayiib'.
   We were the ones who wanted the tortillas to be left behind by the sellers.

4. Kachokon le kolob' chqeech; chaak'amaa loq.
   The rope is useful to us; bring it here.

VOCABULARY

kowinem	(IVS)	to be able
chokonem	(IVS)	to be of use
kanajem	(IVS)	to remain
ajawaxik	(TVD)	to be wanted, loved
-aa-		Active Voice root
-ajawa-		Root for Simple Passive, Completed Passive, and Agent-Focus Antpassive Voices
loq (la–)	(ADV)	here, in this direction
b'iik (b'i–)	(ADV)	away, out from here, away from here
kanoq (kan)	(ADV)	behind
k'amik	(TVR)	to be received + *loq* "to be brought here"
		to be received + *b'iik* "to be taken away"
ya'ik	(TVR)	to be given + *kanoq* "to be left behind"

K'ICHEE' TO ENGLISH

1. Qak'amaa b'i le tz'i'. Xa kaqasipaj chee le qachalaal.
2. Janipaa chi ix qaajnaq la waraal pa tinamit?
3. Karaj le achi kuutij uwaa chaaniim; chaak'amaa loq.
4. La kaj la kab'ee la quk' pa muqunik?
5. Xkanaj kan le achi jee la' pa taq'aaj. Na xuuq'i' ta chik xpee quuk'
6. Na xeekowin ta le winaq xeekik'am la le kalk'u'aal waraal pa kunaxik.
7. Kachokon le laq chwee; utz kiiyaa kanoq.
8. Rajawaxik kayaa la qawaa rumal le aj-'iik.
9. Kuutij nu'b'i le uwaa le wachajiil, k'atee k'u ri' kab'ee pa chaak.
10. Janipaa kakowin la katzalij chi lu'loq?
11. Na kojwa' ta chik. Xtijtaj la le qeech chuwa ja.
12. Le yawaab' xresaj kan le reqa'n aretaq xuumajij paqaleem chuwa le juyub'.

ENGLISH TO K'ICHEE'

1. Do you (laal) want to take the dog away with you?
2. I was not able to bring my friend here today.
3. Leave (alaq) the dried ears of corn in the house.
4. If the marimba is useful to the marimba players, we'll bring it here tomorrow afterward.
5. I'm not sad for the man (b'isoxik uwach); he is the one who wanted to suffer.
6. The child left from the house (in this direction).
7. It is necessary that the money be returned here to its owner.
8. I'm going to eat my food before going (nu'b'iik).
9. The man did not want me to take his son to be cured.
10. We are not able to help you (alaq) because we have to leave from here today.
11. Do you (ix) want to help me take away from here the fresh ears of corn?

USEFUL EXPRESSIONS

1. K'a jan taq pa kapeetik.
   From time to time he comes.

2. K'o ri kapeetik, k'o ri na kapee taj.
   At times he comes, at times he does not come.

3. Jun tziij kimb'eek.
   I am going for good.

4. Na tziij ta chee.
   It isn't important to him.

5. Na tziij taj chi xuub'ano.
   It's not true that he did it.

   Tziij chi xuub'ano.
   It's true that he did it.

K'ichee' to English Vocabulary

aa

    aab' (N) hammock
    aaj (N) reed
    aak' (N) type of grain (*chan* in Spanish)
    aal (PN) woman's child; (ADJ) heavy
    aanimajem (IVS) to run away, flee
    aaq (N) pig
    aaq' (PN) tongue
    aaq'anem (IVS) to climb up
    aataam (ADV) early
    aatinem (IVS) to bathe

a

    a- (POSS PRO) your (SING-FAM)
    ab'aj (N) rock, stone
    ab'iix (N) corn plant
    achajiloom (PN) husband; **-achajiil** (possessed form)
    achalaal (PN) sibling, near relative
    achi (N) man; **achijaab'** (PL) men

achik'axik (TVD) to be dreamed about

achi'iil (PN) companion, friend

aj (N) fresh corn

ajaaw (PN) owner, lord

ajawaxik (TVD) to be wanted, loved
   -aa- active voice root
   -ajawa- root for Simple Passive, Completed Passive, and Agent-Focus Antipassive voices (see lesson 38)

ajchaak (N) worker; **ajchakiib'** (PL) workers

ajch'a'ooj (N) fighter, soldier; **ajch'o'jiib'** (PL) fighters, soldiers

ajiij (N) sugar cane

ajiil (PN) price (of something)
   kapaki' rajiil "its price goes up"
   kaqaaj rajiil "its price goes down"
   -ajiil -tz'aqaat (PN) relatives (term of endearment)

ajk'aay (N) seller; **ajk'ayiib'** (PL) sellers

ajlaxik (TVD) to be counted

ajq'iij (N) diviner, Mayan priest, day keeper; **ajq'ijaab'** (PL) diviners, Mayan priests, day keepers

ajq'ojoom (N) merimba player; **ajq'ojomaab'** (PL) merimba players

ajtiij (N) teacher, instructor; **ajtijaab'** (PL) teachers, instructors

ajxojoloob' (N) dancer; **ajxojoloob'** (PL) dancers

ajyuuq' (N) shepherd; **ajyuq'aab'** (PL) shepherds

aj'iik' (N) maid, servant paid by the month; **aj'ik'aab'** (PL) maids, servants

ak' (N) chicken

ak'aal (N) child; **ak'alaab'** (PL) children

ala (N) boy; **alab'oom** (PL) boys

alaj (ADJ) small (see *la'j*)

alanxax (N) orange, orange tree

alaxik (TVD) to be born (to give birth to); (N) relatives, siblings (e.g., *oj alaxik* "we are siblings")

alaq (PER PRO, PLU-FORM) you; (POSS PRO) your (PLU-FORM) (see lessons 7 and 8)

ali (N) girl; **altomaab'** (PL) girls

alkalte (N-SPAN) mayor

alk'wa'laxeel (PN) child (man's, couple's); **alk'wa'laxelab'** (PL) children
   -alk'u'aal (possessed form)

am (N) spider

amaq'el (ADV) always

amoolo (N) housefly

anaab' (PN) sister (male's)

anima (N-SPAN) heart, soul

aninaq (ADV) quickly

apanoq (apan-) (ADV) over there (at a determined distance)

aqanaaj (PN) foot (feet)

aq'ab' (N) night, early morning
   nik'aj aq'ab'—midnight
   chaaq'ab'—at night
   nimaq'ab'—in the morning

aq'anoq (aq'an-) (ADV) up, up above

aree (see *are'*)

aree chi (CONJ) in order that

aree chi' (ADV) at that time; (CONJ) and so

aree la' (DEM) that there is it, that there is — — (see lesson 25)

aree ri' (DEM) that is it, that is — — (see lesson 25) **aretaq** (CONJ) when

aree wa' (DEM) this is it, this is— (see lesson 25)

are' (aree-) (PER PRO) he, she, it, him, her

asaron (N-SPAN) hoe

at (PER PRO) you (SING-FAM)

ati't (PN) grandmother

atz (PN) older sibling

atz'aam (N) salt

atz'iyaq (N) clothing, cloth

aw- (POSS PRO) your (SING-FAM) (see lesson 8)

awaas (N) taboo

aweex (N) corn planting

a'ree (see a're')

a'ree la' (DEM) those there are they, those there are — — (see lesson 25)

a'ree ri' (DEM) those are they, those are — — (see lesson 25)

a'ree wa' (DEM) these are they, these are — — (see lesson 25)

a're' (a'ree-) (PER PRO) they, them

b'

b'aalam (N) jaguar

b'aaq (ADJ) thin; (N) bone, needle

b'aqik (TVR) to be washed (hair)

b'aatz' (N) day in Mayan ceremonial calendar

b'a' (b'aa-) (EXCLAM) well, oh!

b'a (N) gopher-like animal

b'ajixik (TVD) to be nailed, screwed on, put on tightly

b'alixik (TVD) to be loaded, filled up

b'alkatixik (TVD) to be rolled over

b'alka'teem (IVS) to roll over

b'aluk (PN) brother-in-law

b'anik (TVR) to be made, done

b'aqilaal (PN) body

b'aq'wachaaj (PN) eye(s), eyeball(s)

b'atz' (N) thread

b'ayi's (N) rat

b'a'ik (TVR) to be masticated, chewed

b'eenaam (IVS) to go

b'enaq'iij (ADV) in the afternoon

b'eeyik (TVR) to be delayed

b'e (N) road, trail

b'elejeb' (NUM) nine

b'e'eel (PN) one's own road (i.e., exclusively); ub'e'eel correctness

b'iik (b'i-) (ADV) away, out from here, away from here

b'iineel (N) traveler

b'iineem (IVS) to walk, travel

b'iiq'ik (TVR) to be swallowed, gulped

b'iis (N) sadness

b'iit'ik (TVR) to be torn

b'irireem (IVS) to roar (as the ocean, a car motor)

b'isoxik (TVD) to be sad about

b'it' (N) a tearing sound

b'ixaxik (TVD) to be sung

b'ixik (TVD) to be said

b'i'aaj (PN) name (s)

b'oolik (TVR) to be roasted in fire

b'ooqik (TVR) to be pulled out by roots

b'ochi'xik (TVD) to be courted, comforted, coaxed, pacified (a baby)

b'o'j (N) clay cooking pot

ch

chaaj (N) ash

chaak (N) work

chaaniim (ADV) right now, quickly

chaj (N) pine tree, pine pitch

chajixik (TVD) to be taken care of, guarded

chakach (N) basket

chakuxik (TVD) to be worked (as land)

chapik (TVR) grab, catch, detain, begin

chaqijem (IVS) become dry

chaqijsaxik (TVD) to be dried

chaqi'j (ADJ) dry

chaq' (ADJ) fat, cooked, ripe

chaq'ajeem (IVS) to become fat, cooked, ripe

chaq'ajsaxik (TVD) to be cooked, ripened, fattened

chaq'ixeel (PN) younger sibling (same sex)

chaq'ixelaab' (PL) younger siblings (same sex)

chaaq' (poss form of *chaq'ixeel*)

chayik (TVR) to be chosen, selected (irregular; see lesson 30)

cha' (**chaa–**) (IVS-IRREGULAR) to say (quotatative)

Incomplete Aspect

kincha'	I say
katcha'	you say
kacha'	he says
kachaa la	you say
kojcha'	we say
kixcha'	you say
keecha'	they say
kacha' laq	you say

Completed Aspect

xincha'	I said
xatcha'	you said
xcha'	he said
xchaa la	you said
xojcha'	we said
xixcha'	you said
xeecha'	they said
xcha' laq	you said

(Also used in Imperative and Perfect Aspects)

ch_ee (ch) (PREP) to — —, for — —, from — —

chwee (ch)	to me
chaawee (ch)	to you
*chee (ch)	to him
chee (ch) la	to you
chqee (ch)	to us
chiiwee (ch)	to you
chkee (ch)	to them
chee (ch) alaq	to you

***chee** (chi) = with (instrumentally)

e.g., *Xkamisax chi ch'iich.* "He was killed with a machete."

chee' (N) tree, wood, jail; (ADJ) stiff, rigid

che'rem (IVS) to become rigid, stiff

ch_iij (PREP) behind − −, over − −, around − −

Chwiij	behind me
Chaawiij	behind you
chrij (chiij)	behind him
chij la	behind you
Chqiij	behind us
Chiiwiij	behind you
Chkiij	behind them
chij alaq	behind you

chiim (N) wooven bag

chi (CONJ) that

chi (PREP) with (see *ch_eech*)

chik (chi−) (ADV) again, now

chikop (N) animal, insect

chi'iij (**chi'aaj**) (PN) mouth, opening, edge; *uchi ja*, door of the house

ch_naqaaj (PREP) near

chnunaqaaj	near me
chaanaqaaj	near you
chuunaqaaj	near him
chnaqaj la	near you
chqanaqaaj	near us
chiinaqaaj	near you
chkinaqaaj	near them
chnaqaj alaq	near you

chookik (TVR) to be contracted (some work)

choolik (TVR) to be lined up, put in order

choom (adj, n) fat, fat one; **choma'q** (PL), fat ones

cho (N) lake, pond

chokoneem (IVS) to be of use

chokonsab'exik (TVD) to be used

chomaal (N) fatness

chomaal (N) meeting, plan, intention

chomaxik (TVD) to be thought about, planned, arranged

choqon (N) tickling, ticklish

choqonaxik (TVD) to be tickled

choqonaneem (IVS) tickles

cho'lem (IVP) to loosen

ch_paam (PREP) inside of − −

chnupaam	inside of me
chaapaam	inside of you
chuupaam	inside of him
chpam la	inside of you

chqapaam	inside of us
chiipaam	inside of you
chkipaam	inside of them
chpam alaq	inside of you

chuun (N) lime, limestone

chuupik (TVR) to be put out, extinguished (as a fire or light)

chu (ADJ) smelly

chub'aaj (PN) saliva, spittle

chub'axik (TVD) to be spit on; Absolutive Antipassive Voice: **chub'anik** spit

chuchi' (PREP) at the edge of it, at; alternate form: **chii'** (**chii–**)

chulaaj/chula'j (PN) urine

chuqe' (**chuqee–**, **chuq–**) (ADV) also, in addition

ch_wach (PREP) before ___, in front of ___

Chnuwach	before me
Chaawach	before you
chuwach (chuwa)	before him
chwach la	before you
Chqawach	before us
Chiiwach	before you
Chkiwach	before them
chwach alaq	before you

chwe'q (ADV) tomorrow

ch_xee' (PREP) under ___, below ___

chnuxee'	under me
chaaxee'	under you
chuuxee'	under him
chxee la	under you
chqaxee'	under us
chiixee'	under you
chkixee'	under them
chxee' alaq	under you

ch_xo'l (PREP) among, between

chuuxo'l	among them (nonliving)
chqaxo'l	among us
chiixo'l	among you
chkixo'l	among them
chxo'l alaq	among you

ch'

ch'ab'al (N) language, Christian doctrine

ch'aab'exik (TVD) to be spoken to, visited

ch'aajik (TVR) to be washed; two Antipassive Voice forms:
  ch'ajanik — wash oneself,
  ch'ajo'manik — do laundry, menstruate
ch'aakik (TVR) to be won, earned, guessed
ch'aat (N) bed
ch'aweem (IVS) to talk, speak
ch'ajch'oj (ADJ) clean, unblemished, pure
ch'ajo'n (N) laundry, washing
ch'am (ADJ) acidic, sour
ch'ami'y (N) walking stick, staff, cane
ch'aqab'axik (TVD) to be made wet
ch'aqaleem (IVP) to become wet
ch'ayaneel (N) hitter
ch'a'ik (TVR) to be complained about
ch'a'k (N) sores on skin
ch'a'ooj (N) fight, dispute, war
ch'iich' (N) car, machete, any metallic object
ch'iitik (TVR) to become worse (sickness)
ch'oob'ik (TVR) to be comprehended, announced
ch'oolik (TVR) to be peeled, skinned
ch'oop (N) pineapple
ch'o (N) mouse
ch'o'jib'exik (TVD) to be fought over
ch'o'jineem (IVS) to fight
ch'o'jixik (TVD) to be fought over
ch'ok (N) a type of black bird
ch'uch'uj (ADJ) smooth, soft
ch'uuqik (TVR) to be covered
ch'umiil (N) star(s)
ch'uti'n (ADJ) small; ch'uti'q (PL) small (ones)

d

Dyoos (N-SPAN) God

ee

_ee (ch) (POSS PRO)

wee (ch)	mine
awee (ch)	yours
ree (ch)	his
ee (ch) la	yours
qee (ch)	ours

iwee (ch)	yours
kee (ch)	theirs
ee (ch) alaq	yours

eek' (N) a type of tree parasite

eera (N) a place where wheat is thrashed

e

elaq' (N) theft, stealing

elaq'axik (TVD) to be robbed, stolen
Antipassive Voice: **elaq'ik**
Agent-Focus Antipassive Voice: **elaq'anik**

elaq'oom (N) thief; **elaq'omaab'** (PL) thieves

elem (IVS) to leave, go out

elesaxik (TVD) to be removed, taken out, taken away

engañar, b'anik (TVR, SPAN) to be deceived (see lesson 30)

engaño (N-SPAN) deceit

eqaneel (N) carrier, backpacker

eqaxik (TVD) to be carried on the back

eqa'n (N) load, cargo

erexik (TVD) to be hauled

etaal (N) sign, mark

etaxik (TVD) to be measured

eta'maxik (TVD) to be learned, known;
Positional Aspect: **eta'aam** (_eta'm–) (see lesson 32)

etzelaxik (TVD) to be hated

etz'ab'a'l (N) toy, plaything

etz'ab'exik (TVD) to be played with

etz'aneem (IVS) play

ii

iib' (REFLEXIVE PRO) self

wiib'	myself
awiib'	yourself
riib'	himself
iib' la	yourself
qiib'	ourselves
iwiib'	yourselves
kiib'	themselves
iib' alaq	yourselves

iij (PN) covering, skin, back; (N) measles

iik (N) chile, a dish or bowl of food

iik' (N) moon, month

i

i- (POSS PRO) your (PLU FAM) (see lesson 7)
ichaaj (N) edible herbs, greens, vegetables
ikaj (N) ax
ikiraxik (TVD) to be carried on the head
ilawachixik (TVD) to be observed
ilik (TVR) to be seen, watched
in (PER PRO) I, me
inuup (N) ceiba tree
itzeel (ADJ) evil, bad
iw- (POSS PRO) your (PLU FAM) (see lesson 8)
iwir (ADV) yesterday
ix (PER PRO) you (PLU FAM)
ixiim (N) dry kernels of corn
ixoq (N) woman; ixoqiib' (PL) women
ixoqiloom (PN) wife; _ixoqiil (poss form)
iye'xik (TVD) to be waited for; Absolutive Antipassive Voice: iye'nik or iye'b'ik
iyoom (N) midwife

j

jaaqik (TVR) to be opened
jaalik (TVR) to be changed, exceeded (go past the correct place or measure)
jaamik (TVR) to be vacated, emptied
ja (N) house, building
jab' (N) rain
jab'uxik (TVD) to be scattered
jacha' (jachaa-) (PREP) like, as
jachinaq (jachin__) (INTER) who, which one
    jachin chqee (ch)   which one of us
    jachin chiiwee (ch)   which one of you
    jachin chkee (ch)   which one of them
    jachin cheech alaq   which one of you
jachikee (jachin chkee) (INTER PRO) what (one), which (one), (PRO) whatever
jach' (N) corn harvest
jal (N) dried ears of corn
jampa' (jampaa-) (INTER, ADV) when, how much
janipa' (janipaa-) (INTER) how many, how much
jas (jasa) (INTER) what; (PREP) as, like (jasa . . . jee', as . . . so; e.g., *Jasa kaqab'an oj, jee kiib'an ix.* "As we do, so do you.")
jas chee (INTER) why
jas chemna (INTER) why . . . not
jastaq (N) thing(s)

jat (IVS) go! (see *b'eenaam* — irregular second person sing imperative form)

jat'ixik (TVD) to be tied

jawi' (**jawi–**) (ADV) where

ja' (N) water, liquid, liquor

ja'ee (ADV) alright, fine, okay

ja'ii' (ADV) no

jee la' (MANNER, DIR) that way, like that, over there (see lesson 25)

jeek'ik (TVR) to be pulled

jee ri' (MANNER, DIR) like that (see lesson 25)

jee wa' (MANNER, DIR) this way, like this (see lesson 25)

je' (**jee–**) (ADV) yes, like, in such a manner, in such a way; *jee . . . jasa,* "so . . . as"; e.g., *Jee kib'an ix, jasa ri kimb'an in.* "So do as I do."

je'lik (**je'l–**) (ADJ) pretty, lovely, beautiful, attractive

jii' achi (PN) father-in-law

jii' ixoq (PN) mother-in-law

jia'xeel (PN) son-in-law; **jia'xelaab'** (PL) sons-in-law; **_ji'** (poss form)

jiq'ik (IVS) to choke, drown

jitz'axik (TVD) to be strangled, hanged

jooj (N) crow

jook'ik (TVR) to be ground (as coffee)

jolomaaj (PN) head(s)

jok'o'm (N) a meal of whole beans prepared in a ground corn broth

jorob'eem (IVS) to become cold

jororeem (IVS) to feel pleasant or fresh feeling (as temperature)

joron (ADJ) cold; (N) cold water

josq'ixik (TVD) to be cleaned

jo'ob' (**job'–**) (NUM) five

juumuul (ADV) one time

juun (NUM) one; (indefinite article) a, an

jub'iik' (ADV) a moment, a little, a gulp (literally)

juch'iin (ADV) a bit, a moment

jul (N) hole

junaam (ADJ) equal, same; *junaam _uk'* = equal with __, same as __

junelik (ADV) unending, eternal

jupuleem (IVP) to lie face down

juyub' (N) mountain, hills

k

k- (POSS PRO) their (see lesson 8)

kaabiij (ADV) the day after tomorrow

kaamuul (ADV) two times

kanajeem (IVS) to remain

kanoq (kan-) (ADV) behind

kaa' (N) grinding stone

kajib' (NUM) four

kajmaxik (TVD) to be served

kamik (ADV) today

kamulixik (TVD) to be done a second time

kamyon (N-SPAN) truck

kandiil (N-SPAN) kerosene lamp

karna't (N) passion fruit (*granadia* in Spanish)

karne'l (N) sheep; karne'laab' (PL) sheep

kayexik (TVD) to be bitten (as by a dog)

ka'yeel (N) watcher

ka'yeem (IVS) to see, look, watch

ka'yexik (TVD) to be looked at, watched

kab'ijiir (ADV) the day before yesterday

kameel (N) one who dies

kameem (IVS) to die

kaminaq (ADJ) dead; (N) dead one; kaminaqiib' (PL) dead ones

kamisaneel (N) killer

kamsaxik (TVD) to be killed

kape (N) coffee

kaq (ADJ) red

kaqiiq' (N) wind, air

kar (N) fish

kaxlan (ADJ) foreign

kaxlan wa (N) bread

keej (N) horse

keem (N) weaving

keemik (TVR) to be woven

ketzal (N-SPAN) Guatemalan monetary unit

ke'eb' (keb'-) (NUM) two

ke'eem (PN) soaked kernels of corn ready for grinding; _ke' (poss form)

ke'xik (TVD) to be ground (as corn)

b (N) blood; _kik'eel (poss form)

kiirik (TVR) to be untied

ki- (POSS PRO) their (see lesson 7)

ki (N) maguey plant

kinaq' (N) beans

ki'koteem (IVS) to be happy

ki'kotirsaxik (TVD) to be made happy

koojik (TVR) to be placed, put, put on, believed

koolik (TVR) to be saved, defended

kook' (ADJ) finely ground

kooseem (IVS) to become tired

ko (adj, adv) strong, hard; strongly, loudly

kochixik (TVD) to be received as a gift

kojeej (ADV) in four days

koloneel (N) savior, defender

kolob' (N) rope

kompesanto (N) cemetery

korob'axik (TVD) to be loosened

koroneem (IVP) to loosen

kotz'i'j (N) flower, candle

kowineem (IVS) to be able

kowixik (TVD) to be hurried

ko'k (N) wooden box used for packing objects, jail

ko'lik (ADJ) small; ko'koj (PL) small ones

koj (N) lion

kon (ADJ) stupid

koq (ka-) (ADV) in, inside, in close

kuuk (N) squirrel

kuuyik (TVR) to be pardoned

kumatz (N) snake

kunab'al (N) medicine

kunaxik (TVD) to be cured

ku'lem (IVP) sit

k'

k'aajeem (IVS) (no meaning alone)
    k'aajeem wachaaj to learn a hard lesson (won't do it again)

k'aak' (ADJ) new

k'aamik (TVR) to be received, gotten
    k'aamik loq — to be brought here
    k'aamik b'iik — to be taken away

k'aaqik (TVR) to be thrown, shot, struck

k'aat (N) cargo net

k'aateem (IVS) burn

k'aatik (TVR) to be burned

k'a (ADJ) bitter

k'a (ADV) still, yet

k'ab'ak'ik (ADJ) gaping (mouth)

k'aj (ADJ) pulverized; (N) wheat flour

k'ajoloxeel (PN) son (male's); k'ajoloxelaab' (PL) sons; -k'ajool (poss form)

k'ajsaxik (TVD) (no meaning alone)
    k'ajsaxik wachaaj, to be taught a hard lesson (won't do it again)
k'amal b'e (N) guide, marriage broker
k'amo (N) thanks
k'amowaxik (TVD) to be given thanks for
k'asleem (IVP) to be alive, be awake
k'aslemaal (N) life
k'astajeem (IVS) to wake up, resurrect
k'asuxik (TVD) to be awakened
k'at (N) a day in Mayan ceremonial calendar
k'atan (N) hot liquid; (ADJ) very hot, burning, scalding
k'ate' (**k'atee-**) (ADV) as of, first time, after
    k'atee wa' — as of this time, this is the first time
    k'atee la' — as of that time, that is the first time
    k'atee ri' — as of that time, after that
    k'atee k'u ri' — and after that
k'ax (ADJ) difficult, painful; (N) suffering difficulty, pain
k'axeel (N) replacement, exchange, namesake (child named after grandparent)
    k'e'x — alternate form
k'ayib'al (N) marketplace
k'ayixik (TVD) to be sold
k'a'aam (N) vine, string, one cuerda (measure of land)
k'a'n (ADJ) mean, ill-tempered
k'a'naal (N) meanness
k'a'nareem (IVS) to become angry
k'eexik (TVR) to be changed, exchanged
k'el (N) type of green parrot
k'imuul (ADV) many times
k'iiseem (IVS) to end, terminate, finish
k'i (ADJ) many, much, a lot
k'im (N) thatch
    k'ima ja, thatched-roof house
k'isiis (N) cedar tree
k'isik' (N) goat
k'ook' (ADJ) fragrant
k'oleem (IVP) be (in a place), to exist, have (see lesson 34)
k'oolik (TVR) to be put away, stored
k'ootik (TVR) to be dug
k'ojoxik (TVD) to be patched
k'olib'al (N) place, dwelling place
k'olok'ik (ADJ) spherical
k'otixik (TVD) to be dug out

k'uul (N) blanket
k'uulik (TVR) to be met
k'uutik (TVR) to be shown
k'uch (N) buzzard
k'ulaneem (IVP) to marry; (N) marriage
k'ulaxik (TVD) to be met, accepted
k'ulel (N) enemy
k'ulub'axik (TVD) to be married off
k'ulula'xik (TVD) to be despised
k'ut (**k'u-**) (CONJ) and, but
k'utuneem (TVR, Absolutive Antipassive Voice) to appear
k'u'ik (TVR) to be hidden
k'u'xaaj (PN) heart, core

l

la (interrogative particle) (see lesson 6)
laal (PER PRO, SING-FORM) you
lamna (INTER) negative question word (see lesson 31)
laatz' (ADJ) crowded; *laatz' nuwach* "I'm busy"
laatz'ob'eem (IVS) become crowded
lawalo (ADJ) seriously ill
la (POSS PRO) your (SING-FORM) (see lessons 7 and 8)
lajuuj (NUM) ten
laq (N) clay dish
la' (DEM PRO) that there, that one there (visible to the speaker or spoken of as if it were) (see lesson 25)
la'j (**alaj-**, **laj-**) (ADJ) small
la' le (DEM PRO) that — there
le (DEM ART) the (that one there); (REL PRO) that one there who, that one there which (see lesson 24)
lej (N) tortilla
leejik (TVR) to be made tortillas
leemik (TVR) to be put in order, in line
leme't (N) bottle
lik'ilik (ADJ) spread out
lool (N) grasshopper
looq'ik (TVR) to be bought; Absolutive Antipassive Voice: **loq'o'manik**
lo (ADV) perhaps
loq (**la-**) (ADV) here, in this direction
loq'oxik (TVD) to be loved
Luu' (N) Pedro

m

maaj (IVP) (negative form of of verb *k'olem* in positional aspect) he isn't, there isn't (see model conjugation in lesson 34)

maajik (TVR) to be taken hold of, grabbed, begun

maam (N) grandfather

maataam (ADV) late

Maax (N) Thomas

maayik (TVR) to be wondered at, to be marveled at, to be surprised at

ma (CONJ) because

maja' (**majaa–**) (ADV) not yet

makaaj (PN) sin

makaleem (IVP) to become weak

makuxik (TVD) to be sinned against

maltyoox (N) thanks

maltyoxixik (TVD) to be given thanks for

mas (ADV-SPAN) very, a lot, much, very much

masaat (N) deer

matzaleem (IVP) be quiet, still

Ma't (N) Magdalena

mayestr (N-SPAN) teacher

meejik (TVR) to be bent, doubled

meesik (TVR) to be swept

meb'aa' (ADJ) poor; (N) poor person, orphan; **meb'a'iib'** (PL) poor people, orphans

meb'a'iil (N) poverty, belongings (a polite way of saying "one's riches" by emphasizing how slight they are)

me's (N) cat

miich'ik (TVR) to be pulled (hair, whiskers), to be plucked

miiq'ik (TVR) to be warmed

miinik (TVR) to be forced into, crammed into

miq'in (ADJ) warm; (N) warm liquid

miq'saxik (TVD) to be made warm, warmed up

moolik (TVR) to be gathered

mookik (TVR) to be hired

moox (ADJ) mentally unbalanced

moxiib' (PL) mentally unbalanced people; (PN) left hand (e.g., numoox — my left hand)

mooxireem (IVS) to become mentally unbalanced

mooy (ADJ) blind; (N) blind one, twilight; **moyiib'** (PL) blind ones

mooyireem (IVS) to become blind

muul (ADV) times

    Juumuul   one time

kaamuul   two times

oxmuul   three times

k'iimuul   many times

muuqik (TVR) to be buried

mulaneem (IVP) to gather together

mulixik (TVD) to be gathered together

myeer (ADV) earlier today

n

naab'e (NUM) first; (ADV) at first (see shortened form: *na*)

naab'eyajeem (IVS) to go first

naan (N) ma'am (direct address); (PN) mother (see *nanaxeel*)

na (ADV) first, still, yet, later, for a while, have to (see *naab'e*); **na k'ut** (**na k'u–**) oh, well, yes

naj (ADV) far, a long way, a long time, for a long time

nanaxeel (PN) mother; **nanaxelaab'** (PL) mothers; **_naan** (poss form)

na . . . ta (j) (PART) negativizer (see lesson 13)

naqaaj (ADV) near, nearby, close by, near (in time)

na'ik (TVR) to be felt

nee' (N) baby, infant

ne' (**ne–**) (ADV) actually, really

nik'aj (N) half, rest of, remainder of, other half; (ADJ) middle of; **nik'aj aq'ab'** at midnight (literally, middle of the night)

niim (ADJ) big; **nima'q** (PL) big (ones)

nimaal (N) bigness, size

nimaq'ab' (ADV) in the morning

nimaq'iij (N) fiesta

nimareem (IVS) to become big, enlarged, become proud

nimatajeem (IVS) to become sicker; worsen

nimaxik (TVD) to be obeyed, respected

noojeem (IVS) to become filled

noojsaxik (TVD) to be filled up

no'jiim (**no'jimaal**) (ADV) slowly

nu– (POSS PRO) my (see lesson 7)

nuumeen (IVS) to be hungry

oo

ooj (N) avocado

ok'oweel (N) passerby

ok'oweem (IVS) to pass by

oopaneem (IVS) to arrive in another place

o

ochoch (o'ch) (PN) house, home

oj (PER PRO) we, us

ojer (ADV) in past times; *ojer kanoq* "a long time ago"

okeem (IVS) to enter, become

onojeel (ADJ) all of __, each of __, every one of __; **ronojeel**, all of them (nonliving); each, every (e.g., *ronojel winaq kakamik* "every person will die")

Qonojeel	all of us
Iwonojeel	all of you
Konojeel	all of them
onojel alaq	all of you

oqataxik (TVD) to be chased

oq'aab' (N) an edible green

oq'eej (N) act of weeping, act of crying (nominalized form of *oq'eem*)

oq'eem (IVS) to cry

oq'exik (TVD) to be cried about, cried over

ora (N-SPAN) hour, time

owaxik (TVD) to be hidden

oxiij (ADV) in three days

oxib' (NUM) three

oxjiir (ADV) three days ago

oxmuul (ADV) three times

oyowaal (N) anger; *kape oyowaal* "get angry"

o'ch (ochoch) (PN) house, home

p

paajik (TVR) to be weighed

paamaaj (PN) stomach, interior, diarrhea; **upa ja** the interior of the household, family

paar (N) skunk

paas (N) sash

paatzik (TVR) to be packed (clothes, etc.), to get dressed up

pa (PREP) in, into, toward, to, from, at

pach'uxik (TVD) to be braided

pak'aleem (IVP) to lie face up

palajaaj (PN) face(s)

paqaleem (IVP) to go up

paqchixik (TVD) to be pushed, shoved

pa q'iij (ADV) at noon, in the daytime

pataan (N) service, use

patanixik (TVD) to be served

patan (N) head strap used for carrying loads (*mecapal* in Spanish)

patzapik (ADV) shaggy

patz'an (N) dried plant stalk

paxeem (IVS) to break (dish, bottle, etc.)

paxixik (TVD) to be broken (dish, bottle, etc.)

pay (ADJ) stupid, incompetent; (N) stupid person; **payiib'** (PL) stupid people

payireem (IVS) to become stupid, incompetent

payu (N) handkerchief, bandana

pa'ixik (TVD) to be divided, broken in half

pa'k (N) cracked hands

peepe (N) butterfly, moth

peeteem (IVS) to come

piilik (TVR) to be butchered

piim (ADJ) thick

piirik (TVR) to be broken into pieces (bread, tortillas)

piisik (TVR) to be wrapped up

piitz'ik (TVR) to be pressed down, pushed in

pine (CONJ) although, even though

pinemna (CONJ) even though . . . not, although . . . not

poom (N) copal

poop (N) straw mat

pooy (N) scarecrow

poqon (ADJ) hot (spicy)

poq'oweem (IVS) to boil

poroxik (TVD) to be burned

powi' (**pawi'**) (N) hat

po'j (N) type of coastal tree

po't (N) woven blouse

pruta (N) banana

pwaq (N) money

puuch' (N) matter from eyes

puum (N) dove

puupu (N) balloon, bladder

p_wi' (PREP) on, on top of

panuwi'	on top of me
paawi'	on top of you
puwi' (chuwi')	on top of it
pawi' la	on top of you
paqawi'	on top of us
piiwi'	on top of you
pakiwi'	on top of them
pawi'alaq	on top of you

puyixik (TVD) to be pushed

q

q- (POSS PRO) our (see lesson 8)
qaajeem (IVS) to go down
qaajik (TVR) to be borrowed
qaajoq (qaj-) (ADV) down, down below
qaasana' (N) baptism
qa- (POSS PRO) our (see lesson 7)
qib'eem (IVS) to draw near
qoolik (TVR) to be scratched or skinned
qumuxik (TVD) to be drunk

q'

q'aajeem (IVS) to break (as a bone)
q'aajik (TVR) to be broken (as a bone)
q'aaq' (N) fire, light, heat
q'aatik (TVR) to be stopped, broken off, cut off
q'aaxeem (IVS) to pass by, pass from one place to another
q'aayeem (IVS) to rot
q'ab'aaj (PN) hand (s)
q'ab'areel (ADJ) drunk; (N) drunk person; q'ab'arelaab' (PL) drunk people
q'ab'areem (IVS) to become drunk
q'ab'axik (TVD) to be blamed for
q'alaaj (N) clear, visible
q'alajineem (IVS) to become clear
q'alajsaxik (TVD) to be made clear, visible
q'aluneel (N) one who holds in the arms; godparent in baptism
q'aluxik (TVD) to be held in the arms
q'an (ADJ) yellow
q'apooj (N) young woman, maiden; q'apoj a'li adolescent girl; q'apojiib' (PL) adolescent girls, maidens
q'ataleem (IVP) to stop, block
q'ataneem (IVS) to pass by
q'atb'al tziij (N) courthouse, law, government
q'atexik (TVD) to be blocked, hindered
q'atuxik (TVD) to be inspected
q'axexik (TVD) to be passed from one place to another; q'axexik tziij translate into another language
q'ayees (N) weeds, undergrowth
q'a'leem (IVP) to lean, recline; q'a'lem k'u'xaaj to be consoled, confide (literally, heart leans)
q'eq (ADJ) black
q'e'leem (IVP) to be turned sideways, be transversed

q'iij (N) day, sun, importance

q'iilik (TVR) to be corrected (in a disciplinary manner)

q'inoom (ADJ) rich; (N) rich person; **q'inomaab'** (PL) rich ones

q'inom (N) cashew fruit

q'inoomareem (IVS) to become rich

q'inomarsaxik (TVD) to be made rich

q' i'ik (TVR) to be borne, tolerated, withstood

q'i'tajeem (Absolutive Antipassive Voice) become bored

q'oochik (TVR) to be wrinkled

q'ojoom (N) marimba, music

q'ojomaxik (TVD) to be played (as a musical instrument, especially a marimba)

q'ooq' (N) a type of squash

q'oolik (TVR) to be picked (coffee, beans, etc.)
Absolutive Antipassive Voice: **q'olowik**

q'oxoom (N) pain, ache, soreness

    q'oxoom jolomaaj   headache

    q'oxoom pamaaj   stomachache, etc.

q'oyoleem (IVP) to lie down

q'o'ik (TVR) to be embroidered, adorned
Absolutive Antipassive Voice: **q'o'wik**

q'o'ooj (N) embroidery, adornment

q'or (ADJ) lazy; (N) lazy one; **q'oriib'** (PL) lazy ones

q'orixik (TVD) to be lazy about

q'uuq' (N) quetzal bird

q'ulixik (TVD) to be scalded, burned

q'u'aaj (PN) blanket, covering; **nuq'uu'** (POSS) "my blanket, covering"

q'u'xik (TVD) to be covered up with

r

r- (POSS PRO) his, her, its (see lesson 8)

raamik (TVR) to be cut

rajawaxik (nominalized Simple Passive Voice form of **ajawaxik**, to be wanted) necessary, necessity

ramixik (TVD) to be cut off, cut down

Ramuux (N) Domingo, Dominga

rapaxik (TVD) to be whipped

raqixik (TVD) to be broken open, burst open

rayixik (TVD) to be desired

rayi'n (N) desire

rax (ADJ) green, unripe, uncooked

retrato (N-SPAN) picture, photograph

ri (DEM ART) the (that one not present); (REL PRO) that, who, which (not present) (see lesson 24)

riiqik (TVR) to be found, met, reached, encountered; *kuurik tyeempo chee — —* "time arrives for — —"

riki'l/rikiil (N) dish of food that accompanies tortillas

ri' (DEM PRO) that one, that very one (not present to the speaker, a future past or hypothetical event); those (PL) (see lesson 25)

ri'j (ADJ) grown, mature; (N) grownup
  ri'jaab' (PL) grownups

ri'job'eem (IVS) to become old, mature, grown up

ri' ri (DEM PRO) that very (intensifies the object spoken of even though it is not present); those very (PL) (see lesson 25)

rook'ik (TVR) to be scratched

rumal ri (CONJ) because

S

saacheem (IVS) to get lost, disappear

saachik (TVR) to be forgotten, lost, pardoned

sachaleem (IVP) to become absent, unconscious

sak'aaj (ADJ) industrious; (N) industrious one; **sak'ajiib'** (PL) industrious ones

saneyeb' (N) sand

sanik (N) ant

sa'ik (TVR) to be dried out by sunning or over fire, to be aired out

sa'leem (IVP) to be sunned, aired out

saq (ADJ) white, clear

saqiil (N) whiteness, clearness

saqmo'l (N) egg

saq'uul (N) plantain (a type of banana)

siik'ik (TVR) to be picked up (as something lying about or lost), to be found

siiqik (TVR) to be smelled, sniffed

siin (N) bamboo

siip (N) wood tick

sipaxik (TVD) to be given as a gift

sii' (N) firewood

sib' (N) smoke

sib'alaj (b'alaj) (ADV) very

Sika' (N) Francisca

sik'ixik (TVD) to be called, invited

Si's (N) Francisco

slab'axik (TVD) to be moved

slab'eem (IVP) to move

sokaaj (PN) nest, bed

solixik (TVD) to be visited
suub'ik (TVR) to be deceived
suuq (N) scum on water
suutz' (N) cloud(s), fog
sub' (N) corn tamales
sub'uneel (N) deceiver
suk'umaxik (TVD) to be straightened out, repaired
sutixik (TVD) to be turned around, rotated, spun around
su'ik (TVR) to be wiped
su't (N) scarf
swaan (siwaan) (N) gully, canyon

t

taaqik (TVR) to be sent, ordered, commanded
taasik (TVR) to be separated
taat (N) sir, mister
tajkiil (N) errand
tak'aleem (IVP) to stand
tak'ale'xik (TVD) to be stood on, walked on
Taliin (N) Catarina
tanab'axik (TVD) to be stopped
tanaleem (IVP) to stop, to cease
tap (N) crab
tapa'l (N) a type of fruit
taq (PART) pluralizer (see lesson 5)
taqchi'xik (TVD) to be tempted, persuaded; *taqchi'x chee maak* "to be tempted to sin"
taqo'n (N) emissary, one who is sent
taq'aaj (N) coastal plain
tatab'exik (TVD) to be listened to, heard
tataxeel (PN) father; **tataxelaab'** (PL) fathers; **_taat** (poss form)
tayik (TVR) to be heard, asked (irregular, see lesson 30)
teem (N) chair, bench
teeq' (ADJ) torn
teew (N) cold
teq'etobeem (IVS) to become punctured, torn open
teq'uxik (TVD) to be punctured
terne'xik (TVD) to be followed, continued
tewechi'xik (TVD) to be blessed
Te'k (N) Diego
te'l (ADJ) torn; (N) opening, tear
te'leem (IVP) to become open

tiijik (TVR) to be eaten, drunk; Simple Passive Voice: tiijik or tijowik

tiikik (TVR) to be planted, created Antipassive Voice: tikonik or tiko'nijik

tiitz'ik (TVR) to be stuffed, forced into

tijoxeel (N) student, disciple, pupil; tijoxelaab' (PL) students, disciples, pupils

tijoxik (TVD) to be instructed, to teach someone

tiko'n (N) cultivated plot, creation

tinamit (N) town, nation, community

ti'iij (N) meat; _ti' (poss form — meat to eat; e.g., nuti' my meat)

ti'ik (TVR) to be bitten (by an animal, insect)
  Antipassive Voice: tiyo'nik, bite, bark

ti'jaal (PN) flesh

toojik (TVR) to be paid, paid for

toorik (TVR) to be opened

toloneem (IVP) to become empty; tolon wachaj, unoccupied

toq'ob' (N) favor, mercy, poor (to be pitied); toq'ob' uwach ri achi, the poor man

toq'ob'saxik (TVD) to be pitied, to be looked upon mercifully

to'ik (TVR) to be helped; Antipassive Voice: tob'ik or tob'anik

tuuj (N) steam bath

Tuun (N) Antonio

tuukik (TVR) to be stirred

tukur (N) owl

tuqareem (IVS) to become exhausted

tu' (N) breast, breast milk

t'

t'oot' (N) snail, vagina

t'o'y (N) woven cap

t'uyub'axik (TVD) to be seated

t'uyuleem (IVP) to sit

t'u'y (N) cooking pot

tz

tzaajeem (IVS) to dry up, evaporate

tzaakik (TVR) to be cooked by boiling or steaming

tzaam (N) liquor, aguardiente

tzaaqeem (IVS) to fall, become lost, become stolen

tzaaqik (TVR) to be dropped, made to fall, to be lost

tzalaneem (IVP) to lean sideways

tzalijeem (IVS) to return, go back

tzalixik (TVD) to be returned

tza'maaj (PN) nose(s)

tzatz (ADJ) thick (liquid)

tze'xik (TVD) to be laughed at; Antipassive Voice: **tze'nik**, to laugh

tziij (N) word, truth, true; **b'anik tziij** or **b'ixik tziij**, tell lies

tziijik (TVR) to be lighted, turned on (as a candle or electric light)

tzi (N) hominy

tzijob'exik (TVD) to be spoken to

tzijoxik (TVD) to be told about, talked about, spoken about

tzuuqik (TVR) to be nourished, fed

tzuurik (TVR) to be angered

tzukuxik (TVD) to be looked for, searched for

tz'

tz'aapileem (IVP) to become closed

tz'aapixik (TVD) to be closed, shut

tz'aqaat (ADJ) completed; (N) complement

tz'aqateem (IVS) to be completed in number or quantity

tz'aqatsaxik (TVD) to be completed in number or quantity

tz'iil (ADJ) dirty, unclean, impure; (N) dirt, stain

tz'iilob'eem (IVS) to become dirty, unclean, impure

tz'ikin (N) bird

tz'inileem (IVP) to be motionless, silent, abandoned

tz'inoweem (IVS) to be silent

tz'i' (N) dog

tz'umaxik (TVD) to be kissed; to be sucked
  Absolutive Antipassive Voice: **tz'umanik**, nurse at the breast

tz'u'uum (tz'u'm–) (N) skin, hide; _ **tz'u'maal** (poss form)

uu

_uuk' (PREP) with

wuuk'	with me
awuuk'	with you
ruuk'	with him
uk' la	with you
quuk'	with us
iwuuk'	with you
kuuk'	with them
uk' alaq	with you

uul (N) landslide

u

u- (POSS PRO) his, her, its (see lesson 7)

ub'een (N) tamale with beans inside

uchaxik (IVS) to be told (quotative)

Incomplete Aspect

Kinuchaxik	I am told
Katuchaxik	you are told
Kuchaxik	he is told
kuchax la	you are told
Kojuchaxik	we are told
Kixuchaxik	you are told
ku'chaxik	they are told
kuchax alaq	you are told

Completed Aspect

Xinuchaxik	I was told, etc.

oj (PER PRO) we, us

uk'a'xik (TVD) to be carried, sustained

ukaab' (NUM) second

ukaaj (NUM) fourth

uleem (IVS) to arrives here

ulew (N) land, earth, ground, soil

_umaal (PREP) by, by agency of, because

Wumaal	by me
Awumaal	by you
Rumaal	by him
umal la	by you
Qumaal	by us
Iwumaal	by you
Kumaal	by them
umal alaq	by you

rumal ri = because

rumal k'u ri' = and for that reason

uq (N) woman's skirt (Indian style)

uroox (NUM) third

uroo' (NUM) fifth

us (N) gnat

utiw (N) coyote

utz (ADJ) good, well

utziil (N) goodness, peace

utzireem (IVS) to become better, ready

utzirsaxik (TVD) to be made better, ready

uwach ulew (N) world

uxeem (IVS) to become

uxlaneem (IVS) to rest

w

w- (POSS PRO) my (see lesson 8)

waakax (N) cow, bull

waach'ik (TVR) to be crushed, smashed (as a finger with a hammer)

wa (N) general name for edible substances made from corn

wachaaj (PN) face(s), eye(s), front, eye infection, appearance, class, type, kind, condition, state of being, fruit (of tree)

wachib'al (N) representation (as a picture, statue, etc.)

wachik' (N) dream, dreaming

wachik'axik (TVD) to be dreamed about

wachik'eem (IVS) to dream

wajxaqiib' (NUM) eight

waqiib (NUM) six

waraal (ADV) here

waraam (IVS) to sleep

warab'al (N) sleeping place

wartisaxik (TVD) to be put to sleep

wa' (DEM PRO) this one, these (very close to the speaker) (see lesson 25)

wa'kateel (N) wanderer, traveler

wa'kateem (IVS) to take a pleasure walk, wander, galavant

wa'iim (IVS) to eat; (N) meal

wa'lijeem (IVS) to get up, rise up

wa'lijsaxik (TVD) to be gotten up, to be raised up

wa' we (DEM PRO) this very, this here, these very, these here (see lesson 25)

we (CONJ) if

we (DEM ART) the (this one very close); (REL PRO) this one who (which) (see lesson 24)

Weel (N) Manuel

we ne' (ADV) maybe, perhaps

we nemna (ADV) perhaps not, maybe not

web'al (N) plate (for eating)

wemna (CONJ) if not

We'l (N) Manuela

wiiqik (TVR) to be decorated, adorned, to be set (a bone)

wi (PART) directional particle (see lesson 14)

wikiq'ab' (PN) right hand

winaq (N) person, people

wi'aaj (PN) hair (on head)

wookik (TVR) to be built

woorik (TVR) to be pierced, opened (as a hole in something)

wo'qib'al (N) eating place

wuuj (N) paper, book

wuqub' (NUM) seven

wuqub'iix (ADV) in a week

wuqub'ixiir (ADV) a week ago

wulijeem (IVS) to break apart, fall apart

wulixik (TVD) to be taken down, destroyed

x

xa (ADV) just (contrary to what is expected or hoped for); xa k'u jee ri' (CONJ) and for that reason

xaan (N) adobe; xana ja, adobe house

xab'eem (IVS) vomit

xajooj (N) dance

xaq (ADV) no more than, only, just

xa'ooj (N) vomit, vomiting

xa'r (N) clay cup

xekeb'axik (TVD) to be hung up

xekeleem (IVP) to hang

xewi (xeu-) (ADV) only (of all possibilities, *only* this)

Xe'p (N) Isabela

xe'xik iib' (TVD) to be afraid (commonly reflexive)

xiimik (TVR) to be tied

xib'aal (PN) brother (female's)

xib'ineel (N) ghost, spook; xib'inelaab' (PL) ghosts, spooks

xib'ixik (TVD) to be frightened

xkinaaj (PN) ear(s)

xoot (N) clay tiles for roof, clay griddle for cooking; xota ja, house with tile roof

xojoweem (IVS) to dance

xo'l (PREP) among them, between them (see *ch_xo'l*)

xulaneem (IVP) to go down, to descend

xu'y (ADJ) stingy, selfish

xu'yaxik (TVD) to be stingy about giving (something)

Xwaan (N) Juan

y

y (CONJ-SPAN) and

yaab'iil (N) sickness, disease

yaak (N) fox

yaakik (TVR) to be picked up (as clothing, dishes, etc.)

ya (adv-Span) now

yajik (TVR) to be scolded

ya mero (adv-Span) almost, nearly

yawaab' (ADJ) sick; (N) sick person; **yawab'iib'** (PL) sick people

ya'ik (TVR) to be given; **ya'ik + kanoq** = to be left behind

yoojik (TVR) to be destroyed, wrecked

yojojeem (IVS) to roar (as rushing sound of water or heavy rain)

yowajeem (IVS) become sick

yowajixik (TVD) to become sick with

yo'xik (TVD) to be shooed away, chased away

yuuqik (TVR) to be stretched

yuq'uxik (TVD) to be shepherded, herded

Story

RI KITIKITAJIK RI CHIKOP OJER TYEMPO
The Creation of the Animals a Long Time Ago

Chaniim kaqatzijoj jub'iq'cheri ojer tyempo aretaq xpee le maar. Le winaq aretaq xpee ri mar, ee k'o xkik'ot kijuul, xeeb'ee pa ulew, komo xkito ri maar kapeetik. A're' k'u ri ee nik'aaj xa'q'an aq'an chuwi' chee'; a're' la' xo'k k'ooy.

Now we're going to tell a little about how in ancient times the ocean came. Some of the people, when the ocean came, dug their holes and went into the earth because they heard the ocean was coming. But others climbed up on top of the trees; they became monkeys.

Pero le joron katajin kanimarik, entonse k'o xeek'asi' chkee, pero na xee-winaqir taj. Xaq si xu'x chikop. Le ee nik'aaj xu'x ib'ooy. A're' la' xkikoj poop, xkimuq kiib' pulew. Xkib'ot kiib pa sin poop. Komo le staq ib'oy keqil oj chi jeri k'o poop le kiq'u'uum. Jun wi ub'anom le staq kiij. Entonse na xu'x ta chi winaq. Xaq si xeechikopir wi.

But the water was expanding, so some of them survived, but they did not become (remain) people. They really became animals. A portion of them became armadillos.

They were the ones who used petates (woven mats) and buried themselves in the ground. They wrapped themselves up in petates. Just like the armadillos we see, it's as if they cover themselves with petates. Their shells/skins are odd (jun wi). And so they didn't become people anymore. They just turned into animals.

Entonse ee q'at b'a mismo ee winaq ojer. Entonse ri a're' kwando xpee le maar xa pa ulew xeek'oji' wi. Xkichomaaj chi na keeriqitaj ta rumaal le joron. Entonse ri maar maataam xtzaajik. Entonse ri a're' xa si b'enaam xkib'an pa ulew. Na xeewinaqir ta chi wi. Ee k'ask'oj, pero xa ee chikop chik. Na ee winaq ta chik.

And also the gophers were people a long time ago. But when the ocean came they were under ground. They thought that they wouldn't be reached by the water. But it took a long time for the ocean to dry up, so they went forever under the ground. They did not become people anymore. They were alive, but they were now animals. They weren't people anymore.

Are' la' b'antajinaq ojer arechi' xpee le maar. Xkimuq kiib' pa taq ri ulew. Xkitzukuj kik'olib'al. Xeek'oji' pa taq jul. Entonse pa kiwach ri a're' keekolotajik. Xeek'asi' na k'ut pero xa ee ib'ooy chi xo'k wi. Xa keetijow chik. K'oo chi kipoop xkiq'u'uj. Are' la' le sin kiij, jee ri k'oo poop kaqil oj.

That's what happened a long time ago when the ocean came. They buried themselves in the ground. They looked for their places. They stayed in holes. They thought they would be saved. They did survive, but they turned into armadillos. They are just eaten now. They cover themselves with petates. We see that their shells are like petates.

Are' wa' ri xb'antaj kan ojer tyempo. Xa na k'u qatoom kitzijom kan ri ojer taq winaq ri ee kaminaqiib' chik.

This is what happened a long time ago. We have just heard what the elders who are dead now have told.